'A charming historical journey of fruit and veg in all their glorious variety . . . oozes trivia and taste notes.'

Daily Mail

'Gardeners and allotment-holders take note! This superb guide to Britain's traditional, but fast-disappearing fruit and vegetables sounds a clarion call to all of us . . . A very detailed and interesting guide to the history and idiosyncrasies of these truly unforgettable fruits and vegetables.'

Good Book Guide

'Fresh insight into Britain's natural and social history, with inspiration for gardeners in spadefuls.'

National Trust Magazine

'A fascinating work of natural and social history as well as a bit of a reminder of favourites from your childhood that have lost popularity! What's really interesting about this book is that it gives you the chance to grow history in your very own garden, producing Victorian favourites, or classic greats from the 1500s.'

Country Kitchen

'Considers the origins of unusual varieties but imparts far more along the way about their place in the social fabric of Britain.'

Amateur Gardening

'If you love the titbits and tales behind the varieties, you're in for a treat . . . This book has more facts than you can shake a stick at, and certainly more than enough to bore countless friends and acquaintances with next time you're down the pub (or on the allotment perhaps).'

Garden News

'This gem of a book is learned and you will be able to disarm your guests with erudite lore on the social history of vegetables.'

Country House

'If you want to grow a bit of history in your garden, get a taste of something truly different or find out about British rural life over the centuries, *Forgotten Fruits* makes irresistible reading.'

Folio

'This superbly written book reveals the stories behind our fruit and veg in an attempt to rescue the best survivors from obscurity.'

Countryfile Magazine

'Stocks's mix of fascinating history and literary references is bound to inspire, whether you have a garden or not.'

Waitrose Food Illustrated

'Beguiling . . . Packed with facts and stories, it's a great source on how to grow your own rarities.'

Sainsbury's Magazine

'A fascinating new book called *Forgotten Fruits* which creates a definitive guide to Britain's traditional fruit and vegetables and their significance to our past.'

Eastern Daily Press

'A huge amount of research has gone into selecting varieties to focus on and the result is an extremely informative and interesting look, not only at the produce itself, but also at the people who developed and grew these varieties.'

Essex Life

'A fascinating account of our horticultural history.'

Dorset Echo

'A good read for everyone, gardener or not.'

Oxford Times

Forgotten Fruits

Praise for *Forgotten Fruits*

Shortlisted for the André Simon Book Awards 2008

Runner-up for the 2008 Garden Media Guild's Inspirational Book of the Year: 'Christopher Stocks's passion for, and research of, his subject makes *Forgotten Fruits* a fascinating read – and not just for experts.'

'This is my favourite book of the year. Written with passion and real knowledge of his subject, Stocks celebrates the story behind our favourite fruit and veg . . . you will be inspired.'
Monty Don, *Daily Mail Weekend*

'The names of Christopher Stocks' *Forgotten Fruits* carry an extraordinary cargo of memories and he unpacks this baggage in the course of his captivating book . . . written with a wonderfully light and assured touch.'
Anna Pavord, *Gardens Illustrated*

'Handsome and readable . . . full of intriguing facts . . . This book will be enjoyed by people interested in the diversity of British fruit and vegetables and the stories behind their development.'
Joy Larkcom, *The Garden*

'A scholarly and fascinating study of rare traditional varieties of British fruit and vegetables that conjures a lost world from the humble gooseberry, leek and apple.'
Jane Shilling, *The Times*

'I have . . . added the excellent *Forgotten Fruits* to my ever-growing pile of gardening books, and it is proving to be a great source of inspiration for future projects.'
Simon Tiffin, *Daily Telegraph*

'Meticulously researched, wonderful descriptions, lots of anecdotes, lots of practical advice . . . a serious work and fascinating read.'
Juliet Roberts, editor of *Gardens Illustrated*, on Radio 4,
Gardeners' Question Time

Forgotten Fruits

The stories behind Britain's traditional fruit and vegetables

CHRISTOPHER STOCKS

⚜ WINDMILL BOOKS

To Roy and my parents

Published by Windmill Books 2009

2 4 6 8 10 9 7 5 3 1

Copyright © Christopher Stocks 2008

Christopher Stocks has asserted his right under the Copyright, Designs and Patents Act, 1988, to be identified as the author of this work

First published in Great Britain in 2008°by
Random House Books
Random House 20 Vauxhall Bridge Road,
London SW1V 2SA

www.rbooks.co.uk

Addresses for companies within The Random House Group Limited can be found at: www.randomhouse.co.uk/offices.htm

The Random House Group Limited Reg. No. 954009

A CIP catalogue record for this book
is available from the British Library

ISBN 9780099514749

The Random House Group Limited supports The Forest Stewardship Council (FSC), the leading international forest certification organisation. All our titles that are printed on Greenpeace approved FSC certified paper carry the FSC logo. Our paper procurement policy can be found at www.rbooks.co.uk/environment

Contents

Introduction

Sandwiched between Heathrow airport, the Queen Mother reservoir and the M25, Colnbrook is one of those unexpected scraps of pre-twentieth-century London that, against all the odds, has survived into the twenty-first. Once an important staging post on the road to Bath, it was bypassed in the late 1920s, with the result that the narrow village street still runs, much as it must have done in quieter days, past brick-built cottages and the ancient, half-timbered Ostrich Inn, where in medieval times (so the story goes) the landlord and his wife murdered around sixty of their guests by pitching them, one after another, into a barrel of boiling beer.

Yet, the most interesting building in Colnbrook is not the Ostrich Inn, but a deeply uninspiring block of modern low-rise flats a little further east along what's now called the Old Bath Road. It might not be much to look at, but then what's interesting about The Lawns, as the block is known, is not its architectural distinction (or lack of it) but its incongruously bucolic name. It is called The Lawns because it stands near the site of a nineteenth-century villa of the same name. And as an address, The Lawns, Colnbrook, occupies a surprisingly important place in British history – or rather it would if we took the story of our food as seriously as we take the story of our kings and queens and country houses.

In the early nineteenth century Colnbrook was still a small country village that combined rustic charm with easy access to Windsor and the capital. It was just the kind of place where a comfortably-off Londoner might choose to spend his twilight years, and in the early 1820s a retired brewer from Bermondsey took a lease on The Lawns (or Lawns Cottage, as it was sometimes known) along with two acres of orchards and gardens. Around 1825 he planted some seeds of a Ribston Pippin apple, and a few years later the seedlings that came up bore fruit for the first time. Like most apples grown from seed they were quite different from their parent, and one in particular stood out for its wonderful flavour. In 1836 he gave some grafts of the young tree to one of his neighbours, a nurseryman called David Small, who lived at Nursery Cottage on Colnbrook High Street. Small and his son James started selling this new variety in 1840, and before long other nurseries took it on and its fame began to spread. By the end of the nineteenth century it had become one of the most popular apples in Britain.

The name of the retired brewer was Richard Cox, and his apple became known as Cox's Orange Pippin. Today it is the most widely grown apple in the world, yet every one of those millions of trees can trace its ancestry directly back to that single seedling, planted by Richard Cox at The Lawns, Colnbrook, in 1825.

Mr Cox's villa and gardens have long since disappeared, replaced by modern housing and a car park. No one thought to preserve them, and the original Orange Pippin tree is said to have blown down in 1911 during a gale. Other than its name, The Lawns today bears no sign of its place in culinary history, which is a shame, though Nursery Cottage still stands. But Colnbrook has not forgotten Richard Cox entirely. Not far away, in Albany Park, a small community orchard was planted in 1992, with Cox's Orange Pippin trees and three metal benches in the shapes C, O and X – a typically imaginative contribution from the charity Common Ground, which works with local communities to enhance the spirit of our everyday places.

Cox's Orange Pippin may be the most successful apple of all time, but for all its fame surprisingly few of us are familiar with its story. And it is only one among hundreds of outstanding varieties of fruit and vegetables of which this country can boast. Many of them have histories at least as long and equally interesting, yet we hardly ever see them for sale in the shops, on restaurant menus or in cookery books. Some, which were once as celebrated as Cox's Orange Pippin, have since been almost entirely forgotten or altogether lost. Others are still relatively easy to find, at least if you know where to look.

This book is an attempt to rescue the best of the survivors from undeserved obscurity. Some, such as the May Duke cherry or the Martock bean, may well be hundreds of years old. Others have close connections to a particular region, village or town; sometimes even to a specific house, like the Pitmaston Duchess pear. There are onions named after islands, redcurrants named after castles, even a parsnip named after a popular song. Many varieties commemorate individual people: brilliant professional gardeners and gifted amateurs, as well as ordinary folk – such as George Crook, who in 1833 stumbled across the Yellow Egg plum growing wild in a Worcestershire wood – who just happened to be in the right place at the right time. A number of varieties deserve to be grown for their names alone: who could resist a gooseberry called Hero of the Nile, a plum called the Warwickshire Drooper or a turnip that glories in the name of Orange Jelly?

The damp, temperate British climate allows us to grow a wider range of fruit and vegetables than virtually anywhere else on earth, and the history of their introduction, adoption and improvement has mirrored the transformations in British society from the Roman conquest right through to the present day. Fashions in food have changed just as radically over the centuries as fashions in clothing, but the former tend to be less well known, perhaps because food fashions change so much more slowly. Our forebears would have thought us crazy to eat tomatoes, which were considered fit only for decoration; mind you, they would have thought us mad to eat just about anything raw, including apples, pears, plums and celery, the majority of which, until the mid-eighteenth century, would have gone straight into the cooking pot. Brussels sprouts were once regarded as fashionable upper-class delicacies; cucumbers were believed to be fatal in any quantity; and potatoes were treated with grave suspicion – though at least they were never actually illegal in this country, as they were in France between 1748 and 1772.

International upheavals had unforeseen consequences too. Without the Spanish Inquisition our carrots might never have been orange, while the French Revolution was at least partly responsible for the triumph of British strawberries in the nineteenth century. Even the humblest root crops have their claims to fame: beetroot, for example, is in part responsible for the abolition of slavery, while swedes helped lay the foundations for the Industrial Revolution; carrots did their bit towards winning the Second World War in their guise as an undercover secret weapon, and there would not be so many Irish-Americans in the United States if it wasn't for a potato.

Changes in the kind of crops we grew, and the way we cooked with them, have usually emerged in the wake of major historical events like these, but a few pioneering individuals have revolutionised our fruit and vegetables too. This select band of horticultural heroes includes Richard Harris, a kind of British sixteenth-century Johnny Appleseed; the French spy and fireworks aficionado Amédée-François Frézier, without whom our strawberries would be much smaller; John Tradescant, who probably grew this country's first blackcurrants and runner beans in his Lambeth garden; Joseph Myatt, another south Londoner, who first persuaded the British public to stop treating rhubarb as a medicine and start eating it instead; and a solitary heroine, Charlotte Knight, who with her father bred one of the finest cherries of all, the magnificent Waterloo.

Given this rich and ancient inheritance it's chastening to discover how many old varieties have been lost over the years. Some of them simply died out, victims of gradual decline, inherent feebleness or the cumulative effects of disease; others were superseded by improved varieties, which had greater drought resistance or fuller flavour. Others again proved unsuitable for modern farming, and are no longer grown on a commercial scale. Many old varieties of vegetables were lost simply because no one cared enough about them; partly, I suspect, because vegetables lack fruit's instant visual allure, but mainly because they lead far briefer lives than fruit trees, some of which can survive for anything up to 300 years. We grow most vegetables as annuals, which means that they have to be planted each year from fresh stocks of seed. If their seed isn't carefully collected at the end of every season, or different varieties are allowed to interbreed, an ancient variety can be lost within a couple of years.

Other developments have had unintended consequences. Perhaps the most notorious was the introduction of European Union legislation during the 1970s and 1980s governing the legal use and distribution of vegetable seeds. Currently, only those varieties that are registered on what's known as the National List may be sold as legally certified seed; to sell unlisted vegetable varieties, however ancient or widely grown they may be, is technically illegal. (By a quirk of genetics, fruit escaped inclusion in the list, as most fruit trees and bushes are propagated from cuttings and grafts rather than from seed.) Though intended to protect small-scale producers and, to some extent, to preserve particular local varieties, the National List has had a massive effect on less commercially valuable vegetable varieties, since the process of registering them is long and expensive. At the time of writing it costs £365 to register each variety on the National List, plus an £800 charge for testing and a 'Reference Varieties' fee of £350. Both the testing and Reference Varieties fees are repeated in the second year, which means that to register a single variety will cost £2,665 in the first two years. As a result, hundreds of once-popular varieties have been lost.

Although the period between the late 1970s and the early 1990s was in many ways a low point for older and more unusual varieties of vegetables and fruit, fortunately it was not the end of the story. For one thing, many more varieties survived than one might have expected. People have always treasured old fruit trees and collected seed of favourite kinds of vegetables for their own use or the pleasure of their family and friends. Others were unwittingly preserved, in gardens and hedgerows, on the sites of former nurseries and market gardens, or as overlooked remnants of once-productive orchards, grubbed up decades ago. Still others were saved by enlightened organisations such as Garden Organic (formerly known as the Henry Doubleday Research Association), which set up its Heritage Seed Library in 1975 specifically to safeguard vegetable varieties that had been dropped from the National List (or had never been added to it), and the National Fruit Collection at Brogdale in Kent, whose priceless living collection of fruit trees and bushes includes 1,880 varieties of apples as well as hundreds of plums, pears, cherries and other fruit.

For all the losses – and there have been plenty – what's remarkable is how many old varieties have actually survived. And in fact it seems possible that we may not have lost quite the number that has sometimes been claimed. Many writers have commented on the astonishing wealth of varieties in nineteenth-century seed catalogues, which make their modern-day equivalents look pretty impoverished by comparison. One leading seed company today, for example, offers twelve different kinds of peas, which sounds quite impressive until you turn to the same firm's catalogue from 1852, which listed fifty-three, along with thirty-seven varieties of lettuce and forty-two different kinds of cabbages. Fruit varieties came in similar abundance. In the 1860 edition of his classic *Fruit Manual*, Robert Hogg lists at least twenty-four varieties of apricot (all of them grown in Britain), not to mention a similar number of nectarines and sixty-two kinds of peach, including such delights as George the Fourth, Old Newington, Mountaineer and the legendary Têton de Venus, 'surmounted', in Hogg's words, 'by a large turgid nipple'. Faced with such an embarrassment of riches, our present poverty of choice may seem disheartening, but some of the longest lists of Victorian varieties should probably be taken with a pinch of salt. Our nineteenth-century forebears might have had hundreds more varieties to choose from than we do, but what's less often noted is that the literature of the period was awash with complaints about similar varieties being passed off under several different names. In the days before the Trade Descriptions Act, unscrupulous seedsmen would buy the stock of one variety, change its name and then sell it on as if newly introduced. But the duplication was not only the result of sharp practice: before efficient transport and instant communication it was not uncommon for the same varieties to acquire their own local names in different parts of the country. Sorting out this mess was one of the principal aims of the Horticultural Society of London, founded in 1804 and later to become the Royal Horticultural Society, but as quickly as duplicates could be identified yet more 'new' varieties spilled on to what was, after all, a completely unregulated market. The potato Up to Date offers a particularly arresting example. Less than thirty years after it was launched by the great Scottish grower Archibald Findlay in 1894, it was being sold under 200 alternative names.

It was somehow rather appealing to discover, in researching this book, how many old varieties had been found entirely by chance. Novel varieties of fruit trees seem to have had a habit of turning up in cottage gardens; a new redcurrant was found, appropriately enough, beneath a gooseberry bush. As for apple seedlings, they seem constantly to have been popping up in the most unexpected places: unearthed from rubbish heaps, dug out of roadside verges and liberated from humble front gardens, even on one famous occasion found growing on a roof. Now that scientists and multi-national companies have a virtual monopoly on crop development, what's also striking about these stories is how many of our old varieties were raised by perfectly ordinary people. Few things better illustrate the thrifty and practical outlook of our forebears than the speed with which they took up any chance opportunity that came their way. To them we owe some of our finest kinds of fruit and vegetables, but what also became clear was that they rarely acted entirely on their own. Story after story revealed that every small town (and even many villages) could boast its own local nursery, whose enterprising owners more often than not seized on each new find, quickly building up stocks and then marketing the new variety with energy and imagination. So while the people who made the original discoveries certainly deserve great credit, it was almost invariably the nurserymen who named them . . . and who usually made the money.

Most of these nurseries – the greatest of them, sometimes covering hundreds of acres, as well as the tiny one-man-bands – have long since disappeared beneath modern housing and industrial estates, but even today they continue to haunt us. Not only in the names they once so proudly gave to their own varieties, whose euphonious litany (Kirke's Blue, Laxton's No. 1, Lane's Prince Albert, Williams' Bon Chrétien . . .) echoes down the years, but also in affectingly corporeal ways. Strawberries and radishes still come up in Brompton cemetery, built on the site of a nineteenth-century market garden, and one wonders how many back gardens in Worcester, say, or Berkhamsted, where famous nurseries once stood, unwittingly preserve unusual old fruit trees and lost varieties of vegetable. Fruit trees in particular have an admirable habit of hanging on to life, sometimes for hundreds of years, and almost every week while compiling this book newspaper cuttings would arrive, recording yet another discovery of a long-lost variety of apple or a venerable plum. Set against the terrible destruction of Britain's fruit orchards during the twentieth century, stories like these offer grounds for minor celebration.

When it came to selecting varieties to include, there were several criteria I wanted to apply. First of all, although many are now quite rare, all of the varieties I've chosen can still be found for sale, mostly from specialist nurseries and seed companies, whose contact details can be found at the end of the book. Unfortunately autiquity is no guarantee of quality, so I have tried to include only those varieties that have been personally recommended, or that are generally agreed to be worth growing – usually for their excellent flavour, but often also for their appearance, their vigour, their drought-resistance or some other useful quality. Some were chosen for their fascinating history; others for their long-standing connections with a specific place. A few I couldn't resist including simply because they have such wonderful names. All too many varieties have little or no recorded history, although one of the most enjoyable aspects of my research has been to fill in a few of the gaps, and to confirm (or in some cases correct) many of the dates of introduction, which often prove earlier than previously thought. Some of the stories in these pages are being told for the first time in 150 years; others occurred just about within living memory. Perhaps the most surprising were those stories that have been told many times before, but which turned out on closer examination to be completely unsubstantiated, or in a few cases just plain wrong. Needless to say, any remaining errors are my own.

This is the first attempt to tell the history of so many individual varieties of British fruit and vegetables, and as such it should perhaps best be regarded as a work in progress; as an introduction rather than an encyclopedia. In some ways the most exciting stories are those that remain incomplete, their details often maddeningly vague. Many fascinating mysteries remain to be solved. Who was the Dan immortalised by the gooseberry called Dan's Mistake, and what on earth did he do wrong? Where did the Victoria plum really come from? What, where or who was the Bascombe Mystery? The answers may lie in the pages of crumbling magazines, or hidden away in county record offices, waiting for patient, sharp-eyed local historians to discover them. For these stories are, more than anything else, the stories of local people and particular places, and like the story of The Lawns, Colnbrook, they deserve their own special niche in our common heritage.

Apples

There is no kind of Fruit better known in England than the Apple, or more generally cultivated. It is of that Use, that I hold it almost impossible for the English to live without it, whether it be employed for that excellent Drink we call Cider, or for the many Dainties which are made of it in the Kitchen: In short, were all other Fruits wanting to us, Apples would make us amends.

Richard Bradley, *New Improvements of Planting and Gardening, Both Philosophical and Practical* (1739)

G iven that this country has something like 2,000 varieties of eating and cooking apples alone, it would be easy to write an entire book on the subject – and indeed several people already have. Of all the kinds of fruit and vegetables we have, apples are perhaps the best loved and also, in many ways, the most emotive, so choosing a small selection of the best varieties will always be a contentious exercise. Since one of the aims of this book is to encourage people to try growing things themselves, I have limited myself to those apples that can easily be grown in an average-sized garden (at least on a dwarfing rootstock) and that will repay the effort of growing them. Sadly that counts out several hundred varieties of cider apples, which are best grown in larger groups, but whose inclusion would anyway make this chapter unconscionably long. For a more comprehensive account than there is room for here, the best place to start is with Joan Morgan and Alison Richards' magisterial *New Book of Apples*, published in 2002 and still, happily, in print.

Britain's love affair with apples started early on. Small, sour crab apples are thought to be indigenous to Britain, and the word for apple (*abhal* in Celtic and *aval* in Cornish and Breton) found its way into a number of ancient place-names such as Avalon – the Isle of Apples, legendary burial-place of King Arthur. Although crab apples were, presumably, widely used, and probably made into cider to drink, they were no match for the far larger, sweeter domestic apple that appears to have been introduced, like so many other kinds of fresh fruit and vegetables, during the four long centuries of Roman occupation. The domestic apple's ancestral home is far away, in the ancient Tian Shan fruit forests, which stretch from the edge of the Gobi Desert to the mountains of Uzbekistan. In this area of extraordinary biodiversity wild apples have flourished and interbred since time out of mind, both naturally and, later, thanks to human intervention. (For an absorbing and up-to-date account of apples' genetic origins – part history, part adventure story – see *The Story of the Apple* by Barrie E. Juniper and David Mabberley. Barrie Juniper, Reader Emeritus in Plant Sciences at Oxford University, has raised the intriguing probability that domestic apples are, in fact, descended from a single wild ancestor, *Malus sieversii*, which can still be found growing on the borders between present-day China and Kazakhstan.) Indeed, today's apples have so many different ancestors in their genetic make-up that seedlings almost never come up 'true to type' – which is why named varieties are invariably propagated by grafts and cuttings rather than by seed. By the same token, new varieties are constantly springing up from seed. The vast majority of them, of course, are mediocre at best and worthless at worst, but just occasionally a fine new variety will arise, as it were, from nowhere, such as Bramley's Seedling or the now-ubiquitous Cox.

Like other Roman introductions such as pears, domestic apples may have fallen almost entirely out of cultivation during the Dark Ages, especially if the skills involved in grafting them were lost. Like pears, too, old varieties may have survived in monastery orchards, to be joined by hundreds of new varieties from the continent that began flooding into Britain from the time of Henry VIII. The oldest varieties to survive into the present day probably date from this period: the Winter Pearmain, for example, which is still available now, was mentioned by John Gerard in his famous *Herball* of 1597, when it was apparently thriving in his London garden, between Chancery and Fetter Lanes.

Foreign imports were slowly supplanted by home-grown varieties, and by the early eighteenth century apple-breeding had become something of a British mania. In 1739, a slightly exasperated Richard Bradley noted in his *New Improvements of Planting and Gardening, Both Philosophical and Practical* that 'To set down the several various Names of Apples, would be a Work almost impossible, seeing how many various Kinds are yearly produced from the Kernels, in almost every County in England; and where they happen to prove good, either for making Cider, or Table-use, have Names given them according to the Mind of the Person that raised them.'

If the eighteenth century was the age of unbridled interbreeding, the nineteenth was when apples, like so many other crops, became the subject of scientific enquiry and careful categorisation. When it was founded in 1804, one of the main aims of the Horticultural Society of London was to clear up some of the confusion that had arisen over the years in the naming of apple varieties. Among the hundreds of varieties already available, many were known by different names in different areas, or had been renamed by canny nurserymen in the hope of persuading their customers that they were buying something novel when in fact all they were doing was purchasing a hoary old variety under a brand-new name.

The nineteenth century also brought a rising interest in dessert (rather than cooking) apples, which helps explain why Britain is the only country in the world that distinguishes between the two types. Before this time most varieties of apple were considered to be dual-purpose – that is, suitable both for cooking and, to a lesser extent, for eating raw, although uncooked food of any kind was regarded with some suspicion in the days before clean washing water was widely available and the importance of hygiene in food preparation was universally understood. As food standards improved, raw fruit became not just safe to eat but also extremely fashionable, and few kinds of fruit were more patriotically appreciated than apples, which is one reason why so many of our finest eaters have nineteenth-century origins.

In fact the Victorian love of apples was so widespread, so enthusiastic and so well informed that, in retrospect, the late nineteenth century seems like apples' golden age – something that throws their subsequent decline into dramatically high relief. In some ways apples could be said to be a victim of their own success. While connoisseurs, professional nurserymen and gifted amateurs could happily spend months arguing over the relative merits of, say, Ribston Pippins over Blenheim Oranges, relatively few of the thousands of varieties then in cultivation were suitable for growing on a large enough scale to satisfy the demand for fresh apples from a rapidly growing population. It might even be said that the seeds of our current mass-market monocultures were already set by the time Queen Victoria died in 1901, although their effects were not to be felt until the end of the First World War.

The ever-accelerating destruction of this country's apple orchards during the twentieth century is almost too well known to repeat, but, however one looks at it, the figures are sobering.

According to Common Ground, the charity whose launch of the annual Apple Day in October 1990 kick-started the current apple renaissance, something like two-thirds of English orchards were lost between 1950 and the Millennium. In some areas the story is even worse: around 90 per cent of Devon's orchards, for example, have disappeared since 1945. Yet despite these losses, the twentieth century also saw the first systematic attempt to preserve as many varieties as possible before they disappeared for good. In 1922 the Royal Horticultural Society established its Commercial Fruit Trials at Wisley in Surrey, and began assembling a notable collection of apple varieties around a core collection that had come from the former RHS trial grounds in Chiswick, some of which dated back to the early nineteenth century. After the Second World War, responsibility for the fruit trials passed to the Ministry of Agriculture, and in 1952 what had by then become the National Collection was transferred to its present location at Brogdale in Kent, although the RHS retained many of its own trees at Wisley (which gives the RHS collection a strong claim to be the oldest in the country).

Although we continue to import almost three-quarters of the apples we eat, the last decade has seen more and more people becoming aware of the traditional British apple's plight. Annual Apple Days have sprung up around the country, community orchards are flourishing and specialist suppliers have widened the range of old-fashioned varieties for sale; at least at the local level the picture looks rosier now than it has done for the last fifty years.

With so many unusual and historic varieties to choose from, this chapter can only hope to scratch the surface, but here are a few British apples that deserve to be far better known. There are apples for every kind of orchard and garden, and there's hardly a county in Britain that doesn't have its own local variety, so with a little research (and the help of the sections at the back of the book) there's plenty of choice for everyone.

Ashmead's Kernel
c. 1700

Hugh Fearnley-Whittingstall is only the latest gourmand to wax lyrical about the taste of this small, rather odd-looking, late-ripening apple, which is one of the finest of all eating apples, yet one of the least well known. Its slightly rough russet skin belies its delicious flavour – 'exploding with champagne-sherbet juice infused with a lingering scent of orange blossom' (*Guardian Weekend* magazine, September 2006). Back in 1927 the author, architect and oenophile Morton Shand (who was also, incidentally, best friends with Le Corbusier and grandfather of Camilla Parker Bowles) was equally enraptured. 'What an apple,' he enthused in his *Book of Food*, 'what suavity of aroma. Its initial Madeira-like mellowness of flavour overlies a deeper honeyed nuttiness, crisply sweet not sugar sweet, but [with] the succulence of a well-devilled marrow bone. Surely no apple of greater distinction or more perfect balance can ever have been raised anywhere on earth.' Less elevated commentators say that its flavour reminds them of acid drops (a peculiarity shared by its most likely parent, the ancient Nonpareil).

All of which begs the question: if Ashmead's Kernel is such a prodigy, why have so few people ever heard of it? The answer, unfortunately, seems to be that we have grown accustomed to judging food first and foremost by its appearance – and there are prettier (and larger) apples than Ashmead's Kernel. It's also a rather erratic cropper, which may irritate commercial growers, although this is less likely to discourage the discerning amateur. That it remains a rarity is a shame, not only because of its inherent quality but also because its history most probably stretches right back to the early 1700s. Like many old varieties its exact origins are not entirely clear, but it may have been named after William Ashmead, who was clerk to the city of Gloucester in the mid-eighteenth century and who died in 1782. Ashmead is said to have grown it in his garden in Clarence Street, later the site of Ashmead House and, less romantically, the office of the municipal gasworks. Certainly Ashmead's Kernel is most commonly found in old Gloucestershire gardens, which suggests that it originated within the county.

Its past may be obscure, but the future of this delectable apple looks more promising: in 1993 its outstanding qualities were recognised with an Award of Garden Merit from the Royal Horticultural Society, and it has become increasingly popular with gardeners in Britain and the USA.

Bardsey
before 1998

The newest 'ancient' cultivar was discovered in 1998 on the island of Bardsey, off the remote and beautiful Lleyn peninsula in North Wales, by Ian Sturrock, a nurseryman and former lumberjack. It may be the last survivor of an ancient monastic orchard – or perhaps a random seedling. Either way, being the only one of its kind it is undoubtedly unique, and more usefully it also appears to be resistant to canker and scab, diseases which Welsh apple trees are particularly prone to suffer from. Sturrock, who has been described as 'a horticultural cross between Inspector Morse and Mr Incredible', rescues old trees from threatened orchards, taking grafts and raising them at his nursery near Bangor (for details see www.bardseyapple.co.uk).

The Bardsey apple is creamy coloured, often streaked with red, and has an appealing lemony smell and a sweet, juicy taste; it also cooks well without sugar.

Bascombe Mystery
before 1827

Few apples have quite such a captivating name as the Bascombe Mystery (sometimes spelled Bascomb or described as Bascombe's Mystery), but who, what or where Bascombe was, and why it should be a mystery is a mystery in itself: no one seems to know. Could it have something to do with the ancient Bascombe family of Boscombe in Wiltshire? Or could it have been found near Bascombe Road, at Galmpton in Devon, which was renowned for its apple orchards until the Second World War? It is usually said to date from around 1831, but it obviously pre-dates the 1830s by some time: in an 1827 edition of John Claudius Loudon's *Gardener's Magazine*, for example, the 'Bascomb Mystery apple, from Mr John Bridgman, FHS', is mentioned without comment in a list of plants distributed by the Horticultural Society of London (possibly John Bridgeman, listed as a member of the Horticultural Society in 1820; he lived in Wigmore Street, London). The apple evidently needed no introduction, nor is it described as a new variety, which suggests that it was well known even then. For now, at least, its origins remain as mysterious as its name, and all that we can be reasonably sure of is that this late dessert apple was widely planted in Kent by the mid-nineteenth century. It was grown commercially as late as the 1930s. The medium-sized, pale-green fruit may not be much to look at, but they are refreshingly crisp and sweet; given careful storage they have been known to keep for anything up to sixteen months.

Beauty of Bath
before 1864

Once the most important commercially grown early-ripening eating apple in Britain, Beauty of Bath is now rarely seen in the shops, for the simple reason that it does not keep. Yet eaten straight from the tree it is one of the best early apples of all. Its origins are uncertain, although it seems to have first turned up in the village of Bailbrook, by the banks of the River Avon on the north-east side of Bath. Originally called Bailbrook Seedling, it was introduced to cultivation around 1864 by a well-known local nurseryman called George Cooling, and won a first-class certificate from the Royal Horticultural Society in 1887. By the 1930s it was planted in commercial orchards all over England.

As a tree it is moderately strong-growing and spreading in shape; it has small leaves whose edges are finely serrated. It blossoms early, which makes it vulnerable to frosts in cold areas, but it is relatively resistant to scab. The fruit, which can often be picked as early as July, is handsome and shapely, small but regular, with yellow skin heavily striped with bright-red streaks; it also has a delicious fragrance. The variety's only drawback, apart from the fact that its fruit have to be eaten fresh, is that it tends to drop its apples before they're quite ripe, so wily Beauty of Bath-lovers carpet the ground around each tree with straw. The flesh is white, juicy, sweet and slightly acid, with a distinctive individual flavour. As late as the 1950s it was still the earliest apple to arrive in the shops, though those who remember those days are not always complimentary: according to one correspondent they were 'tasteless, mealy and generally revolting', although perhaps that says more about its short shelf-life than its intrinsic quality.

Blenheim Orange
1781?

Possibly the only apple whose taste has been described as addictive, Blenheim Orange is a connoisseur's delight, and if there is one variety that deserves to be reintroduced to a wider market it is this. Its story is well known, and was widely recorded in the nineteenth century, often wreathed with romantic embellishments. The seedling – probably the pip from a discarded apple core – was found by a tailor called George Kempster, growing against the drystone wall that encloses Blenheim Palace, the Duke of Marlborough's vast house in Oxfordshire. Kempster lived in Old Woodstock, just outside the park, and he transferred the seedling to his garden, where it thrived. Its large, delicious and attractive fruit soon began attracting attention, and according to Robert Hogg's rather purple account of 1851, before long 'thousands thronged from all parts to gaze on its ruddy, ripening, orange burden; then gardeners came in the spring-tide to select the much coveted scions, and to hear the tale of his horticultural child and sapling'. At first it was known as Kempster's Pippin, but around 1804 it was renamed Blenheim Orange in honour of the Duke. This date, as well as the fact that it does not appear to have entered cultivation until 1807 –

the first record of its commercial introduction is an 1807 advert for 'the new scarlet nonpareil, and the new Blenheim orange apple, as in high estimation' by a nurseryman called James Biggs (whose premises were at 27 Mealcheapen Street in central Worcester) – makes one wonder whether Kempster's discovery of the original tree might not have been rather later than the

Blenheim Orange apple

usually quoted date of 1740: if Kempster's tree was the prodigy that Hogg suggests, would it really have taken more than sixty years for anyone else to try growing it? Hogg himself admits that it was 'not noticed in any of the nursery catalogues of the last [i.e. eighteenth] century', which seems surprising given how quickly new varieties were propagated even then. These circumstances give more weight to the claim, reported in the American magazine *Horticulture* in 1853, that the first Blenheim Orange 'was raised, or first brought into notice, in the year 1781'.

Whatever the exact date of its origins, Blenheim Orange apples were being exhibited at the Horticultural Society of London by 1822, when they won a prestigious Banksian Medal. Around the same time they were drawn by the botanist William Hooker, although curiously Hooker's drawing differs in many details from another illustration, also entitled 'Blenheim Orange', in Thomas Andrew Knight's *Pomona Herefordensis* of 1811. (In their fascinating book *The Story of the Apple*, Barrie Juniper and David Mabberley suggest that one is actually a mutant version, or sport, of Kempster's tree, and it is this sub-variety – informally known as the Broad-Eyed Blenheim Orange – which is commonly sold today.) By the late nineteenth century it was the best-loved apple in Britain, and its apotheosis was reached in 1883 at the Royal Horticultural Society's famous Apple Congress, when it was the single most exhibited variety. It also proved a remarkable hybridiser, and Bramley's Seedling, Cox's Orange Pippin and Newton Wonder can be counted among its likely offspring.

Although it declined in commercial popularity from the 1930s on, the 'true' Blenheim Orange can still be bought from specialist nurseries, and it is well worth seeking out, not only for its great size but also for its flavour, which is distinctly nutty and sweet. It is good eaten raw and excellent for cooking, keeping its shape when baked, and producing a thick purée. The rotten, hollow stump of Kempster's original seedling finally expired in 1853, and that same year *Horticulture* magazine recorded that 'The only sound piece of wood remaining was preserved by a horticultural enthusiast to make a snuffbox, to serve as a memorial of the past, and to recall visions of him "who first planted the tree".' Could that snuffbox still exist?

Bramley's Seedling
c. 1813

As most people already know, Bramley's Seedling should, by rights, be known as Brailsford's Seedling, as the first tree was grown from seed by Mary Brailsford, in the pretty Nottinghamshire town of Southwell, between 1809 and 1813. But then any number of other chance seedlings should probably be known by other names: Williams' pear, for example, should really be called Wheeler's or Stair's, since it first grew in a garden owned by a Mr Wheeler and, later, a Mr Stair. In Bramley's case it just so happened that the first grafts from the original tree were taken in 1876, twenty-four years after Mary Brailsford's death, by which time her cottage was owned by the local butcher, Matthew Bramley. It was Bramley who allowed Henry Merryweather (whose descendants still run a nursery on Halam Road in Southwell) to take the grafts from the tree; hence the name. In 1883 Merryweather won a First Class Certificate for Bramley's Seedling at the National Apple Congress in Chiswick, held by the Royal Horticultural Society; with its reputation firmly established, the first commercial Bramley orchards were planted in 1890, at Loddington Farm, near Maidstone in Kent, which rather cheeringly still grows Bramley's Seedlings today. What is said to be Mary Brailsford's original tree in Southwell is, remarkably, still standing, if 'standing' is the right word, since around 1900 it blew over in a storm and the present tree grew up from a toppled branch. But is it really the original? Apple trees are notorious for assuming an appearance of great age when they are, in fact, only a few decades old, and Henry Merryweather himself (who almost equally remarkably lived until 1932) cast a shadow of doubt on its actual antiquity. Writing in 1925, he noted that 'My attention was drawn to this variety and I went to see it in 1876; but I could not definitely state whether the tree was the original or not.' Whatever the truth, Bramley's Seedling has proved its quality over the years, and now accounts for around 90 per cent of all the cooking apples sold in Britain. Home-grown Bramleys, unsurprisingly, are rather different beasts from the hard, green monsters most of us are accustomed to: left to ripen properly they are far sweeter than their commercial cousins, and if stored until the spring they make a good – if still quite sharp – eating apple too.

Cornish Gilliflower
c. 1800

The intensely fragrant Cornish Gilliflower was first brought to the notice of the Horticultural Society of London in 1813 by one of its learned members, Sir Christopher Hawkins of Trewithen, who sent cuttings of:

a new sort of Apple, said to have been discovered about ten, or fifteen years since, by a gentleman in a cottage garden, near Truro; who having purchased some of the fruit, afterwards took grafts from the tree. It goes by the name of the July flower Apple, probably from the pleasant smell it gives out when cut. The fruit has a long conical shape, and is of a yellowish green colour, with red towards the sun. The fragrance of the smell when cut, and the excellence of the flavour, render it one of the best of modern Apples.

The society was evidently impressed, awarding Sir Christopher a silver medal for his find. Like so many of the best-tasting apples it is not much to look at, being more oval than round and rather knobbly to boot, but its flavour is remarkable: rich and so intensely fragrant that it smells almost flowery when ripe, with refreshingly crisp, creamy coloured flesh. ('Gillyflower' was the old English name for the carnation, which shares the Cornish Gilliflower's clove-like scent.) Sir Christopher was interested in many fields apart from horticulture: he was also a geologist, and in 1811 he commissioned Richard Trevithick to build him the first ever steam-powered threshing machine, which has been preserved for posterity in the Science Museum.

Cox's Orange Pippin
c. 1825

Arguably the most famous apple of all, Cox's Orange Pippin owes its existence to Richard Cox, who retired to Colnbrook, a village then in the countryside outside London but now uncomfortably close to Heathrow airport, in the early 1820s. Cox had made his money as a brewer in Bermondsey, then a scattered settlement that looked across the River Thames to the City of London. In the late eighteenth century the area was well known for its breweries and noxious-smelling tanneries, and though the site of Cox's brewery has never been identified, a painstaking examination of John Fairburn's 1801 'Plan of Westminster and London' reveals, sandwiched between Hay's Wharf and Battle Bridge Stairs, a tiny area called Cox's Wharf. Could this have been where Richard Cox's business was? If so, the wharf seems to have been destroyed by the construction of Hay's Dock a few years later, and today the site lies beneath Hay's Galleria shopping centre.

Cox's Orange Pippin apple

The legendary Orange Pippin started life as a seed from one of the most popular apples of the day, the Ribston Pippin, and the seedling tree produced its first fruit around 1825. (Less well known is the fact that Richard Cox grew a second seedling alongside the Orange Pippin, which never really caught on – except, for some reason, in Sweden – although it is still available from specialist nurseries. Its name is Cox's Pomona, and it is an attractive cooking apple, which is good for baking and makes a sweetish yellow purée.) Cox's local nursery, run by David Small and his son James, started selling Orange Pippins in 1840, but it was not until the 1850s, when they were taken up by the Royal Nurseries in Slough and Queen Victoria's head gardener, Thomas Ingram, that their fame began to spread – too late, tragically, for old Mr Cox, who died on 20 May 1845 at the age of seventy-nine.

Apples were at the peak of their popularity by this time, and the British Pomological Society was founded in 1854, under the presidency of Sir Joseph Paxton. Its secretary was Robert Hogg, whose *Fruit Manual* became the standard reference work of the time, and its council members included the leading professional nurserymen Thomas Rivers and James Veitch. Though the society only lasted for ten years, its work did a great deal to establish Cox's Orange Pippin as the best-known new variety of its day. At the Royal Horticultural Society's Grand Chrysanthemum and Fruit Show in November 1861 Cox's swept the board, taking first, second and third prizes in the dessert apple section. (Thomas Ingram came first, with Lady Molyneux of Slough in second place and Charles Turner of the Royal Nurseries coming third.) Commercial cultivation soon expanded from around London to Kent and the Vale of Evesham, though Cox's primacy was never as completely assured as it might seem today: in the early twentieth century its popularity slumped because of its susceptibility to disease, but the introduction of new fungicides in the 1920s returned it to widespread use. Today something like 50 per cent of Britain's remaining orchards are devoted to Cox's Orange Pippin trees.

It may be the best-loved apple in the world, but as we saw in the Introduction Richard Cox has never received the credit he deserves. His original Orange Pippin tree is thought to have been destroyed by a gale in 1911, and the site of The Lawns, his house in Colnbrook, is now occupied by a depressing block of low-rise flats. Apart from a small community orchard off Colnbrook high street, which was laid out in 1992 with apple trees and benches spelling C, O and X, the only real memorial to Richard Cox's memory is his rather sombre tomb, which can be found, unvisited and uncelebrated, in the graveyard of St Mary's church in Harmondsworth.

Crawley Beauty
c. 1870

Rarely have the words 'Crawley' and 'beauty' come together more convincingly than in this useful all-round apple, which is sufficiently acid for cooking but mellows in storage to become sweet enough for eating raw. The story goes that it was found, in 1870 or thereabouts, in a cottage garden in the village of Tilgate, which has since been absorbed by modern Crawley's southern sprawl. It was first sold by John Cheal, who established Lowfield Nurseries in Crawley with his brother Alexander in 1871, and Crawley Beauty has been a favourite local variety ever since. Crawley Beauty is particularly good for frost-prone areas, for it often flowers as late as June, after the risk of frost has passed. Round and green with broken red stripes, it has rather soft, sweet white flesh. John Cheal died in 1896 at the age of ninety-six, but Cheals Garden Centre still serves Crawley's gardeners today, and the borough council recently planted several Crawley Beauty trees in the walled gardens of the town's Tilgate Park.

D'Arcy Spice
c. 1785

Despite its romantic name, D'Arcy Spice has nothing to do with Jane Austen's Mr Darcy, and in the flesh, so to speak, is something of a disappointment. Like many late apples (it was traditionally picked on Bonfire Night) it has tough, coarse skin and a dull, greenish yellow appearance. But what it lacks in looks it more than makes up for in flavour, which as its name suggests is spicy, with a slightly peppery taste and a distinct fragrance of nutmeg. It was found around 1785 in the gardens of D'Arcy Hall, an ancient moated house in Tolleshunt D'Arcy, Essex, but it doesn't appear to have been sold commercially until 1848, when a nurseryman called John Harris of Broomfield, near Chelmsford, began selling it as the Baddow Pippin. Its delicious taste brought it widespread popularity, especially in Essex and East Anglia, whose long days of autumn sunshine helped it develop its finest flavour; it still grows better there than anywhere else. If picked in November it can be stored until April or May the following year, although its flavour is at its most intense between February and March. D'Arcy Hall still stands beside the village church in Tolleshunt D'Arcy, and an avenue of D'Arcy Spice apple trees lines its drive.

Dumelow's Seedling
c. 1790

Long before Bramley's Seedling had ever been heard of, Dumelow's Seedling was this country's favourite cooking apple. It was raised in the late eighteenth century by Richard Dummeller, a farmer from Shackerstone, near Market Bosworth in Leicestershire, who died around 1813; 'Dumelow' was the local pronunciation for Dummeller. Known locally as Dumelow's Crab, it was planted in the gardens of nearby Gopsall Hall, whose owner, Richard Curzon-Howe, seems to have introduced it to Richard Williams (of Williams' pear fame), who ran the well-known Turnham Green Nursery near London. Williams in turn introduced the new apple at a London Horticultural Society show in 1818 under its original name of Dumelow's Crab, but around 1819 it was renamed Wellington, presumably in honour of the Duke, whose triumphant return to Britain that year was widely celebrated, and it is still sometimes known as Wellington today. By the second half of the nineteenth century it was one of the most admired and widely planted cooking apples in the country, and though Dumelow's was overtaken commercially by Bramley's Seedling in the twentieth century, its 'brisk' flavour and creamy texture are far superior, both for mincemeat and as one of the best baking apples of all.

Howgate Wonder
1915

This famously enormous cooking apple was raised during the First World War by George Wratten, who lived at Hope Cottages, in Howgate Lane at Bembridge on the Isle of Wight. The original Howgate Wonder was a cross between two of the finest old varieties, Blenheim Orange and Newton Wonder, but it was not until 1929 that Mr Wratten entered it in the National Fruit Trials at Wisley, where it won an Award of Merit. It was first marketed in 1932 by the Enfield firm of Stuart Low, but it never won wide commercial success, perhaps because its flavour, while pleasant enough, cannot compare with Dumelow's or Bramley's. What it lacks in complexity of flavour, though, it can make up for in size, a fact that has commended it to amateur enthusiasts and won it many prizes at horticultural shows. In 1997 a Howgate Wonder apple weighing 1.67kg (3lb 11oz) was recorded by the *Guinness Book of Records* as the largest apple ever grown.

Irish Peach
c. 1819

Popular among Victorians and Edwardians but rarely seen today, the Irish Peach was first brought to the attention of the Horticultural Society of London by John Robertson in 1819. Robertson, who ran a nursery in Kilkenny, was a Fellow of the Horticultural Society, as well as being an early convert to the fertilising wonders of soot and liquid manure. The original Irish Peach was said to hail from Sligo, but its delicious flavour – sharp, juicy and sweet – made it a popular dessert variety, and it flourished around London and in Kent. By 1830 *The Gardener's Magazine* was describing it as 'among the best table apples of August', a position it retained for many years. That it is no longer common today can be put down to the fact that this most delectable of apples neither keeps nor travels well: to enjoy it at its best it must, like a peach, be eaten straight off the tree.

Irish Peach apple

Keswick Codlin
c. 1790

Despite its raffish origins – the original seedling was discovered around 1790 growing on a Cumbrian rubbish tip – the Keswick Codlin is a stylish tree, beautiful in flower and remarkably heavy in fruit, and as hardy as its geographical origins suggest. It was found behind a wall at Gleaston Castle, a ruin in a field that stands between Ulverston and Barrow-in-Furness, and was first sold in

Keswick Codlin apple

1793 by the nurseryman John Sander of Keswick, who seems to have come up with its name (a codlin being a cooking apple ideal for coddling, like an egg). Its fruit are long, pale green and angular, and their flavour is especially suited to tarts and apple jelly, needing little extra sugar when cooked.

Lane's Prince Albert
before 1841

One of the finest cooking apples, Lane's Prince Albert bears the name of the nurseryman John Lane, once a major employer in the Hertfordshire town of Berkhamsted. But the original tree grew in the front garden of Thomas Squire, who lived with his wife and three daughters in a large house on the high street. According to one version of events, Squire (who according to the 1841 census was a gentleman of independent means) had planted the young tree in 1841, on the very day that the recently married Queen Victoria and Prince Albert visited Berkhamsted, and in a fever of patriotism he named it 'Victoria and Albert'. John Lane is said to have noticed the compact shape of Squire's growing tree, and the heavy crops it bore of orange-striped apples, which turned yellow as they ripened, and he began selling it around 1850 under its new name of Lane's Prince Albert. Lane showed it at the 1857 exhibition of the newly formed British Pomological Society, which must have done wonders for the variety's public profile; in 1872 it won a First Class Certificate from the Royal Horticultural Society. By the 1880s it was widely grown, both by amateur gardeners and in commercial orchards – not only in Britain but also as far away as Eastern Europe.

A small, late-flowering tree with pale green leaves and colourful blossom, it is susceptible to mildew and tends to give good crops only every other year, but its flavour is excellent, cooking to a lemony purée; if picked in mid-October and stored until the following March it makes a refreshing (if rather acid) eater, too. Berkhamsted is still a pleasant place to visit, but Lane's large nursery has long since gone: its site, off Park Street between the high street and the Grand Union Canal, is now occupied by modern housing and a car park. Thomas Squire's original tree could still be seen in a garden in the high street as recently as 1958, but his house was demolished and the old tree was, presumably, destroyed alongside.

Newton Wonder
c. 1870

Many of our best apples originated in chance seedlings, but few of them turned up in quite such peculiar circumstances as the Newton Wonder. According to legend, the original seedling was found, around 1870, by William Taylor, landlord of the Hardinge Arms in King's Newton, Derbyshire, growing in his thatch. It's a lovely story, but like so many others it seems to have been gingered up over the years. In a less romantic version of events the seedling is said to have been discovered growing in a gutter, which seems more likely, given that the roof of the present Hardinge Arms is tiled, not thatched (though perhaps it was in the nineteenth century; thatched houses aren't uncommon in the locality). Nor, it turns out, was William an innkeeper. According to the 1901 census, it was William's elderly mother, Sarah, who actually kept the village beer-house, later to become the Hardinge Arms, and while William appears to have been sharing the house with her and his crippled sister Bessie, he is described as a market gardener, not a publican. Bearing in mind his profession, one does begin to wonder whether the Newton Wonder was found entirely by chance, or whether William Taylor hybridised some seedlings himself; it is said to have been a cross between Dumelow's Seedling and Blenheim Orange, which suggests that someone knew its parentage, unless these were the only other trees growing close enough to have produced cross-pollinated seeds.

If we can believe the rest of the tale, Taylor transplanted the seedling to the orchard behind the pub, and it grew quickly into a sturdy tree with unusually smooth bark, whose large, round, yellow-green apples turned out to cook to a deliciously sweet and fluffy purée. The apples can be picked from mid-October on, but they will keep until the following March or April, and after a few months of careful storage they make an appealingly sharp-flavoured eating apple too. Aptly christened the Newton Wonder, it was introduced commercially in 1887 by J. R. Pearson & Sons of Chilwell, Nottingham, and received a First Class Certificate from the Royal Horticultural Society later the same year. It became one of the most popular of all cooking apples, being less acidic than Bramley's Seedling (which coincidentally was found just a few miles away at Southwell). Newton Wonders are at their best by December, making them perfect as a Christmas ingredient for mincemeat and turkey stuffing.

Although widely grown until relatively recently, in the last half-century the Newton Wonder has steadily lost ground to the now-ubiquitous Bramley, perhaps because of its biennial tendencies: like Lane's Prince Albert, it often has a heavy crop one year but bears fewer fruits the next. It's a very vigorous and easy tree to grow, although the fruit can be prone to suffer from bitter-pit. The Royal Horticultural Society gave the Newton Wonder a second seal of approval as recently as 1993, when it won a coveted Award of Garden Merit.

William Taylor's original tree lived until at least the 1940s, when it was mentioned in *The Apples of England* by the presumably unrelated H. V. Taylor, but while the Hardinge Arms is still going strong, its orchard disappeared beneath new houses in 2004. As for William Taylor himself, he was still (just) alive in 1905, when the *Gardener's Chronicle* reported that it was 'sorry to say that Mr William Taylor, the raiser of Newton Wonder, is very seriously ill, and has not left his bed for several months'. He died the same year at the age of sixty-six.

Nonpareil
before 1696

The first documentary record of Nonpareil dates from 1696, when it was listed by the Brompton Park Nursery in London. This makes it one of the oldest apple varieties still grown, despite wild claims that are occasionally made for others – such as the endlessly recycled tale that Decio dates back to the time of ancient Rome, although there is precious little evidence to indicate that it pre-dates the early twentieth century. As its name suggests, Nonpareil could well have been French in origin, like many apples of the time, although as the Victorian fruit expert Robert Hogg pointed out, its name is puzzlingly absent from seventeenth-century lists of apples compiled in France. The first British description appeared in 1724: writing in *The Practical Fruit Gardener*, Stephen Switzer recorded that 'It is no stranger in England; though it may have its original

Nonpareil apple

from France, yet there are trees of them about the Ashtons in Oxfordshire, of about a hundred years old, which (so they have it by tradition) was [*sic*] first brought out of France and planted by a Jesuit in Queen Mary or Queen Elizabeth's time.' A dessert variety with cinnamon-russet skin, it does best in southern counties, as its full flavour takes time – and lots of late sunshine – to develop. But it is worth waiting for if you want to experience the taste that was so highly esteemed by our seventeenth- and eighteenth-century ancestors: with a fragrance most often compared to fruit drops, its flavour is sharp yet sweet, with firm, almost leathery flesh. The fruit keeps well whether picked or left on the tree, and Hogg records a Mr Fairchild of Hoxton in London who 'has now (February) one of the Nonpareile [*sic*] apples upon a small tree, in a pot, which seems capable of holding good till the blossoms of this year have ripened their fruit'.

Norfolk Beefing
before 1780

If you wanted a quick mid-afternoon pick-me-up in the early nineteenth century, instead of popping out to buy a KitKat or a Mars bar you would probably have scooted over to the local confectioner's and bought yourself a Norfolk Beefing (or Biffin, as they were more commonly known). These leathery, thick-skinned cooking apples, usually eaten cold, were hugely popular, and they were cooked in cooling bread-ovens once the daily bread was done; after many hours of slow baking they developed a rich, spicy taste. They turn up in many books of the time, usually with comic connotations, suggesting that they were considered to be rather down-market, as Charles Dickens evidently regarded them in *Dombey and Son* (1844–6): 'The fruit laboriously gathered from the tree of knowledge by this latter young gentleman, in fact, had been subjected to so much pressure, that it had become a kind of intellectual Norfolk Biffin, and had nothing of its original form or flavour remaining.' If their disappearance from popular literature is anything to go by, they began to lose favour in the second half of the nineteenth century, though the occasional Biffin could still be found at Norwich market as late as the 1950s. The original slow food, healthy and sustaining, they surely deserve a revival. Although their origins are lost in the mists of time, Norfolk Beefings are known to date back to at least the late eighteenth century, and there is an intriguing if inconclusive mention of a 'Beefing' in a fruit notebook which dates from 1698, owned by the Walpole family of Norfolk. There are actually two types: the original Norfolk Beefing and the Striped Beefing, a larger kind – presumably a natural 'sport' or mutation – that was discovered in the Norwich garden of one William Crowe around 1794. The original variety has pale green skin which flushes to an apoplectic purple in the sun, and is a superb keeper: if picked in mid-October and stored carefully it can be kept till the following June.

Pitmaston Pine Apple
1785?

Yet another apple with rather convoluted origins, the wonderfully named Pitmaston Pine Apple seems to have first been shown at the Horticultural Society of London in 1845 by the notable fruit breeder John Williams of Pitmaston House in Worcester. Although Williams raised many other varieties, including the Pitmaston Duchess pear, the Pine Apple is said to have been originally grown around 1785 by a Mr White at Witley Court, just a few miles north-west of Worcester. White was steward to Lord Foley, owner of both Witley and Stoke Edith, a grand mansion east of Hereford, which has confused several writers into stating that it was raised in

Herefordshire rather than Worcestershire. If it really dates back to 1785 then it's hard to understand why such a remarkable variety, with its distinctive pineapple fragrance, should have taken around sixty years to come to public attention, for news of new varieties normally spread fast, even back then. We will probably never know the full story of the Pitmaston Pine Apple, although it's conceivable that the Foley estate papers in the Herefordshire Record Office might contain an explanation. A small, late-ripening dessert variety with finely russeted skin, at its best it has sweet, crisp yellow flesh with a nutty flavour and a wonderful pineapple scent, although its quality can be variable.

Ribston Pippin
c. 1709

Before the rise of Cox's Orange Pippin, no eating apple was more popular or more widely planted than the Ribston Pippin. It originated at Ribston Hall, the Goodricke family's imposing mansion near Knaresborough in North Yorkshire, though its ancestors may have come from Normandy – at least according to an undated letter written by a Miss Clough, who spent her early years at Ribston Hall. She recorded that:

Ribston Pippin apple

These pippins were sent to Sir Henry Goodricke (4th Bart.) from Normandy about the year 1709, only one of them succeeded, and from that all the Ribston Pippins have descended. The Ribston Pippin came from Normandy about the beginning of last century; my great grand-father Sir Henry

Goodricke, had a friend abroad who sent him three pippins in a letter, which being sown two came to nothing; the present old tree at Ribston is the produce of the third of these pippins, and have been transplanted into all parts.

Like most new varieties it appears to have been first taken up by a local nursery, in this case rather a smart one, run by William Perfect, later Mayor of Pontefract. Perfect supplied plants to large estates in the north of England, and the first recorded mention of Ribston Pippins is in his 1769 catalogue. By 1775 Ribstons were being sold by the Brompton Park Nursery, London's leading horticulturalists, and during the course of the nineteenth century they were planted all over the country and their fame spread as far as New Zealand and Nova Scotia.

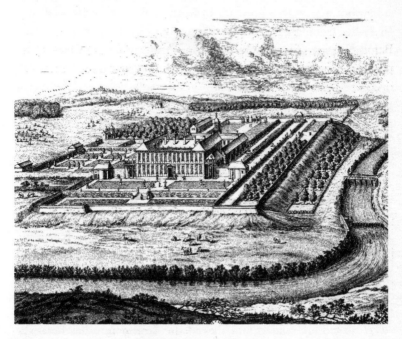

Ribston Hall and its orchards c. 1715

So what made the Ribston Pippin so universally popular? Its flavour, which is the true taste of the nineteenth century: rich and complex, like an especially good dessert wine. Though it looks quite similar to the Cox's Orange Pippin, the Ribston's flavour is far more intense (Cox's Orange is thought to have had a Ribston Pippin in its parentage), and it is slightly less juicy when fully ripe, but far more aromatic, a quality that was particularly prized by our Victorian forebears.

Ribston Hall still stands, though it was sold to the Dent family in 1836, and within a fenced enclosure in the grounds an offshoot of the original Ribston Pippin tree still grows. Its predecessors had an unfortunate tendency to succumb to the powerful gales that Ribston Hall is evidently prone to: the primal tree was blown flat in 1810, but branches grew up from its prostrate trunk. It was dead by 1835, but a new tree grew up from the base, which by 1906 was sixty-five feet high; this survived intact until 1928, when along came another storm and flattened it. From this second tree, which clung on to life until 1932, grew the trunk of the present tree.

Tom Putt
1700s

Though mostly used for making cider, this much-loved old West Country variety makes a crisp, refreshing eating apple and cooks well too. There are two stories about its origins. It seems to have been raised in the late eighteenth century, either by the Reverend Thomas Putt, who was rector in the pretty village of Trent (then in Somerset but now in Dorset) from 1802 until around 1835, or by his uncle, Sir Thomas Putt, a barrister and owner of the Combe House estate at Gittisham, near Honiton in Devon. The fact that the Putts were so closely related and shared the same name has been the source of endless confusion since, especially as the Reverend Putt was one of many family members to inherit a life interest in the Combe estate after his uncle's death in 1787; he was living at Combe House in the year of the 1841 census, by which time he was eighty years old. Although both accounts seem equally plausible, it may be suggestive that the 1889 Ordnance Survey map of Trent shows the rectory surrounded by orchards, and the 1915 edition of the long-running *Notes and Queries for Somerset and Dorset* noted that 'In the S.E. corner of the garden at Trent Rectory, Somerset, now in the Administrative County of Dorset, is still to be seen an old Tom Putt apple tree.' On the other hand, an 1891 map of Gittisham shows numerous orchards too, so the evidence remains frustratingly inconclusive. One could hazard a guess that the Reverend Tom either found the apple at Gittisham and introduced it to Trent, or raised it there and brought it back to Combe, but unless the Putt family records (preserved in the Devon Record Office) reveal the truth, a guess it must remain.

The variety's popularity can be ascribed not only to its versatility, but also because Tom Putts make small but hardy trees, bearing heavy crops even in wet and windy situations. The red-striped apples are attractive to look at, too. Combe House is now a smart hotel, while Trent has changed little since 1935, when the entire village and its surroundings were bought by the Ernest Cook Trust, which still owns it today.

Worcester Pearmain
c. 1870

Brilliantly coloured and deliciously fragrant at its best, the Worcester Pearmain is one of our most attractive apples. Like Beauty of Bath and Irish Peach, it is an early ripener, and like them it is markedly scented, with rather soft flesh, often flushed with pink. It was first marketed by the firm of Richard Smith and Company, which had good claim, in the nineteenth century, to be the largest nursery in the world. Based in St John's, just across the River Severn from Worcester, it extended to 157 acres on either side of Malvern Road, almost completely surrounding Pitmaston House, home of the Pitmaston Pine Apple and the Pitmaston Duchess pear. The St John's Nurseries were founded by Thomas Smith, but it was his son and grandson, both called Richard, who built up the business from the 1820s on. At its peak the nursery employed 200 staff and boasted twenty-eight kilometres (eighteen miles) of pathways, several acres of greenhouses and a central avenue more than two kilometres (2,300 yards) long.

The Worcester Pearmain appears to have turned up as one of two seedlings around 1870, in a small market garden at Swan Pool (now Swanpool Walk), said to have been owned by William Hale. (Some accounts say John Hale, but William seems most likely: William Hale is listed in the 1861 census as a 52-year-old head gardener, living at 4 Bush Lane (now Bush Walk), across the road from Swan Pool; there are no records of a John Hale, Hales, Hailes or any similiar surname in the Worcester area for the mid- to late nineteenth century.) Swan Pool was midway between St John's Nurseries and the main bridge across the Severn into Worcester, so Richard Smith must have passed Hale's gardens regularly, and it isn't hard to imagine how the trees – one of which had yellow apples, the other brilliant red – caught his eye, even if Smith and Hale were not already known to one another. The story goes that Richard Smith offered William Hale £10 in return for exclusive rights to take grafts from the tree with bright red fruit. It must have sounded like a good deal to Hale, but Smith made an excellent return on his investment. The Worcester Pearmain, as Smith named it ('pearmain' apples have a slightly pear-like shape), was an immediate success, winning a First Class Certificate from the Royal Horticultural Society in 1875, and it became one of the most popular eating apples of its time; in 1876 Smith was selling the young trees for a guinea each. Although it is still fairly widely available, the Worcesters that appear in the shops today in early to mid-September have usually been picked when they are under-ripe, which is why they often taste bland and characterless. A real, tree-ripened Worcester is a very different thing: with its intense colour and wonderful strawberry scent, it is one of those apples that really repays the trouble of growing your own.

Richard Smith and Company continued trading into the twentieth century, although the firm slowly sold off its land for housing, and finally closed for ever in 1993. But the Worcester Pearmain lives on, in other apples too, for it has proved to be an excellent parent: among the modern varieties bred from Worcester stock are Elton Beauty, Lord Lambourne and Discovery.

Beetroot

Shiryaev's short, fat neck turned suddenly red as a beetroot.
The colour mounted slowly to his ears, from his ears to his
temples, and by degrees suffused his whole face.

Anton Chekhov, *The Wife* (1895)

lthough people have been eating beetroot leaves (often
called leaf beet) for thousands of years, swollen-rooted
beetroots seem to have been unknown – or at least unmen-
tioned – before the sixteenth century. The first clear descriptions of
what we would recognise as beetroot date from the 1530s, and even
forty years later they were still being referred to as new and rare.
Large-rooted beetroot may have originated in Italy, at that time a
great centre for fruit and vegetable cultivation, and certainly the
earliest widely grown variety was known as Roman Beet, which
suggests Italian origins. In his famous *Herball, or Generall Historie of
Plantes*, first published in London in 1597, John Gerard mentions both
'white' (that is, leaf) beet and 'another sort . . . that was brought unto
me from beyond the seas', whose 'red and beautiful root (which is to
be preferred before the leaves, as well in beautie as in goodnesse) I
refer unto the curious and cunning cooke, who no doubt when hee

had the view thereof, and is assured that it is both good and whole-some, will make thereof many and divers dishes, both faire and good'. Gerard's account suggests that his contemporaries were not yet familiar with root beet, but by the time John Parkinson was writing in 1629 he was able to report that 'The roote of the common red Beete with some, but more especially the Romane red Beete, is of much use among Cookes to trimme or set out their dishes of meate, being cut into divers formes and fashions, and is grown of late dayes into a custome of service, both of fish and flesh.'

Beetroot was taken up with particular relish in Germany; in fact some accounts suggest that the root varieties actually originated there, rather than in Italy. Whatever the truth of this, we do know that from Germany it spread north and east, into Scandinavia, Russia, Poland and Ukraine, where it was to have an important influence in cooking (most notably in borscht, the delicious beetroot soup). Despite John Parkinson's enthusiasm, beetroot seems to have been rather slow to catch on in Britain. Before 1800 only two varieties were available in this country, the Red Roman and the Long Red, and according to the biologist, film critic and all-round beetroot expert Stephen Nottingham, it was regarded as something of a novelty until the nineteenth century; he mentions an intriguing eighteenth-century recipe for red beetroot biscuits, which must be ready for a revival.

Beetroot may not have made much of an impression on eighteenth-century cuisine, but in its own way it did help to end slavery, which is more than can be said for most vegetables. In the 1740s a German chemist, Andreas Sigismund Marggraf, examined the crystals that formed in beetroot syrup and realised that they were identical to the sucrose crystals obtained from sugar cane. It was an exciting discovery, because it offered a chance to break the monopoly that France and Britain then held over sugar production, which came from their hugely profitable slave plantations in the West Indies. Although Marggraf's beetroot syrup yielded far less sucrose than sugar cane, one of his students, Franz Achard, managed to increase sugar yields from beetroot to an economically viable level by the early years of the nineteenth century. He did this in two ways: by improving the extraction process, but also by raising a new variety of beetroot that contained more sugar than previous kinds, the Weisse Schlesiche, or White Silesian (still the ancestor of most sugar beet grown today). In the end, though, the biggest boost to the sugar-beet trade came, ironically, from France, not Germany. In response to the British blockade of French shipping from the West Indies during the Napoleonic Wars, Napoleon backed a move to increase sugar-beet production in France and the areas of Germany then under French control. Although this had little immediate impact on the British monopoly, by the time the wars were over a combination of over-production, increased sugar-beet output and the growing disquiet over the slave trade led to a collapse in cane-sugar prices, and the eventual break-up of the slave plantations. By the end of the nineteenth century, beetroot supplied more than half the international market in sugar, and although cane sugar has since made something of a comeback, sugar beet still accounts for something like two-fifths of the global supply.

While sugar beet was doing its bit for emancipation, culinary beetroot was gradually infiltrating the kitchen. The Victorians found it particularly to their liking, cutting it into fancy shapes for salads and even rinsing their hair in beetroot juice (something some people still do), and many new varieties were developed, most of them for use through the winter; summer beetroot was largely a twentieth-century innovation. As so often, nineteenth-century cooks could choose from a far wider range of shapes and sizes than are generally available today, from the squashed-looking Egyptian Turnip-Rooted and the long-rooted Cheltenham Green Top to the decorative, curly-leaved Bull's Blood.

Bull's Blood
before 1900

With its striking deep-red leaves that verge on black, Bull's Blood was often planted in ornamental bedding schemes (and indeed still is at Osborne House on the Isle of Wight), but its tender young roots have an excellent flavour of their own – although like many kinds of beetroot it becomes woody and fibrous with age. This variety certainly pre-dates 1900, and the heritage seed specialist Thomas Etty believes it could be synonymous with Blood Red Hamburgh, which was sold from the late 1870s by Sutton's Seeds. Its broad, curly-edged leaves are good for eating too, either used young in salads or steamed – they have a notably sweet taste when cooked. It withstands hot conditions better than many other old cultivars, which have a tendency to bolt in unseasonably warm weather.

Cheltenham Green Top
before 1883

In the late nineteenth century the plain around Cheltenham was covered with market gardens, which utilised the rich soil to grow all kinds of produce, not just for local use but also for the large urban markets within easy reach thanks to the opening of the Bristol and Birmingham railway. Beetroot was an important winter crop by this time, and an 1889 report in the *Gardener's Chronicle*, recorded by Thomas Etty, describes the Cheltenham Green Top as 'a very valuable variety of beet . . . scarcely any other is grown in the market gardens around Cheltenham'. Its long ruby-red roots give it the look of an embarrassed parsnip, but its pink-stemmed green tops are more reminiscent of the puzzlingly fashionable Swiss chard (which of course is botanically the same plant). Although the Cheltenham Green Top can be maddeningly slow to raise from seed, it crops well on decent soil. It is one of the sweetest varieties, although some people consider the texture of its deep-pink flesh a little coarse.

Egyptian Turnip-Rooted
before 1849

This curling stone-shaped beetroot may well have originated in Egypt, and was first noted by the famous French seed firm Vilmorin in 1849; by the 1870s it was well known in Britain too. With its low profile and modest leafage it seems perfectly designed for growing in cold frames, and its relatively shallow roots make it especially suitable for growing on thin soils – although it also needs watering more than most varieties. But the extra effort is worth it, for the Egyptian Turnip-Rooted is fast to grow and has intensely deep-red flesh with a delicious flavour, either for cooking or using raw in salads. It is not to be confused with Crosby's Egyptian, which is round in shape and American in origin.

Egyptian Turnip-Rooted beetroot

Rouge Crapaudine
before 1856

Despite its slightly unfortunate name, Crapaudine is an excellent if slow-growing old French beet, which was already being sold in Britain before the end of the nineteenth century. Like the Egyptian Turnip-Rooted beetroot it pre-dates the 1850s, making it one of the oldest varieties known. In France it is sometimes known as Rouge Ecorce au Crapaudine, after its craggy, blackened, pitted and warty-looking skin. But don't be discouraged by its eccentric appearance and its often misshapen roots, for its bright-red flesh is firm and very sweet.

Broad Beans

Hallo, old bean . . .
P. G. Wodehouse, *Indiscretions of Archie* (1921)

B road beans are very, very old. So old, in fact, that they seem to have outlived their wild forebears, for no wild ancestor has ever been found and it has almost certainly long been extinct. They were probably domesticated between five and seven thousand years ago, somewhere in the Middle East, and by the earliest days of recorded history they were being grown as far apart as Greece, Germany and Spain. Ancient broad beans were black, but paler kinds began to appear in Roman times – which was handy, as the Romans used beans to cast votes in their elections: white for yes and black for no. The Romans (or their minions) also seem to have developed the larger beans that we recognise today.

Broad beans had everything going for them. They were easy to grow, productive, nutritious, tolerant of a wide range of conditions, from the Nile delta to the upper reaches of the Rhine, and they could also be dried and stored for use right through the winter. Their ubiquity, in the centuries before other kinds of beans crossed the Atlantic from America, is hard to imagine now, but they were a staple food for millions, and their wind-producing effects must have contributed their own individual fragrance to the rich olfactory mix of the past. By the eighteenth century, British gardeners had many named varieties to choose from, roughly divided into 'Windsors' and 'Long Pods' – Windsor pods normally containing two to four beans and Long Pods between five and eight – but a field trial conducted by the Horticultural Society of London in 1831 revealed that 'only eleven kinds of Beans can be distinguished amongst forty-three reputed varieties'. This was a common problem right through to the early twentieth century, and not just among beans.

Considering their immense antiquity, surprisingly few really old varieties of broad bean are still with us, with the notable exception of Martock, which, if the stories are true, may date back to the Middle Ages, making it the oldest single cultivar in this book.

Bunyard's Exhibition
before 1880s

Grown in the kitchen gardens at West Dean and the Lost Gardens of Heligan, Bunyard's Exhibition is a tall, heavy-cropping long-pod variety with up to eight pale-green beans in each pod, which have a good sweet flavour. When it acquired its current name is uncertain, but it may be an 'improved' form of an older variety called Johnson's Wonderful, which dates back to the 1830s. Bunyard's was one of the leading Victorian fruit nurseries, based at Allington, near Maidstone in Kent. Founded in 1796, it became famous especially for its apples, including such favourites as the Christmas Pearmain. Edward Bunyard, who inherited the family firm in the late nineteenth century, became a noted gourmet, but his love of wine, fruit and roses – which he wrote enthusiastically about in a series of books – drew him away from business and increasingly into debt. On 19 October 1939, on the brink of bankruptcy, he blew his brains out in his room at the Royal Societies Club in London.

Crimson Flowered
1700s

Said to date back to the late eighteenth century, the Crimson Flowered broad bean sounds remarkably similar, if not identical, to the Red Blossomed bean described in the 1831 report of the Horticultural Society of London, even as far as its variable flowers:

Stem about four and a half feet high. Blossoms varying, sometimes of a light red, at others of a dark crimson colour. Pods short and much pointed, seldom containing more than three Beans, which are small, short, and thick, of a rusty white colour when ripe. This is only fit for ornament; it is but a moderate bearer, and will not keep long after gathering, as it soon turns black.

As an ornamental, indeed, it makes an appealing addition to the flower border, but that is not to say its edible qualities should be ignored. Perhaps our nineteenth-century predecessors were more picky, or the plants that have come down to us represent an improved strain, but 'modern' Crimson Flowered beans have a surprisingly delicate flavour, as long as they are picked young. Experimental cooks might like to try its tender young leaves and flowers, too.

Green Windsor
before 1754

Another old variety, Green Windsor gets its name from the colour of its beans, which stay green even when they are mature. Although some of the beans sold as Green Windsor today have long pods, the pods of the true Green Windsor are short, and each contain just three or four large beans. There are numerous 'improved' versions of Green Windsor, but few can match it for flavour, which surely accounts for its long survival. It was well known by the early eighteenth century, and was recommended by Philip Miller in the 1754 edition of his

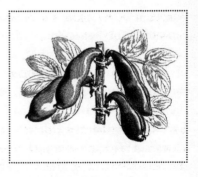

Green Windsor bean

Gardener's Dictionary. 'The Windsor Bean', Miller writes:

is allowed to be the best of all the Sorts for the Table: when these are planted on a good Soil, and are allowed sufficient room, their Pods will be very large, and in great Plenty; and when they are gathered young, are the sweetest and best tasted of all the Sorts: but these should be carefully saved, by pulling out such of the Plants as are not perfectly right; and afterward by sorting out all the good from the bad Beans.

Good advice, and still worth following.

Martock
1200s?

The line between fact and fiction, as every historian knows, tends to become blurred over the centuries, and the history of the Martock bean is as puzzling as it is alleged to be long. It is said that it dates back as far as the thirteenth century, and that it was once widely grown in Somerset – the Martock of its name is an ancient one-time market town west of Yeovil. It certainly looks old: a short but upright plant with white flowers and variable blotches of purple, it bears small, rather unappealing brown beans. The oft-repeated story goes that, while it disappeared from common cultivation, a few ancient Martock beans survived in the gardens of the Bishop's Palace at Wells, where they had been grown since the Middle Ages as a food for passing travellers; in some versions the beans were given as a thank you to those who donated funds for the cathedral. It's a cheery yarn, but sadly I have failed to find a scrap of evidence to support it, either at the Bishop's Palace or in the Somerset county archives. The story's origins, for now at least, are as mysterious as the bean itself, although the paper trail appears to point towards the late founder of Garden Organic, Lawrence Hills. What does seem true, though, is that the town of Martock was always famous for its beans. In a manuscript written in the 1730s (now in the Somerset county archives) the antiquarian and pioneering geologist John Strachey, of Sutton Court near Stowey, recorded that 'Beans are more abundant in the marshy parts more particularly about Martock where 'tis a proverb, "Take a Martock man by the collar and shake him, and you will hear the beans rattle in his belly", which being told to one of that country he readily replyed [*sic*] it might be true but twas but few that could trye the experiment.' Whether the proverb holds true today, I cannot say.

The Sutton
1923

A cross between two older varieties, Exhibition Longpod and Beck's Green Gem, The Sutton (also known as Sutton Dwarf) was introduced in 1923 by Sutton's Seeds of Reading. Hardy, fast growing and early to mature but only thirty centimetres (one foot) tall, this bushy bean is ideal for growing either where space is limited or in exposed places where wind would damage taller crops.

It bears dependably heavy crops of medium-sized pods, each containing five or six small but tender beans. The Sutton won an Award of Garden Merit from the Royal Horticultural Society in 1993, which was reconfirmed after further field trials in 1999.

Brussels Sprouts

During rehearsals for *Peter Pan*, J. M. Barrie ordered Brussels sprouts every day for lunch, but never ate them. When his friend, the painter William Nicholson, asked him why, Barrie explained: 'I cannot resist ordering them. The words are so lovely to say.'

William Nicholson (painter and set designer for the
original production of *Peter Pan*), *The Sunday Referee*
(5 December 1931)

Although you wouldn't think it to look at them, Brussels sprouts descend from the same species of wild cabbage, *Brassica oleracea*, as cauliflower, broccoli, kohlrabi and kale. Their differences may be striking, but let any of these crops go to seed and their common ancestor reappears. Left to open, broccoli and cauliflower heads turn out to have been just densely packed cabbage flowers all along, while Brussels sprouts unfurl to reveal that they are nothing more than cabbage leaves in tight bud. The process also works (after a fashion) in reverse: cut the top off a regular cabbage and lax little 'sprouts' will form down the stem.

The history of the Brussels sprout is maddeningly vague. Some authorities claim that Brussels sprouts have been around practically for ever, citing references that date back, in some cases, to the thirteenth century. Others have unhelpfully pointed out how ambiguous these references are, and given that there are no clear botanical descriptions of what we'd recognise as sprouts until the mid-eighteenth century, it seems most likely that they were developed then – probably as a chance mutation from a savoy-type cabbage or what's now called Cottager's Kale. What's fairly certain is that they originated around Brussels and were hardly known outside France and Belgium until the nineteenth century: as late as 1875 a popular British gardening encyclopedia could claim that 'Of this excellent vegetable we have only one pure sort.' It took several decades for sprouts to catch on in this country, and it wasn't until the early twentieth century that they established themselves across the Atlantic. In their early days they were regarded as something of a delicacy, which may seem odd to anyone who hated Brussels sprouts as a child, and even now some residual snobbery attaches to their size. Gourmets claim that smaller sprouts are more tasty, with a nutty flavour that is lost in larger specimens; their flavour is also supposed to be enhanced by frost. According to research conducted by the University of Georgia, refined Europeans like their sprouts to be around 1.25cm (half an inch) in diameter, while size-obsessed Americans prefer theirs to be between 2.5 and 5cm (one to two inches).

Several British varieties were developed in the late nineteenth and early twentieth centuries, but most of the older, open-pollinated varieties have since been supplanted by F1 hybrids. (F1 hybrids are varieties whose characters can be guaranteed, as they are the result of a first-generation cross between two different but stable varieties, giving the same resulting hybrid each time.) This is not just an example of pointless modernisation: as Charles Darwin noted, brassicas of all kinds readily interbreed, and to keep seed of one variety pure it must be isolated from other brassicas nearby – so saving seed can be a tricky business, especially when the recommended 'isolation distance' between different varieties of brassicas is between 500 metres and one kilometre. Luckily a few old varieties still survive, preserved by careful growers. Unlike F1 varieties, whose sprouts are ready to harvest at the same time, open-pollinated sprouts mature from the bottom of the stem to the top, which is useful if you are growing them for your own use.

Bedford Fillbasket
before 1925

Sandy soil, the Great Northern Railway and, it is said, gargantuan heaps of virtually free horse-manure from London combined from the 1860s onwards to make Bedfordshire one of the great market gardens of Britain, and Brussels sprouts – then still quite a novelty – rapidly became one of the county's major exports, steadily supplanting onions. It has been estimated that by 1926 around 40 per cent of Britain's Brussels were being grown in Bedfordshire, where they were often interplanted with potatoes and provided a useful winter income. Although Worcester and Hertford became important Brussels-growing areas too, Bedford's domination of the British sprout market continued right up until the Second World War, with 10,332 acres devoted to the crop – double the second-largest acreage, in Worcestershire. Bedford Fillbasket dates from these glory days, and although there seems to be no record on its introduction, it certainly pre-dates 1925. Its longevity can be ascribed to several things: as its name suggests, this long-stalked variety produces a heavy crop of extra-large sprouts, which, despite their size, stay solid and retain their flavour.

Evesham Special
before 1926

Second only to Bedford in the sprout-growing stakes, Worcestershire also boasts light soil and direct rail connections to the London markets, but in the days when early crops commanded the highest prices it had an added advantage: the sheltered microclimate in the Vale of Evesham, giving its market gardeners the chance to harvest ahead of the competition. Evesham Special, however, is noted for its hardiness, and grows into a sturdy plant of middling size which bears a heavy crop of large, firm sprouts. It was first listed by the long-established nursery firm of Watkins & Simpson in 1926, and assessed by the Royal Horticultural Society at their Wisley trial grounds two years later. Although no longer grown on a commercial scale, it remains a popular garden variety.

Wroxton
1895

Wroxton dates from the period when the sprout was still a gentleman's vegetable. It was originally developed by Lord North's head gardener, Mr Findlay, who ran the kitchen gardens at North's Jacobean country house, Wroxton Abbey, near Banbury in Oxfordshire. Introduced to the wider market in 1895, Wroxton quickly made its name as one of the first so-called dwarf varieties: given that it grows over a metre tall, standard Victorian sprouts were obviously huge. A talented head gardener, Findlay also introduced the Wroxton onion, but the Norths were less successful than their sprouts: the family fell on hard times and had to sell up. Since 1965 Wroxton Abbey has been the British campus of the New Jersey-based Fairleigh Dickinson University.

Cabbages

'Eat your greens!'
Unpopular saying

Of all the vegetables in this book, cabbages are perhaps the least glamorous, with the possible exception of turnips. Maybe this explains why the history of individual varieties is so sparse: while the introduction of a delicious new apple might be cause for general rejoicing, the launch of a new type of cabbage is unlikely to generate such widespread celebration. Which is a shame, since cabbage, as every mother knows, is one of the healthiest vegetables you can eat. What it isn't – and what it has probably never been – is fashionable. Cheap, nutritious and capable of being grown right through the year, cabbage was for centuries a staple food of the poor, and its association with poverty seems to have sunk deep into the collective unconscious. Its strong taste and unsociable after-effects are unlikely to have helped either.

Yet the wild cabbage, *Brassica oleracea*, is an extraordinary beast. For this rather unremarkable-looking plant, which you can still see growing wild on the cliffs of North Wales, Dorset, Sussex and Kent, has given us cabbages, kale, Brussels sprouts, broccoli, cauliflower and kohlrabi, all thanks to several hundred years of careful cultivation. Yet each of these strikingly different crops will revert to wild cabbages within a generation or two if their pollen is allowed to mix, undoing centuries of painstaking selection in a matter of months – a sobering demonstration of just how important it is to conserve the wealth of varieties we have inherited from the past, and how easily they can be lost.

Like so many other crops, cabbages were probably brought to Britain by the Romans, who certainly recognised their health benefits. At least until the sixteenth century, and probably well beyond that, the cabbages that most people grew are likely to have been more like lax-headed kale than the solid-hearted cabbages we're accustomed to today. But there were new developments abroad. Germany's long-standing importance as a centre of cabbage culture is attested by the vast range of cabbage-related recipes still in general circulation there, and it's thought that both red and white varieties were being grown in the region in early medieval times. Savoy cabbages, whose wrinkly leaves have a disconcerting resemblance to tripe, may also have originated in Germany in the early sixteenth century, although it is possible that they are much older. Their name suggests a French or northern Italian origin, and they were growing in France by the 1540s, owing, it is said, to Henri II's Florentine queen Catherine de Medici, whose cooks also imported such delicacies as garden peas and artichokes – an appealing story, even if it has only the most tenuous connection to historical fact.

Although there must have been much low-level cabbage breeding in Britain, their cultivated cousins don't appear to have been introduced to this country until the sixteenth century. Writing in 1699, John Evelyn, the diarist and heir to a gunpowder fortune, claimed: 'Tis scarce an hundred Years since we first had Cabbages out of Holland. Sir Anth. Ashley of Wiburg [*sic*] St. Giles in Dorsetshire, being (as I am told) the first who planted them in

England.' As loose-leafed kale-like cabbages were already widely grown (and had been described by William Turner in 1551), Evelyn must be referring to more sophisticated cabbages such as savoys, but either way, Sir Anthony Ashley's role in cabbage history is an intriguing one. Secretary to the Council of War under Elizabeth I, he joined the Earl of Essex in the spectacular sack of Cadiz in 1596, and it is perfectly possible he brought back new varieties of cabbage with him, either from Spain or from his travels elsewhere, to be grown in his gardens at Wimborne St Giles in Dorset. His canopied tomb (erected by his son-in-law, the first Earl of Shaftesbury) is tucked behind the altar screen in the village church, and includes an extremely unusual feature: a polyhedron, supported by a pair of mailed hands, which projects from the foot of Sir Anthony's effigy. It has long been taken locally to represent a heraldic cabbage. While it's a tempting idea, a less romantic – and, let's face it, rather more plausible – interpretation maintains that it commemorates Ashley's interest in geometry and navigation.

By the nineteenth century there were many different varieties of cabbage, such as Atkin's Matchless, Battersea and Enfield Market, though as *The New Practical Gardener and Modern Horticulturalist* pointed out in 1875: 'The seedsmen's catalogues exhibit a number of names more than we have enumerated . . . but it is to be questioned whether they do not merely exist in name only.' Charles Darwin was fascinated by cabbages as by so much else, and warns of their wanton promiscuity in *The Variation of Plants and Animals Under Domestication* (1868), noting that 'great care must be taken to prevent the crossing of the different kinds. To give proof of this: I raised 233 seedlings from cabbages of different kinds, which had purposely been planted near each other, and of the seedlings no less than 155 were plainly deteriorated and mongrelised; nor were the remaining 78 all perfectly true.' Darwin makes the interesting observation: 'It may be doubted whether many permanent varieties have been formed by intentional or accidental crosses, for such crossed plants are found to be very inconstant.' In other words, unlike many other kinds of vegetables and fruit, distinct varieties of cabbages are almost certain to have been the result of sustained and careful selection, rather than having appeared by happy accident in the form of chance seedlings. That we now have so many different types – drum-headed or flat; round, oval, pointed or conical; winter, spring, summer, autumn; red, white, green; savoy – is a testament to generation after generation of dedicated gardeners. Few of us give cabbages a second thought, but it is actually a minor miracle that a handful of old varieties have survived at all.

Brunswick
1800s

Also known as Early Dutch and Early Drumhead (an example of the multiple names that so irritated *The New Practical Gardener*), Brunswick has been grown in Britain since at least the early nineteenth century. Its name suggests German origins – Brunswick being the former name of the north German city and region of Braunschweig, east of Hanover – but like many varieties it may well have arrived via Holland, which would account for one of its alternative names.

Brunswick is a short, easy-to-grow, hardy cabbage with dark green leaves and a 'flat' or drum-headed shape, and does well in a wide range of soil types and climates. If its seed is sown in February and the plants are cosseted it can grow to a giant size by September, with huge solid heads weighing three to four kilograms each. Brunswick stores well, and like many cabbages its

Short-stemmed Brunswick cabbage

flavour is said to be improved by a touch of frost. An excellent variety for both sauerkraut and coleslaw.

Christmas Drumhead
c. 1880

Despite its name, this small but fast-growing cabbage is a hardy late variety, which can generally be harvested from October onwards. Introduced at some time in the late nineteenth century, it is one of the most popular 'heritage' varieties, being dependable and easy to grow, with solid, flattened heads (like a drum, hence its name) and blue-green leaves. More than that, unfortunately, it is impossible to say, for like all too many cabbages its earlier history remains obscure.

January King
before 1867

This pan-European cabbage was introduced from France in the second half of the nineteenth century, where it was known as Pontoise or chou Milan de l'Hermitage. January King is a large, sweet-flavoured winter cabbage with attractive blue-green, almost metallic leaves, often tinged with red and crimped around their edges like a savoy. Among the hardiest of all varieties, it is virtually impervious to frost, making it ideally suited to cold, exposed areas. The crisp, compact heads take time to mature, but can usually be harvested between October and February, although they can be left in the ground till March. In Germany it is known as Blaugrüner.

Jersey Walking Stick
before 1830

In the nineteenth century this bizarre-looking kale was grown extensively in the Channel Isles, where it was sometimes induced to reach five and a half metres (eighteen feet) in height with the help of careful tending and liberal applications of evil-smelling seaweed. As its name suggests, it had a practical as well as a gastronomic use: after a year, or sometimes two years of growth – during which time the lower leaves were stripped off and generally fed to sheep – the long, woody stalk was dried, varnished and laboriously fashioned into rather knobbly, hollow walking sticks. More, perhaps, to be regarded as a novelty than a serious crop, it would certainly raise a smile on the average allotment, although the knowledge that its leaves were used as sheep fodder (apparently it gave them lovely silky wool) hardly inspires culinary confidence.

Myatt's Offenham
c. 1897

This dark-green, conical cabbage offers a fascinating if little-known footnote to a remarkable horticultural family, the Myatts of south London. It was raised by James Myatt around 1897, in the village of Offenham, near Evesham in Worcestershire, and has long been highly regarded for its vigour and its resistance to bolting. Myatt had moved to Offenham in 1852 at the age of forty-eight, but he was born in London, in the hamlet of Loughborough, which then stood in open fields between the villages of Camberwell and Brixton and is now commemorated in the names of Loughborough Road and Loughborough Junction station. We have his far-sighted father, Joseph, to thank for the fact that we cook rhubarb as a dessert instead of taking it as a medicine (a story that is more fully told later in this book), although in his own day Joseph Myatt was better known for his strawberries, especially the patriotically named British Queen. The Myatts had market gardens in Deptford and Camberwell, but by the 1840s the phenomenal rate of new house building in the capital was putting ever greater pressure on open fields like theirs. Luckily it seems to have dawned on James Myatt that the equally explosive expansion of the railway network offered a brilliant opportunity to move their business out of London altogether. The coming of the railways meant that, for the first time in history, fresh produce could be grown at long distances from its final market, and Myatt lost no time in seizing his chance. In 1852 he leased twenty-eight hectares (seventy acres) of fertile alluvial land outside Offenham, just months after Evesham station opened on the newly built Worcester to Oxford line, offering easy access to the London market Myatt knew so well. By all accounts the move was a success, and Myatt seems to have concentrated on the high-margin crops his father was already famous for, such as asparagus, rhubarb and strawberries (including, one hopes, his father's own varieties of Victoria rhubarb and British Queen strawberry), but he was obviously not above growing cabbages, for which succeeding generations of gardeners have been duly grateful.

Ormskirk
c. 1899

A fine savoy cabbage with deeply wrinkled leaves, Ormskirk was presumably raised around the ancient market town of Ormskirk in Lancashire, but little more seems to be known about it apart from the fact that it was introduced around 1899. As befits a Lancastrian cabbage, it is tolerant of severe winters and can be harvested later than most other varieties.

Shetland Kale
1600s?

The Shetland Kale – which is actually a hearting cabbage rather than a loose-leafed kale – is perhaps the only British crop to be associated with its own specialist building (with the arguable exception of Yorkshire's brick rhubarb-forcing sheds). The young seedlings were once raised in 'plantie-crubs', small dry-stone-walled enclosures, roughly circular in shape, which protected them from foraging sheep and the salt-laden winds that whip across their exposed and treeless homeland. A scattering of plantie-crubs can still be found across the islands, and Shetland Kale continues to be popular, although some people find its slightly bitter taste (closer to kale than modern cabbage) rather strong. No one is really sure how long it has been grown on Shetland, despite claims that it was introduced in the seventeenth century around the time of Oliver Cromwell, but it is a quite distinct variety, and probably formed the staple vegetable crop on the islands before potatoes arrived in the early eighteenth century. Seeds would be planted in their plantie-crubs in August, then (gales and rogue sheep permitting) the young plants would be transferred to larger, walled 'kale yards' the following spring. There they would stay for another year and a half, for Shetland Kale – while as hardy as one might expect of such a northerly crop – is painfully slow-growing, and only forms its large, dense hearts in the winter of its second year. Most were harvested and cooked or, in the past, preserved in barrels of salt like sauerkraut, but a few of the best plants were always kept for seed for the following year.

Wheeler's Imperial
before 1846

George Wheeler set up a nursery in the small market town of Warminster, Wiltshire, in 1773, supplying the local town and its surrounding gentry (such as the Marquess of Bath at Longleat, just four miles away) with fruit, vegetables and ornamental plants. In 1819 he passed the business on to his son, also called George, and in George Junior's hands the Warminster Nursery prospered for most of the nineteenth century – in the 1860s, for example, he was supplying the pioneering photographer Henry Fox Talbot with plants for his gardens at Lacock Abbey. But like many nurserymen before and since, Wheeler's interest went beyond simply producing plants for sale to actively breeding new varieties, and his introductions included the first double fuchsia and the pretty pale-yellow 'Warminster broom' (*Cytisus x praecox* 'Warminster'), which was first sold around 1867 and remains popular to this day. His cabbage, proudly named Wheeler's Imperial, seems to have been introduced in the early 1840s (it was referred to as 'Wheeler's New Imperial Cabbage' in 1847), and its seed was widely sold both in Britain and overseas. A small spring-harvesting variety with dark-green leaves and solid, conical hearts, it is ideal for smaller gardens and has a sweet, mild flavour. The immature leaves also make excellent winter greens.

Carrots

Sowe Carrets in your Gardens, and humbly praise God for them, as for a singular and great blessing.

Richard Gardiner, *Profitable Instructions for the Manuring, Sowing and Planting of Kitchen Gardens* (1599)

The contemporary carrot – orange, sweet and rampant with carotene – is a wonderful thing, but it's not a British invention. It's not even that ancient, although some varieties can trace their ancestry back to at least the eighteenth century. In fact if it wasn't for John Calvin and some patriotically minded Dutchmen we might still be gnawing on the tough, stringy roots of wild carrots rather than their more cultivated cousins. Wild carrots have been gathered for thousands of years, mainly for their seed although sometimes (presumably in desperation) for their roots, but cultivated varieties seem to have originated in the Middle East, slowly spreading west and north around the Mediterranean. Originally they were coloured purple, yellow, white or red, and it wasn't until the sixteenth century that orange carrots started making their appearance.

Who first had the idea of selecting from red and yellow carrots to make orange ones we don't know, but the most appealing suggestion is that they were bred as a kind of underground resistance symbol in honour of William I of Orange (1533–84) during the Netherlands' long, bloody war for independence from the Spanish occupation. The Low Countries certainly had plenty of the deep, sandy soils that carrots love. Unfortunately they also had the Inquisition, whose less-than-encouraging attitude towards the Protestant followers of John Calvin led to thousands of them fleeing to Elizabethan England from the 1560s onwards. They brought with them not only their skills, but also their carrots. Many of the Dutch landed at Sandwich and Deal in Kent, whose sandy soils turned out by happy chance to be ideal for carrot cultivation. Dutch carrots dominated the field for two centuries or more, led by the redoubtable Long Orange, first mentioned in 1721 and generally considered to be the granddaddy of the main cultivars we grow today.

The Dutch may have got the ball rolling, but we have the French to thank for popular modern varieties such as Nantes and Chantenay – and more particularly the great nineteenth-century French horticulturalist Louis de Vilmorin, whose *Notes sur la création d'une nouvelle race de betterave et considerations sur l'hérédité des plantes* (*Notes on the Creation of a New Race of Beetroot and Considerations on Heredity in Plants*) (1856) is widely credited as having laid the foundations of modern plant breeding. With one or two notable exceptions (such as the unfeasibly long Altringham) there are few authentically British carrots. For reasons that social historians have yet to investigate, carrots never seem to have caught the national imagination in the way that, say, peas or gooseberries did – except during the Second World War, in many ways the British carrot's finest hour. Cheap, nutritious and sweet enough to be used in many recipes as a substitute for scarce imported sugar, carrots could be found in everything from curries to cakes, not to mention being pressed into service in a swede-and-carrot-juice cocktail christened Carolade. Carrots even played their part in the propaganda offensive. When British fighters began shooting down unusually large numbers of German planes, it was put about that our pilots had developed uncannily sharp eyesight after gorging themselves on bunches of carrots, thus deflecting suspicion from the top-secret radar that had been fitted to their planes.

Altringham
1800s

In the nineteenth century the Cheshire town of Altrincham was surrounded by market gardens – sixteen square miles of them – producing fruit and vegetables for the seething metropolis of Manchester, just a few miles' haul by train. Along with neighbouring Timperley it was noted for its onions, rhubarb (see Timperley Early) and carrots, of which the Altringham became the most famous. Keen-eyed readers will already have spotted that this carrot is misspelled – except it's not, because it dates back to some time in the early 1800s, when 'Altringham' was a perfectly acceptable alternative. A rare example of an English carrot gaining widespread popularity in France (under the slightly more poetic title of Carotte Rouge Longue d'Altringham) rather than the other way around, Altringham's most striking attribute is its enormous length – it can grow anything up to a metre (three feet) long. Unfortunately its length is not matched by its girth: Altringham is as slender as it is elongated, so despite a good flavour and excellent productivity, it has never been as widely planted as it might have been, since in all but the lightest, most deeply dug soils it

Altringham carrot

tends to break when pulled. Despite this design flaw, its popularity spread throughout the nineteenth century, not just to France but also to Canada, the United States and North Wales. This elegant, deep-red carrot has one other peculiarity, in that its skin turns purple above the ground.

James' Scarlet Intermediate
1800s

A classic main-crop variety with hefty, tapering roots, James' Scarlet Intermediate is a good all-rounder, suitable for eating fresh (as it is at the Lost Gardens of Heligan) or storing in sand for winter use. Its name appears to derive from a Mr James of Lambeth Marsh (now called Lower Marsh) in London. Until the 1830s Lambeth Marsh was an area of small market gardens, the last of which disappeared beneath Waterloo station in 1848. The renowned James' Longkeeping onion is also said to have originated here around 1793, and although there is no conclusive evidence for a connection, it would be nice to think that the unsung Mr James produced them both.

Long Red Surrey
before 1821

Carrots have an irritating habit of acquiring multiple names, and the Long Red Surrey is one of the worst offenders, also being known as the Long Surrey, the Surrey Carrot and the Chertsey. As its various names suggest, in the early nineteenth century it was the commonest variety grown in the sandy fields of west Surrey for the London market. Its long, slender roots need deep soil and fairly careful handling, and it is no longer raised on a commercial scale, although it is still relatively easy to find as seed. In the late nineteenth century the gardening writer James Anderson described the Long Red Surrey, with its unusual yellow core, as 'a large sort cultivated chiefly for cattle, and by farmers for colouring butter'. These days, by contrast, it is recommended to home growers for its 'exceptional' and 'outstanding' flavour, with the added advantage of being tolerant of drought. It is grown in the kitchen gardens at Calke Abbey and the Lost Gardens of Heligan.

Oxheart
before 1842

Neil Porteous, who helped restore the monumental kitchen gardens at Clumber Park in Nottinghamshire to something like their Victorian glory, has nothing but praise for the satisfyingly chunky Oxheart. 'My all-time favourite,' he enthuses. Short, stubby and shaped like a bright-orange wedge, this fast-growing variety (known in France as Guerande) may look more like a hand-grenade than a conventional carrot, but it produces heavy crops whose sweet, tender flesh, as Neil Porteous says, 'tastes wonderful'.

White Belgium
1600s

Although there is little or nothing by way of documentary evidence, the mild-tasting White Belgium or Belgian White (known in France as Blanche) may well have come from Flanders, and has many similarities to an old variety known in seventeenth-century Britain as the Long White. White carrots were grown long before orange carrots burst on to the scene, and of the few white carrots to survive in cultivation, White Belgium is reckoned to have the best flavour.

A good cropper, even on lower quality soils (though it abhors frost), it makes a novel addition to salads, soups or stews, and would be worth experimenting with for an albino version of carrot cake. In France it is most esteemed as horse fodder.

Cauliflowers

Training is everything. A peach was once a bitter almond; a cauliflower is nothing but a cabbage with a college education.

Mark Twain, *Pudd'nhead Wilson* (1894)

Mark Twain was right, for cauliflower really is nothing but a cabbage – albeit a cabbage with a malformed flower-head, which, bizarrely, is the bit we like to eat. Like broccoli, kale and Brussels sprouts, cauliflowers are directly descended from the wild cabbage, *Brassica oleracea*, which can be seen clinging to its native habitat on cliffs in Dorset, Sussex, North Wales and Kent.

Cabbages with outsized flower-heads are believed to have developed somewhere in the eastern Mediterranean, although their early history is frustratingly obscure. The traditional story is that cauliflowers were first cultivated in Cyprus, from where they made their way to Italy, almost certainly via Venice, which ruled the island from 1489 to 1571. The Moors are also said to have introduced cauliflowers to Spain in the fifteenth century, but whether they came to Britain via Italy, Spain or directly from Cyprus is unclear. There are occasional claims that cauliflowers have been grown in Britain since the 1400s, but it appears more likely that they arrived much later on, at some point in the late sixteenth century. Admittedly there is not much evidence to speak of either way, but it is instructive to note that while John Gerard refers to 'cole-florey' in his famous *Herball* of 1597, cauliflowers are conspicuously absent from Thomas Hill's encyclopedic *Gardener's Labyrinth*, published just twenty years earlier. Could they have quietly crept in during the intervening period? It seems quite possible.

Whatever the circumstances of their arrival, these ancient cauliflowers are thought to have been smaller, rougher, less brilliantly white and far less finely grained than modern hybrid cultivars. To our eyes they would probably have looked more like large, loose heads of off-white broccoli, but the early adopters of the seventeenth century had never seen anything like them, and they quickly became extremely fashionable. They were also quite expensive, as fresh supplies had to be specially imported every year, the British climate being too cold for cauliflowers to produce fertile seed outdoors. Their air of exclusivity was enhanced by their being rather tricky to grow, and for a surprisingly long time they were classed as exotic novelties, like cucumbers and melons, a status confirmed by their immortalisation in the form of the first-ever novelty teapots, produced by Wedgwood from the late 1750s. By 1785 'cauliflower' was, according to Francis Grose's engagingly scabrous *Classical Dictionary of the Vulgar Tongue*, a term for 'A large white wig, such as is commonly worn by the dignified clergy, and was formerly by physicians', but it was not until the early nineteenth century that cauliflowers – the vegetables, that is, rather than the wigs – finally became commonplace. By this time, too, the Dutch had discovered how to persuade cauliflowers to produce fertile seeds, by growing them in greenhouses at temperatures that induced fertile flowers in their second year; this had the result of reducing their price and increasing their availability. The white-headed varieties, incidentally, are only white because they have been protected from the sun, either by their own 'self-blanching' leaves (which naturally wrap themselves around the head), or by the older and more labour-intensive method of tying the outer leaves together with garden twine or rubber bands.

All the Year Round
before 1933

Why this long-popular variety shares its name with a lettuce is not known, and neither are its origins, although it is a relatively modern introduction, first noted in 1933. As its name suggests it can be sown all year, and as long as it is given the rich, open soil that cauliflowers prefer it grows well both under the glass of a cold frame or in the open air. Its large, deep-green leaves curl tightly round good-sized, solid heads, which are ivory white in colour, keep well and have an excellent flavour; the diced and blanched curds also freeze well.

Leamington
c. 1873

Also known as Mr Perkins' Leamington and the Leamington Broccoli, this winter-heading variety is best suited to frost-free gardens, but produces large, solid white heads for harvesting in late March and early April. It was first sold, and possibly raised, by a Mr F. Perkins of Regent Street, Leamington Spa, and won a First Class Certificate from the Royal Horticultural Society in 1873.

Purple Cape
before 1808?

They may look like novelties, but purple-headed cauliflowers are actually among the oldest varieties we have, and Purple Cape is said to have originated in South Africa during the eighteenth century. The story goes that it was introduced to Britain in 1808 by the Hon. Marmaduke Dawnay, who then lived at Bookham Grove, Great Bookham, just outside Leatherhead in Surrey. Dawnay certainly had a fair-sized garden, and seems to have been interested in horticulture, although how Purple Cape made its way from Cape Province to Leatherhead has not, alas, been revealed. To confuse matters further, Purple Cape was often listed as a broccoli in the nineteenth century, which may suggest that the Victorian plant had laxer heads than the tight-headed one we know as Purple Cape today. But then the differences between broccoli and cauliflower (if any) have long been a matter of some debate; botanically speaking they are, after all, the same plant.

It is a hardy variety, ready for cropping in February and March, and has mid-green leaves with purple midribs wrapped tightly round vividly purple heads. They are attractive in themselves and make a colourful addition to crudités, but like many unusually

Purple Cape cauliflower

coloured vegetables they lose their purple tint when cooked and turn green, although they do retain their delicious taste. In 1824 Marmaduke Dawnay left Surrey, having inherited his uncle's Yorkshire estate of Wykeham Abbey. He changed his name to Langley, threw himself into an ambitious round of estate improvements, and died unmarried in 1851. But his Georgian house at Bookham Grove still stands, now split up into flats, and the gardens behind it – where Purple Cape, perhaps, first grew – now form a modest public park.

Snowball
before 1830

Short, stout and productive, Snowball has been a reliable favourite for well over a century. As it rarely grows much higher than thirty centimetres (one foot) it is ideal for growing on smaller plots, and its compact, snow-white heads can be harvested earlier than almost any other variety. It is good for freezing, too. Snowball was originally known as Dwarf Erfurt, and was probably a selected form of a much older German variety. Erfurt cauliflowers – said to have originated in the Thuringian town of Erfurt, famous from medieval times for the quality of its woad and the extent of its market gardens – were particularly hardy, with shorter leaves and smaller heads than other kinds, which made them particularly valuable in the development of dwarf varieties. Snowball's reputation preceded it across across the Atlantic, and it was introduced to the American market in 1888 by the famous New York firm of Peter Henderson.

Veitch's Autumn Giant
before 1871

The Veitch family were giants of Victorian horticulture, with trial grounds in Devon and the splendidly named Royal Exotic Nurseries in the King's Road, London, staffed by attendants in white gloves and frock coats. Their firm, which was founded in 1808 and closed in 1914, was the first to employ professional plant-hunters on a large scale, who scoured the world and introduced hundreds of new shrubs

Veitch's Autumn Giant cauliflower

(such as *Hydrangea macrophylla* 'Veitchii'), orchids and other exotic flowers to British gardens. But they were not too grand to dabble in vegetables, such as Veitch's Red Globe turnip and Veitch's Autumn Giant cauliflower. It is not clear whether Veitch's bred Autumn Giant themselves or, as seems possible, simply rebranded an Italian variety called Gigante di Napoli Precoce (a fairly standard practice in the freewheeling nineteenth century), but either way its winning combination of enormous size and high culinary quality quickly gained it many admirers. Autumn Giant grows around a metre (3ft 3ins) high, with huge white heads that can easily reach thirty centimetres (one foot) across. As its name suggests, it is usually harvested in early autumn.

The Veitch family, giants of Victorian horticulture

Celery

I'm afraid of losing my obscurity. Genuineness only thrives
in the dark. Like celery.

Aldous Huxley, *Those Barren Leaves* (1925)

For an account of wild celery I defer to Mr H. Dyson, head
gardener to Lady Hunloke, whose description appeared in
the March 1835 edition of the *Horticultural Register*:

Celery in its indigenous state is found during the summer months in
shallow water, at the bottom of stagnant drains and ditches, and in other
marshy places on warp, clay and bog soils . . . in its original condition [it]
is a destructive, rancorous poison, both to Man and Cattle, yet when the
plants are removed from their native localities, and cultivated in a garden,
they are divested of their poisonous qualities and become palatable,
salutary and nutritious.

What wild and cultivated celery share is their strong and distinctive
smell, and it is this that appears to have attracted its early adopters.
From ancient times right through to the 1600s celery was used

mainly as a medicinal herb, although its chopped leaves and seeds were also added to soups and stews for extra flavouring; in fact wild celery is still occasionally used in this way (in France, for example, where it is called *céleri à couper*; in Britain it was known as smallage). The development of mild, thick-stalked celery is a relatively modern phenomenon, which seems most likely to have taken place in sixteenth-century Italy. This was a period of great agricultural innovation, especially in the fertile hinterlands of Venice, then at the height of its great trading and maritime empire. Cultivated celery does not appear to have arrived in this country until the mid-seventeenth century, almost certainly through France from Italy: it appears as 'Italian Selleree' in one of the earliest seed lists, published by the London seed-merchant William Lucas around 1677, and until the 1830s the commonest variety was known as Upright Italian Celery.

But perhaps we should really thank John Churchill, first Duke of Marlborough, who captured Marshall Tallard, commander of the French forces, at the Battle of Blenheim in 1704 (along with Tallard's friend, the delightfully named Marquis de Silly). According to a story that did the rounds in the early nineteenth century and still resurfaces from time to time, it was Tallard who first introduced celery 'to the English tables' – an ambiguous claim that may, however, contain an element of truth. For Tallard spent the next few years as a captive, rather bizarrely, at Newdigate House in Nottingham, where he passed at least some of his time in creating a modest French-style parterre, which was still in evidence – if looking rather tatty – when Daniel Defoe visited the town in 1722. Could Marshall Tallard's parterre have been part potager, with carefully clipped celery growing between the lines of box? Sadly we will never know, although I suspect this is one of those many instances of 'fakelore': a legend repeated so many times that it acquires the surface sheen of fact. My suspicion is that, while Tallard is unlikely to have brought celery to Britain, as a highly cultured ex-diplomat he could well have introduced his provincial hosts to the well-established French custom of eating celery raw in salads, rather than crudely cooked in stews.

The famous Neat House market garden in London (which covered two hundred acres between the River Thames and the site of Victoria station) became celebrated for its celery in the late eighteenth century, but it was not until the Victorian era that it was cultivated on a large commercial scale. A bewildering number of new cultivars appeared, although a suspiciously high number of them were virtually identical in all but name. Assessing a recently introduced variety called Cole's Superb Red in his *Book of the Garden* (1855), Charles McIntosh sounded what must have been an all-too-familiar warning when he quoted an expert called Mr Thompson as saying:

Red Solid, alias New Large Red, New Large Purple, New Russian, Cole's Red, Cole's Superb Solid Red, Stripped Solid, Violete de Tours, are the same thing, and so also is the Celeri Violete, the seed of which has been for several years distributed by the London Horticultural Society as the very best red celery. The Manchester Red is believed by him to be scarcely different, and may be considered the same variety, excepting that it has acquired a stronger habit and rounder stalks.

By the mid-nineteenth century celery was being grown all over the country, with important centres of cultivation around London, Manchester, Edinburgh, and Gainsborough in Lincolnshire. At first it was used more for cooking than as a salad ingredient, and as late as 1855 Charles McIntosh was claiming that 'The use of salads is only beginning to be appreciated amongst the middle classes in Scotland, and the natural prejudice against "eating green meat" is daily subsiding – a prejudice, by the way, not altogether unfounded, from the coldness of our climate and habits of the people.' Scottish celery, which grew more slowly in the cooler climate, tended to be small and delicate, but around Manchester the growers were, according to McIntosh, primarily interested in size, having noticed that 'as with asparagus, the larger it is the better it takes in the market'. This Lancastrian obsession with size for size's sake is one of the more peculiar aspects of the Industrial Revolution, but whatever its economic or psychosexual origins it had an enormous impact on the development of British celery, as well as gooseberries and leeks. It certainly stimulated a great deal of horticultural innovation, although this was often at the expense of flavour, as was recognised even at the time. By 1860, when Shirley Hibberd published his *Floral World and Garden Guide*, celery had in his view left the ranks of mere ingredients and joined:

the artistic department of profitable gardening. Like asparagus, melons, cucumbers, and tomatoes, it has a high place in exhibition schedules, and there are not a few celery fanciers in country places where artisans enter into friendly rivalry in the production of enormous samples. As is the case with rhubarb, beet, melons, and a few other similar subjects, the largest celery is not always the most acceptable at table, but being a gross feeder, it is no difficult matter to grow it to almost any dimensions, provided the feeding materials are at hand.

For all the jokes about British cooking, the Victorians were far more knowledgeable and discriminating in their choice of both fruit and vegetables than we are today. They had, of course, far more varieties to choose from, and celery was no exception. They grew white-stalked varieties for the table, as we do, considering them more 'elegant' and finer-flavoured, but they would never have cooked with white celery if they could avoid it, much preferring the red kind for its richer taste; both kinds were universally available. Large 'solid' celery (the kind we know now) was considered far superior to the older, 'hollow' kinds whose small stems tended to be 'piped' with holes. White celery was normally blanched by earthing up the soil around the stems, which stopped them turning green and bitter, but 'self-blanching' varieties began appearing from the 1860s. Although they were less hardy than traditional kinds and their flavour was considered somewhat inferior, they were far less labour-intensive to grow, and self-blanching varieties dominate the market today.

Clayworth Prize Pink
1870s?

Pink-stemmed varieties of celery, such as Pink Solid, have been known since the 1760s, but this often-recommended variety appears to have been introduced around 1870. From the mid-nineteenth century until the 1950s celery was a major crop for the Lincolnshire town of Gainsborough, especially to the south and west of the town, on the low-lying floodplain of the River Trent, whose peaty soil proved perfect for celery cultivation. Clayworth Prize Pink was the most widely planted variety in the area, and was presumably named after the village of Clayworth, which stands about ten kilometres (six miles) west of Gainsborough. A tall, hardy variety with a robust flavour, it has pale pink stems, which keep their colour during cooking. It is sometimes wrongly called Clayworth's Prize Pink, doubtless under the mistaken belief that it was named after a person rather than a place.

Golden Self-Blanching
before 1867

The first of the self-blanching varieties, Golden Self-Blanching originated in France, and is said to have been developed in the Paris area by a Monsieur Chemin at some point before the late 1860s – a supposition given slightly more weight by the fact it was initially known in this country as the Paris Golden Self-Blanching celery. It seems to have arrived in both Britain and the United States in the 1880s, when it was referred to as a new variety, and the seed often came directly from France, but it was considered so revolutionary that it was rapidly adopted, and it could be said to be the first 'modern' variety. Its advantages were twofold: first, it saved the labour of piling earth around the stems to blanch them, and second, it also saved room, since without the piled-up soil the individual plants could be planted much closer together, making it more productive. Smaller and milder in flavour than older varieties, it is earlier to harvest too.

Manchester Giant Red
before 1835

This old red variety has had many names over the years, but was firmly associated with Manchester by the 1830s, when it was first mentioned by the prolific gardening writer John Claudius Loudon. In 1841 Loudon published the results of some field trials he had conducted the year before; among the red varieties he grew was the somewhat tautologically titled 'Manchester Large Giant'. It did not score high marks from Loudon's fellow examiners, who deemed it to be 'coarse, and bad-tasted' and not a patch on Seymour's Solid. But while the latter appears to have disappeared around the end of the nineteenth century, Giant Red survived and was, I imagine, repeatedly 'improved' by selecting particularly good plants and breeding from them, a practice that would account for the number of similarly named sub-varieties. Whether the Giant Red we can still buy today bears much resemblance to the coarse, bad-tasting plant of Loudon's time is open to question, but red celery is worth growing for its attractive stems, strong flavour (better for cooking than salads), vigorous growth and hardiness. Most of the many selected sub-varieties have long since been lost, but Giant Red still occasionally goes under the alternative name of Brydon's Prize; where and when this kind originated is not clear, although it does not seem to have been recorded before the twentieth century. Could it have been introduced by Kent and Brydon, a nursery firm from Darlington in County Durham, which traded from the 1880s until around 1955?

Manchester's pre-eminence in celery cultivation was acknowledged by most nineteenth-century writers, although it clearly puzzled Mr Dyson, the head gardener who introduced this chapter. Searching for a reason in 1835, he wondered why:

The Manchester gigantic Celery has long borne away the palm, and won the laurels of celebrity, throughout England, for its size, weight and quality; – how has my young heart panted to know the reason, or cause of such decided superiority! Situated between the Sea and a bleak mountain ridge, in a northern latitude, with a cold and sterile soil, what advantages can Manchester possess for the growth of Celery? – none, save and except a trifling additional supply of rain water from the clouds, by reason of its proximity to the ocean and mountain ridge. After a close and minute investigation, there appears no just reason to induce another opinion than that the well earned fame of Manchester Celery arises solely from superior cultivation.

Manchester may have been described in more flattering terms elsewhere, but Dyson's attempt to separate horticultural nature from nurture seems admirably clear-sighted even now.

Cherries

Loveliest of trees, the cherry now
Is hung with bloom along the bough
And stands about the woodland ride
Wearing white for Eastertide.

A. E. Housman, *A Shropshire Lad* (1896)

Not many would claim that swedes, say, are as beautiful as they are delicious, but there are few more uplifting sights than a cherry tree in flower. A. E. Housman certainly knew a thing or two about cherries, having been born in Bromsgrove, Worcestershire, whose nineteenth-century prosperity was founded on the historically unusual combination of fruit-growing and the manufacture of nails. As recently as 1964 James Lees-Milne could observe that 'orchards practically surround the town up to its edge', but their days were numbered even then, victims of cheaper foreign imports. It's been estimated that in 1951 there were around 7,000 hectares (18,000 acres) of cherry orchards in the UK; by 2003 that figure had plummeted to a paltry 381 hectares (943 acres). Today over 90 per cent of our cherries are imported from abroad, either by road from Turkey or by air from the West Coast of the USA, and Bromsgrove is surrounded by housing estates and retail parks.

Their decline has been put down to a single factor: size. Sweet cherries are unruly, vigorous trees, and can grow over fifteen metres (fifty feet) high – one of the reasons they were often fantrained against walls, where they could be kept under some kind of control. In open orchards the fruit had to be picked using long, heavy wooden ladders that took two men to carry. It was dangerous and exacting work, not least because it was easy to damage the following season's flower buds, which are hidden beside the cherry stalks. Pickers were sometimes sacked on the spot just for knocking off a few leaves.

Cherries have been a favourite fruit since time out of mind. Wild cherries are found all over Europe. In Britain and Western Europe these were mostly the native bird-cherry, *Prunus avium*, so called for the fairly obvious reason that birds will, given half a chance, quickly strip their fruit. These trees are the ancestors of the sweet cherries we eat today, although their fruit is nothing to write home about. The sour cherries used in cooking are offspring of a different species entirely, *Prunus cerasus* (which itself may be a hybrid of *Prunus avium* and *Prunus fruticosa*, the so-called ground cherry). The origins of *Prunus cerasus* are further east, a clue being hidden in its name: Cerasus was a settlement on the Black Sea coast (now the Turkish town of Giresun) which was famous for its cherries even in the time of ancient Greece.

Cultivated cherries – sweet and sour – were probably brought to Britain, like so much else, by the Romans, and they were widely grown by the Middle Ages, both in monastic and private gardens. Morello cherries (a cultivated form of *Prunus cerasus*) most likely came to Britain via Moorish southern Spain, as their name suggests – Morello supposedly meaning 'Little Moor'. Kent was at the centre of British cherry-growing from the start, partly because of its propinquity to London but also because it offered the well-drained, sandy soil that cherry trees prefer. According to one account, the genesis of the Kentish orchards can be dated to 1533, when they were kick-started by a kind of sixteenth-century Johnny Appleseed. In his *Perambulation of Kent: Conteining the Description, Historie, and Customes of that Shyre*, published just forty years later in 1576, the historian William Lambarde claimed that Richard Harris, who held the title of royal fruiterer to Henry VIII, planted the first orchards of apples, cherries and other fruit trees around Teynham on the instructions of the King. If the seventeenth-century diarist John Evelyn is to be believed, Harris went on to plant orchards round a further thirty Kent towns. Despite their evident popularity and Harris's pioneering efforts, most new varieties of cherries continued to be imported from the continent, at least until the mid-seventeenth century, when some unknown but imaginative orchardist had the bright idea of crossing sweet cherries with the sour Morello kind. The sweet-sour hybrids that resulted became known in Britain as Dukes, although the French called them Anglais in recognition of their origins.

Late eighteenth- and early nineteenth-century cherry cultivation is dominated by one man: Thomas Andrew Knight, a shy, rich but far from idle squire who lived at Elton Hall, near Ludlow in Herefordshire, from his marriage in 1791 until 1809, the year in which his brother gave him Downton Castle and its 10,000-acre estate. One of the founders, and later president, of what was to become the Royal Horticultural Society, Knight has been called the father of horticultural science. His interests in hybridisation were intensely practical, and his experiments – many of them assisted by his teenage daughters – led to many new varieties of strawberries, apples, plums and cherries, including Knight's Early Black, the magnificent Elton Heart, and the delicious Waterloo. Seven of Knight's original trees were found still growing in the orchard at Elton Hall in 1926, and some may even survive today.

Thanks to the efforts of Knight and the hard work of talented nurserymen like Thomas Rivers, the late nineteenth century saw

One of the oldest apples still in widespread cultivation, the original Bramley's Seedling sprang from a pip in Southwell, Nottinghamshire, around 1813. Named after Matthew Bramley, the local butcher, it went on to become the most successful cooking apple of all time.

The Pitmaston Pine Apple may date as far back as 1785, though it was not introduced to a wider public until 1845, when it was exhibited at the Horticultural Society of London by John Williams of Pitmaston House, Worcester. It probably originated at Witley Court in Worcestershire, and got its name from its delicious pineapple scent.

Pitmaston House, on Malvern Road in Worcester, is now owned by the county council, but it originally housed John Williams, one of the leading fruit breeders of the early nineteenth century, who introduced the Pitmaston Pine Apple and the Pitmaston Duchess pear.

An unusually smooth-skinned Rouge Crapaudine beetroot (2) and the Egyptian Turnip-Rooted (3), from a series of chromolithographs published between 1876 and 1882 by the German nurseryman Ernst Benary. The company he founded is still going strong today.

The ill-fated writer and epicure Edward Bunyard (shown here in 1912 at the age of 34) inherited one of the leading fruit and vegetable nurseries of the late nineteenth century, but was more interested in fine food, roses and wine than running the family business. Depressed and virtually bankrupt, he shot himself on 19 October 1939.

Among the finest of all broad beans, Bunyard's Exhibition is a tall Victorian variety whose sweet-scented flowers are followed by heavy crops of long-podded beans.

Shetland Kale – which is actually a cabbage – has been grown on the Shetland Isles for hundreds of years. Young plants are protected from rabbits, sheep and wind in a small stone-walled 'plantie crub', then transferred to a larger enclosure, or kale yard, like this one on the island of Yell.

Wroxton Abbey, near Banbury in Oxfordshire, is less noted today for hunting parties than the Wroxton Brussels sprout, which was raised by Lord North's head gardener, Mr Findlay, around 1895.

The Lost Gardens of Heligan pioneered the rediscovery of Victorian varieties of fruit and vegetables, and the kitchen gardens there are still one of the finest places to see traditional varieties grown in authentic surroundings.

the high point of cherry cultivation, with orchards established wherever suitable conditions could be found. Some were so extensive that they became tourist attractions in their own right. By the early twentieth century the fame of the orchards along the River Tamar in Cornwall was such that, each spring, special boats would ferry tourists up the river from Plymouth to admire the sight of the cherries in bloom. But their days were already numbered, and their decline – precipitated by the shortage of manpower in the Second World War, and continued by the rise of foreign imports – was as dramatic as it was sustained.

Yet there are hopeful signs for the future. Commercial cherry orchards are being planted again, albeit often with smaller trees. Their size once made many varieties of cherry impractical for all but the biggest gardens, too, but modern dwarfing rootstocks such as Colt and G5 can limit their height to a manageable three to six metres (ten to twenty feet) – a fairly acceptable height for an average-sized plot. Given the popularity of those blowsy but barren so-called 'ornamental' varieties, perhaps we can look forward to a time when, once again, cherries are grown for their fruit as well as their flowers, just as they were in A. E. Housman's day.

Two final words of warning. Most cherries aren't self-fertile, and their nomenclature is a mess. To make sure you get fruit it's generally necessary to plant two compatible varieties, thus ensuring pollination (suitable pollinators for each variety are suggested below). The name game is rather more problematic. Over the years the same varieties have been called different names in different areas, with the result that some apparently distinct varieties turn out to be identical. Much work has been done to sort this out, but it still makes sense to buy from a specialist nursery which really knows its stock.

Black Tartarian
c. 1796

This sweet, almost-black dessert cherry has a complicated history. It was introduced to the British market in 1796 by Hugh Ronalds, who had a nine-acre nursery between The Butts and Boston Manor Road in the west London village of Brentford. According to the fruit historian Robert Hogg (who should have known, since he worked for Ronalds early in his career):

The merit of having introduced this excellent cherry is due to the late Mr Hugh Ronalds, of Brentford, who, in 1794, issued a circular, a copy of which is in my possession, in which he signifies his intention of distributing it at five shillings each plant. It was subsequently brought from Russia by the late Mr John Fraser . . . He purchased it from a German, by whom it was cultivated in St Petersburg, and introduced it to this country in 1796.

(John Fraser, who lived in Sloane Square, Chelsea, was a plant hunter of some renown.)

What is striking about Hogg's account, assuming his chronology is correct, is that Ronalds felt able to start advertising his new variety two years in advance of its arrival in the country, which suggests both a sophisticated grasp of marketing and remarkable patience on the part of potential buyers. Its name, Black Tartarian, would have made more sense in the eighteenth century, when the entire eastern half of Russia, including the Caucasus, Siberia and sometimes even Mongolia and Tibet, was known as Tartaria. And indeed a Russian – or more specifically Crimean – origin seems plausible enough, although in 1831 George Lindley claimed that it was 'also said to have originated in Spain, whence it was transmitted to the Russian gardens, and through them into England'. Wherever it really came from, Lindley was in no doubt about its quality, describing it as 'a cherry of great excellence, bearing well on a standard, but doing best on an east or west wall, on which its branches are usually loaded with a profusion of rich and handsome fruit.' It is also unique among cherries in having deeply serrated and distinctly wrinkled leaves. Ronalds' was a leading nineteenth-century nursery, selling exotic plants to Kew Gardens as well as supplying the new cemetery of Kensal Green with 14,000 shrubs in the early 1830s. Hugh Ronalds died in 1833 and was probably buried at St Lawrence's church nearby, but the family nursery was still being run by his son Robert into the 1860s.

Early Rivers
1872

Few cherries are juicier or more delicious than a ripe black Early Rivers picked straight off the tree – and that is exactly how they should be enjoyed, for once they are ripe their soft, meltingly tender flesh does not lend itself to the ordeals of packaging and travel. It was raised in the 1860s by the great fruit cultivator Thomas Rivers, the third Thomas Rivers in a row to run the family nursery at Sawbridgeworth, just north of Harlow in Hertfordshire. It was introduced in 1872 and was an immediate commercial success, winning a Certificate of Merit from the Royal Horticultural Society and quickly establishing itself as one of the most popular of all dessert varieties, almost universally praised for its flavour, productivity and resistance to disease. As its name suggests the fruit ripens early (sometimes as soon as the end of May), starting off a bright shiny red and slowly flushing to the deepest purple-black. Despite its juiciness the fruit rarely splits. Early Rivers was planted all over the world, and still turns up in surprising places: it was one of the commonest cherries to be found, for example, in a 2002 study of orchards in the Czech Republic.

Frogmore Early
c. 1864

The pitfalls of pomological history are many and various, so perhaps it is not too surprising that this attractive yellow cherry should have been wrongly ascribed to William Ingram (it was actually raised by his father, Thomas) and relocated to Frogmore Gardens, Hampstead, when it really began life in the rather grander surroundings of the royal gardens at Frogmore, near Windsor Castle. Yet until the history of food is taken as seriously as the history of, say, music or furniture, minor errors like these will continue to be perpetuated. For Frogmore Early, the facts seem to be these. Writing in the 1880s, the generally reliable Robert Hogg recorded that it was raised around 1864 'by Mr Thomas Ingram, of the Royal Gardens at Frogmore', where, Hogg noted, the original tree could still be found. Thomas Ingram was born around 1796, and according to his daughter entered work in the royal gardens at the age of eighteen. He spent the rest of his life in royal service. By 1816 he was already head gardener to Queen Charlotte at Frogmore, and in 1833 he was appointed overall superintendent of the royal gardens at Windsor, a post he held almost until his death in 1872.

It must have been a demanding but enjoyable job, especially after 1841, when the vast new Royal Kitchen Gardens were laid out. As the *Windsor and Eton Express* reported in October 1842:

The gardens are approached by a neat lodge; central in the gardens is the gardener's house, which is now roofed in; it is a very pleasing erection, in the Elizabethan style, and occupies a frontage of forty-nine feet, containing not only every comfort for her Majesty's head gardener, Mr Ingram, but a small suite of rooms for her Majesty's use whenever she may feel disposed to visit the gardens. On each side of the building, east and west, will be a range of forcing houses; behind, on the north side, extending 822 feet in length, are to be erected fruit rooms, store rooms, seed rooms, and houses for the growth of mushrooms, which will be fitted in a very peculiar and novel style, and various other rooms for the convenience of working the gardens.

By 1851 the gardens had cost £45,000, much (though not all) of which was paid for by laying out a new street in London, Kensington Palace Gardens, whose enormous houses now provide ostentatious pieds-à-terre for embassies and Russian billionaires. Thomas's son, William, was born at Frogmore in 1820, and seems to have worked alongside his father into his twenties, when he left Windsor to become head gardener to the Duke of Rutland at Belvoir Castle.

As might be expected of a gardener with such a high-profile job, Thomas was highly regarded, becoming a Fellow of the Horticultural Society of London and winning prizes at its shows for his fruit. If an 1863 reference to him as 'that indefatigable hybridiser' is anything to go by he was also, like many of his contemporaries, an avid breeder of new varieties, and we have Thomas to thank for both the Frogmore Early cherry and the Frogmore Prolific apple. As for the regal cherry itself, Frogmore Early owes its reputation to its reliability, bearing heavy crops of sweet yellow cherries streaked and flushed with red. They have a first-rate flavour, although the fruit is rather soft, which makes for delicate handling – something that did not deter late nineteenth-century growers, who planted it on a large scale for the London market.

May Duke
before 1665

May Duke is a bit of a conundrum. The fact that it became known in France as the Anglaise Hâtive (the English Early) might indicate that it had British origins, but May Duke may equally be a corruption of Medoc, suggesting that it originally came from France.

Either way it is an ancient variety, and probably the first of the Dukes, produced by crossing *Prunus cerasus* and *Prunus avium*, that became popular in the seventeenth century. It was first mentioned in 1665 by John Rae in his sonorously titled *Flora, seu de Florum cultura* (*Or A Complete Florilege: Furnished with all Requisites Belonging to a Florist*), and was still common in the nineteenth century, although by the mid-twentieth century it had fallen out of favour except in Holland, for reasons best known to the Dutch. Actually the Dutch were quite right, for May Duke is a delicious dessert cherry, with juicy, soft, sweet fruit that starts off bright red and deepens to almost (but never entirely) black, usually ripening in late June. It will set some fruit on its own, but it cross-pollinates well with Waterloo, which generally ensures a heavier crop – although May Duke tends to fruit more heavily in some years than others, a slightly irritating habit that may explain its fall from commercial grace.

Morello
before 1629

One of the oldest cherries still in existence, and among the most delicious, the Morello has been with us so long that it has developed into several very similar varieties that go under the same name, so perhaps it should be regarded as more of a closely related family than a unique variety. The Morello is the sour cherry par excellence, and of all the many varieties that were grown before the Second World War it is one of the few to have survived in fairly widespread cultivation – a testament to its robust constitution, as well as the fine flavour of its fruit. Unlike some cherries it is

Morello cherry

remarkably hardy, and although its blossom is susceptible to frost it grows most happily against a north-facing wall; out of full sun the fruit will often remain on the tree as late as September. Thomas Andrew Knight was a fan. In the address he made to the Horticultural Society of London in 1823, Knight enthused:

As a species of fruit, I consider the Morello cherry to present very strong claims to the attention of the horticulturist. The hardiness of its blossoms, which I have found to be alike patient of heat and cold; the large size of the fruit, with its abundant juice, and power of retaining its soundness and perfection long after it has become mature; and the exuberant produce of the tree in situations where the common cherry succeeds but ill, render it, with all its present imperfections, most valuable.

Although apparently well known by the early 1600s, Morello cherries only became popular during the eighteenth century, perhaps because by then there was a greater availability of cheap sugar to offset its sourness. Its large, dark-red fruit can be eaten raw when fully ripe, although unsurprisingly they are fairly tart, but for cooking they are still among the best.

Waterloo
1815

Widely regarded as the finest dessert cherry of all, Waterloo was raised at Downton Castle near Ludlow by Thomas Andrew Knight with his youngest daughter, Charlotte. Writing to the Horticultural Society of London in 1816, Knight explained that it 'sprang from a seed of the Ambrée of Du Hamel, and the pollen of the May Duke'. The following year, with a nice touch of horticultural chivalry, the sixteen-year-old Charlotte 'very properly was presented with the Silver Medal by the Hort. Soc . . . as a mark of approbation of the fruit'. As the Silver Medal shows, its qualities were quickly recognised, and by the end of the nineteenth century it was planted all over the country; its fame even spread to Canada and the USA. One of its advantages is that, after a spurt of growth in its youth, it settles down to make a compact, leafy, round-headed tree, which makes it perfect for the garden. But what makes Waterloo exceptional is its fruit. Deep, deep red but not quite black, they're so juicy and delicious that the minor fiddle of finding them among the foliage (and protecting them from greedy birds) is repaid many times. It generally flowers around the same time as Early Rivers, which, by happy coincidence, is one of its pollinators. According to Robert Hogg it was given its name from first 'having produced fruit a few weeks after the occurrence of the Battle of Waterloo'. Charlotte Knight, who was born around 1801, deserves posthumous recognition not only for her role in raising one of the greatest cherries we have, but also in acknowledgement of the fact that, of all the hundreds of varieties of fruit and vegetables in this book, Waterloo is the only one *not* to have been created by a man. Charlotte died in 1842, and was buried in the village church at Rous Lench in Worcestershire, but Waterloo lives on.

Thomas Andrew Knight (1759–1838)

Cucumbers

The cucumber, if grown in the home garden and used fresh,
is not in league with the undertaker.

Edward Payson Roe, *The Home Acre* (1887)

B ritain may not occupy the place in the world it once had, but it is, apparently, still famous for the length of its cucumbers. Why ours should be reputedly so much longer than anyone else's is not entirely clear, but Britain certainly has a long history of cucumber cultivation, beginning with the Romans. The emperor Tiberius' passion for parsnips was well known, but he also adored cucumbers, and in order to supply his daily requirements his gardeners came up with an ingenious solution: mobile vegetable-beds, on which the cosseted cucurbits could be wheeled around to capture the best of the sun, then wheeled indoors to keep them warm at night. The Romans also grew them into entertaining shapes with the help of special cucumber moulds, which the growing fruits were placed inside.

The cultivated cucumber appears to be most closely related to *Cucumis sativus* var. *hardwickii*, a wild species that is still quite common in the foothills of the Himalayas, growing between altitudes of 800 and 1,700 metres (2,600–5,500 feet). Their fruit is small and abundant but very bitter, and their domestication, which is thought to have taken place in northern India at some time before 2000 BC, must have involved an interminable process of selecting progressively sweeter varieties. From India they slowly spread both east and west, into China and across to the Mediterranean.

After the Romans abandoned Britain, cucumbers fade from history for hundreds of years, apart from a passing mention by Abbot Aelfric of Cerne in 995 and a reference to 'concumber and gourde' in a seed list compiled for the Archbishop of Canterbury around 1326. It was not until the reign of Henry VIII that they became popular again, and by the time John Parkinson published *Paradisi in Sole Paradisus Terrestris* (which punningly translates as *Park-in-Sun's Earthly Paradise* and is generally regarded as the first great book on British horticulture) in 1629 there were several varieties to choose from, including:

The long greene Cowcumber; The short Cowcumber; being short, and of an equall bignesse in the body thereof, and of unequall bignesse at both ends; The long Yellow, which is yellowish from the beginning, and more yellow when it is ripe, and hath beene measured to be thirteene inches long; Another kinde is early ripe, called The French Kinde; The Dantsicke kind bareth but small fruit; The Muscovie kinde is the smallest of all other, yet knowne.

'Cowcumber' sounds like one of those quaintly archaic turns of phrase, but cucumbers were commonly called cowcumbers as late as the mid-nineteenth century, as keen-eyed readers of *Martin Chuzzlewit* and *Tess of the d'Urbervilles* may recall. Their reputation was not always high: in fact until the eighteenth century many people treated them with outright suspicion. On 22 August 1663 Samuel Pepys recorded the alarming news that 'Mr Newburne is dead of eating cowcumbers, of which, the other day, I heard another, I think Sir Nicholas Crisp's son.' Dr Johnson's opinion of them was not much higher. 'It has been a common saying of physicians in England,' he declaimed, 'that a cucumber should be well sliced, and dressed with pepper and vinegar, and then thrown out, as good for nothing.'

That cucumbers should have aroused such fear and loathing in our ancestors' minds may strike us as odd, but their low standing conceivably may have had something to do with pre-nineteenth-century varieties, which tended to be small, thick-skinned, prickly and more than often bitter-tasting – quite unlike the bland, smooth cucumbers we know today. It was only when gardeners discovered that the fruit from unpollinated female flowers had none of the bitterness of pollinated fruit that the older varieties fell out of favour, and today most commercial varieties are all-female hybrids.

Conqueror
before 1861

A smooth, full-flavoured greenhouse cucumber, Conqueror has rather thick skin, but makes up for that by being hardier (under glass) than most varieties. Its skin is bright green, with crisp white flesh, and like many traditional varieties its male flowers – which can be distinguished by the lack of incipient fruits between flower and stem – should be removed if the fruit is not to have a bitter taste. Visiting Sheffield in 1861, the correspondent of the *Journal of Horticulture* was extremely impressed with the state of local cucumber cultivation. 'Here', he reported, 'I saw and tasted the Conqueror Cucumber', and though he was critical of its appearance (noting that its 'colour . . . is too pale, and the shoulder is too long and small in proportion to the circumference of the other parts of the fruit'), he had to allow that 'for flavour and general cropping it is unequalled'.

King George
1911

Named by Sutton's Seeds of Reading in honour of the newly crowned King George V, this large greenhouse variety was a cross between Matchless (since lost) and Telegraph (see below). It has deep-green skin and tender flesh, and was a popular variety at horticultural shows. Remove male flowers to avoid fruit becoming bitter.

Lemon Apple
before 1894

Spherical and bright yellow with tiny black spines, this looks nothing like your standard cucumber, although its crisp white flesh tastes pretty much identical. Lemon Apple has been grown since the late nineteenth century, mainly as a novelty, but it does have several advantages of its own: it requires less watering than most varieties yet it is also highly productive, and being relatively hardy it can be grown outside as well as in a cold frame or a greenhouse. Its alternative names include Crystal Apple and Lemon Cucumber, although there is some confusion as to whether Crystal Apple is a separate variety, allegedly distinguished by its prickly skin. Lemon Apple may have originated in Australia or New Zealand, but it has certainly been known in Britain for well over a century. Its rather seedy fruits are best picked young, as they can become bitter when mature.

Long Green Ridge
before 1777

Long English Prickly cucumber

The oldest variety still available, Long Green Ridge seems to be synonymous with Long Prickly and Bedfordshire Prize Ridge, which was noted as early as 1777. It has long, dark-green fruit, and although its skin is rather tough and slightly spiny (sometimes referred to as 'ridged' or 'burpy') it has an excellent flavour. Long Green is a good outdoor variety, which stores well and produces heavy crops in good conditions.

Telegraph
before 1861

Rollison's Telegraph cucumber

One of the best of all old greenhouse varieties, the smooth-skinned Telegraph was introduced by the Victorian nursery firm of William Rollison and Sons, which specialised in a wide range of greenhouse plants and published a catalogue of orchids, vines and roses in 1877; the striking burnt-orange potentilla 'William Rollison' was presumably another of their introductions. Telegraph was described as a 'good long sort' by the *Journal of Horticulture* in 1861, and praised by the *Gardeners' Chronicle* in 1868 for its productivity – especially in a heated greenhouse, although it will grow happily enough in a cold frame too. Its large, dark-green fruits have crisp flesh and a refreshing flavour.

Currants

> If there was one sort of work that Johnnie Green had always
> disliked more than another, it was picking currants. Of
> course he didn't object to strolling up to a currant bush and
> taking a few currants for his own use, on the spot. What he
> hated was having to fill pail after pail of currants for his
> mother to make jelly and jam.
>
> Arthur Scott Bailey, *The Tale of Pony Twinkleheels* (1921)

D electable, jewel-like and expensive to harvest on a commercial scale, redcurrants and whitecurrants are actually
among the easiest fruit to grow; blackcurrants, too,
although they are less often seen for sale – perhaps because the vast
majority of them end up being bottled in sugary drinks. Like
gooseberries, which merit a chapter of their own, they all belong to
the *Ribes* family. The blackcurrants we grow are cultivated forms of
the wild *Ribes nigrum*, which grows all over Europe, as well as in
north and central Asia and as far east as Siberia. Cultivated
redcurrants are most closely related to *Ribes rubrum*, which like
blackcurrants grow in northern Europe and northern Asia,
although several other wild species have had a hand in the

development of particular varieties; whitecurrants, for their part, are simply redcurrants with albino genes. Despite their similarities, the histories of blackcurrants and redcurrants in Britain are surprisingly distinct. Although neither has been cultivated for as long as, say, apples or plums, red- and whitecurrants have been grown in British gardens since the 1500s, but we seem to have got by largely without blackcurrants until as late as the eighteenth century.

One sign of their relative youth is that, unlike most fruit and vegetables, currants do not have a unique signifier of their own. Their English name comes from their supposed resemblance to the currants we get from desiccated grapes (which in turn got their name from the Greek city of Corinth, once a major grape producer). The distinction seems glaringly obvious today, but back in 1629 the king's apothecary and pioneering garden writer John Parkinson had to point out to his readers that home-grown redcurrants were different to the dried currants to be seen in grocers' shops. In those days there were few varieties to choose from. The long-lost Common Red was, as its name suggests, the commonest type; its fruits were barely bigger or sweeter than those of wild redcurrants, but by the time Parkinson was writing it was already being supplanted by a Dutch variety, the Great Red, which had been introduced by the great plant collector John Tradescant the Elder in 1611. Tradescant brought it back as part of an extraordinary transcontinental shopping spree which began in 1609, undertaken on behalf of Robert Cecil, secretary of state to both Elizabeth and James I, for Cecil's extravagant new gardens at Hatfield House in Hertfordshire. (Among the thousands of plants Tradescant bought in France and the Netherlands – including more than 20,000 vines and 800 tulip bulbs, then almost worth their weight in gold – were hundreds of varieties of flowers and fruit trees that had never been seen in Britain before; it remains arguably the most important single round of horticultural introductions in British history.) With its aristocratic associations and much-improved flavour the Great Red Dutch quickly became fashion-able, launching a 200-year-long love affair with redcurrants (and to a smaller extent with whitecurrants) that only ended with the arrival of large-fruited 'modern' strawberries and raspberries in the early years of the nineteenth century.

Blackcurrants were never as popular. They seem to have been introduced by John Tradescant at the same time as the Great Red Dutch redcurrant, but the strong smell of their foliage and the robust, almost meaty taste of their berries put many people off. While redcurrants established themselves as a dessert favourite, black-currants were consigned to the medicine cabinet, where they have pretty much remained ever since; in the past they were used to treat gallstones, coughs and chest infections, and even today it could be said that they are prized more for their vitamin C content than their taste. True, those indefatigable improvers the Victorians introduced a number of new varieties, but even so their main interest seems to have been in expanding the currants' girth rather than enhancing their flavour: the nineteenth-century fruit expert Robert Hogg – not a man given to exaggeration – claimed to have seen blackcurrants the size of large gooseberries, although no variety is nearly so big today. Our taste for sweet blackcurrant juice, reinforced during the Second World War when every schoolchild was given a free supply, means that Britain is one of the few countries where blackcurrants are still planted on a relatively large scale; around 90 per cent of the crop is grown for GlaxoSmithKline and ends up as Ribena. In 2006 there were around 2,400 hectares (5,930 acres) of blackcurrants in England and Scotland, mid-way between strawberries (at 3,170 hectares or 7,833 acres) and raspberries (1,430 hectares or 3,533 acres). But global warming is putting the future of British black-currants under threat: their origins, in cold, northern climates, mean that they require cold winters and periods of frost to do well. The race is now on to breed new varieties that are tolerant of warmer conditions. In the United States, by contrast, both black- and redcurrants have only recently been legalised: they were actually prohibited by federal law in 1911 after the forestry industry claimed they spread a virus that damaged white pine trees. The ban was lifted at federal level in 1966, but forty years later some states still have the legislation on their books: in New York, for example, currant cultivation has only been permitted since 2003.

Baldwin
before 1891

Despite its being the most popular blackcurrant for the best part of a century, Baldwin's beginnings have been completely forgotten. It seems to have been a British cultivar, which the fruit connoisseur Edward Bunyard recorded as having been known in Kent since the nineteenth century. Its success can be put down to its vigorous growth and heavy crops of decent-sized, good-flavoured fruit, but it has lost ground commercially to more modern varieties such as Ben Lomond that have better resistance to disease. Its berries freeze well and are delicious fresh; they also make excellent jams and summer puddings.

Houghton Castle
c. 1810

Haughton Castle, as it is known today (Houghton is an earlier spelling) is a splendid fourteenth-century fortress that commands a curve of the North Tyne near Humshaugh in Northumberland, about twenty miles (thirty-two kilometres) north of Hexham. The eponymous redcurrant seems to date from *circa* 1810, around the same time that the Smith family – which had owned the place since 1642 – finally started improving the castle and its estate. According to a story reported in an 1847 edition of the *Gardeners' Chronicle*, it was discovered around forty years before in the kitchen gardens at Houghton by a young apprentice gardener called Robert Charlton, who noticed that the last redcurrant in the row had much larger and better-tasting fruit than the others. His boss, John Gray, had no idea what variety it was, but then remembered that he'd been short of one plant in that row; looking around the gardens he had found a seedling growing under a gooseberry bush, which he'd then dug up and replanted. Charlton went on to become a well-known nurseryman on his own account, establishing his business at Wall, just a few miles south of Haughton, and the redcurrant he named after the castle became one of his best-selling plants. It was one of the best-loved varieties of the nineteenth century, often sold under the alternative names of Raby Castle and Victoria, but it has since become rather rare – although according to Fred Roach, author of the classic *Cultivated Fruits of Britain*, it was still being grown as recently as the 1980s, and indeed it is still listed in the National Fruit Collections at Brogdale in Kent. Haughton Castle, incidentally, played an unusual role in the French Revolution: as part of his estate improvements Captain Smith had built a paper mill in the grounds, which was commissioned by the government to print fake French banknotes in an attempt to devalue the currency. Evidently the experiment was not a success.

Laxton's No. 1
c. 1914

Laxton's No. 1 should by rights be known as Laxton's No. 2, since it was the second variety of redcurrant to be introduced by the once-famous family firm Laxton Brothers of Bedford around the First World War (their first, Laxton's Perfection, was introduced in 1910). It has long been renowned for its dependable and prolific crops of large red berries, which ripen earlier than many other varieties. Reliable, vigorous and adaptable, it remains one of the best garden varieties, although its long, delicate bunches of fruit make commercial harvesting difficult. Both Laxton's No. 1 and Laxton's Perfection are still on the market, the latter being distinguished by its outsize berries.

Wellington XXX
1913

This heavy-cropping blackcurrant was developed by Dr (later Captain) Wellington, the first director of the renowned Fruit Experimental Station at East Malling in Kent, who raised the variety that bears his name before leaving to serve in the First World War. A cross between Baldwin and the Dutch variety Boskoop Giant (the latter dating from 1880 and raised by a Mr Hoogendyk), it was sold commercially from 1927 and is still planted today. Wellington makes a large, fast-growing bush that bears heavy crops of rather thick-skinned but sweetly flavoured berries, although they have an unfortunate tendency to split. It flowers late enough to avoid the worst frosts, and does better than many varieties in hot, dry weather. Like Baldwin, the fruit is good for freezing and acquits itself well in pies and jam. The XXX suffix is a bit of a mystery, but presumably relates to Wellington's size.

White Versailles
1843

Still one of the most popular whitecurrants, White Versailles dates back to 1843, when it is said to have been raised by Monsieur Bertin of Versailles. Also known as Versailles Blanche, it has long trusses of sweet, tasty but rather seedy white fruits on tall stems, which are delicious fresh but also make excellent wine. Unlike redcurrants, they have the advantage of being relatively unattractive to birds, which often strip other soft-fruit bushes bare. White Versailles is one of the earliest varieties to harvest in early July; its fruit are delicate and need gentle handling.

Gooseberries

FALSTAFF: All the other gifts appertinent to man, as the malice of this age shapes them, are not worth a gooseberry.

William Shakespeare, *Henry IV*, Part 2 (1596–7)

The connection between gooseberries and whippets might, on the face of it, seem fairly tenuous, but it would have made a lot more sense if you had been living near Manchester in, say, 1772. It's all a matter of breeding. Lancashire's pre-industrial weavers were a competitive bunch, and in their spare time they bred all manner of things, from whippets and leeks to pigeons and gooseberries. Their preoccupations were surprisingly familiar: speed (dogs and pigeons) and size (fruit and veg). By the 1740s they were mounting annual competitions for the largest gooseberry, run by the many gooseberry clubs that sprang up, first in Lancashire and later across the whole north of England; these reached their peak in 1815, when over 120 shows were held. In 1829 the writer Robert Mudie recorded some of the poignantly humble prizes that were awarded on these occasions, 'adapted', as he said, 'to the manners of the homely people who contend for them. They are often a pair of sugar tongs, a copper tea-kettle, a cream jug, or a corner cupboard.'

In his 1834 miscellany *The Doctor* (which also contains the original fairy tale of 'The Three Bears'), the poet Robert Southey gave an intriguing insight into the lengths gooseberry growers went to in their pursuit of ever-larger fruit. He evidently disapproved, noting that:

In 1830 the largest Yellow Gooseberry on record was shown at Stockport, it weighed thirty-two pennyweights, thirteen grains, and was named the Teazer. The largest Red one was the Roaring Lion of thirty-one pennyweights, thirteen grains, shown at Nantwich; and the largest White, was the Ostrich shown at Ormskirk; falling far short of the others, and yet weighing twenty-four pennyweights, twenty grains. They have been grown as large as Pigeon's eggs. But the fruit is not improved by the forced culture which increases its size. The Gooseberry growers who show for the prizes which are annually offered, thin the fruit so as to leave but two or three berries on a branch; even then prizes are not gained by fair dealing: they contrive to support a small cup under each of these, so that the fruit shall for some weeks rest in water that covers about a fourth part, and this they call suckling the gooseberry.

Their activities fascinated Charles Darwin. For him, as he wrote in *The Variation of Plants and Animals Under Domestication* (1868), 'The most interesting point in the history of the gooseberry is the steady increase in the size of the fruit.' Darwin recorded that wild gooseberries generally weighed around a quarter of an ounce; already in 1786 show gooseberries were being exhibited at double that weight, and by 1852 the winning gooseberry at a Staffordshire show was just short of two ounces. That might not sound much but, as Darwin noted, it equalled the weight of a small apple, or 'between seven and eight times the weight of the wild fruit' – an astonishing feat of genetic engineering. It's been claimed that British breeders developed something like 2,000 named cultivars between the eighteenth and nineteenth centuries, and although only a few of those original varieties survive today, among them are some of the great names of the gooseberry-show past, including London, which beat all comers back in 1852.

The names of the show varieties give us a wonderfully vivid picture of their growers: not only their braggadocio (Roaring Lion, Matchless, Leader, Wellington's Glory, Hero of the Nile, Hampson's Tantararara), but the places they came from (Lancashire Lad, Flixtonia, Glory of Oldham, Warrington Red) and even their wry sense of humour – who could resist Pretty Boy or Dan's Mistake? Remarkably, although most of the old varieties have been lost over the last hundred years – many of them deservedly so, since they were bred far more often for size than taste – a handful of gooseberry shows still survive. Most of them are held in Cheshire, but the most venerable show of all is held at Egton Bridge, on the North Yorkshire Moors just a few miles from Whitby. It celebrated its bicentenary in 2001.

Gooseberries may have lost their former popularity, but they have the longest and most interesting history of all our soft fruit. Part of the reason is simply that gooseberry bushes are unusually long lived (often reaching twenty, and occasionally up to fifty years old), but they're also rather less prone to the viral infections that tend to build up over time in most other kinds of soft fruit, which eventually render older varieties unproductive and unusable. Although they're not now believed to be native to Britain, gooseberries have certainly been grown here since the Middle Ages. Our first record of them dates from 1275, when Edward I's royal fruiterer ordered some gooseberry bushes to plant at the Tower of London: they were despatched from France at a cost of 3d each. By the 1500s gooseberries were commonly grown, and although there don't seem to have been many varieties to choose from, they were put to a far wider range of uses than we're accustomed to today. They were cooked in tarts and sauces, fermented for wine, and, as John Gerard noted in his famous *Herball* of 1597, 'The young and tender leaues [are] eaten raw in a sallad, prouoke vrine, and driue forth the stone and grauell.' They were also pressed, quite literally, into service as a substitute for the grape-juice extract verjuice, which had been a favourite ingredient in English cookery until climate change (manifested as a series of disastrously cold winters) devastated the country's vineyards during the fifteenth century. By the eighteenth century almost every garden seems to have had its gooseberry patch, and the stage was set for the gooseberry shows.

Despite their popularity, gooseberries remained a so-called 'cottager's plant' – that is, they were largely confined to people's gardens and not grown commercially, at least in part because a tax on sugar made the large-scale cultivation of soft fruit uneconomic. The tax was finally repealed in 1876, and the result was an explosion in fruit-growing, with gooseberries planted both for jam and as an industrial source of pectin (the setting ingredient in jam). From then on their fortunes were closely tied to other commercial fruit crops, with a peak before the First World War followed by decades of decline.

Gooseberries have been described as being ideally suited to the British climate, and grow happily from Cornwall to the north of Scotland, where they're sometimes referred to as grozets (a corruption of the French *grosailles*). The only real drawback of the old varieties is their susceptibility to mildew; modern varieties such as Invicta tend to be more resistant.

Crown Bob
before 1812

This large red variety was already being referred to as 'Old Crown Bob' by the 1850s, by which time it was one of the most popular and widely planted of all gooseberries. Where and when it originated is not clear, but it was evidently already well known by the time it won

Crown Bob gooseberry

the Best Red category in the 1812 Mansfield Gooseberry Show, and it was being recommended across the Atlantic to American gardeners as early as 1826. As highly regarded today as it was 200 years ago, Crown Bob is a vigorous if rather droopy-looking bush, which bears heavy crops of outsize, claret-coloured berries with thin, hairy skins and an excellent flavour, both when they are cooked while still green (when they can be picked as early as May) and eaten raw when fully ripe. In 1847 the *Gardener's Monthly* magazine noted that it was 'Considered most profitable and therefore most cultivated by Lancashire Market Gardeners'. It was still planted on a commercial scale a century later, although today it is mainly grown by home gardeners.

Until the mid-nineteenth century it was often called Melling's Crown Bob, and given that gooseberries seem to have most often been named after their originator, rather than the nurseryman who first marketed them, perhaps we have a Mr Melling to thank for this wonderful variety. 'Crown Bob', incidentally, is the name for a particular peal of bells which may date back to the sixteenth century.

Dan's Mistake
before 1853

Who Dan was and why his enormous red gooseberry was such a memorable mistake is a bit of a mystery: it is mentioned in *The Book of the Garden*, by Charles McIntosh, as having been on Holland of Manchester's List of Lancashire Show Gooseberries for 1853, while Robert Hogg's classic *Fruit Manual* of 1860 records it as having been introduced by a Mr Spencer, but gives neither place nor date. The most plausible story I have come across claims that a leading grower – presumably named Dan – chucked out what seemed to be an unpromising seedling, only for a rival (Hogg's Mr Spencer, perhaps) to spirit it away from the compost heap, build it up and go on to win the local gooseberry show under the sardonic name of Dan's Mistake. Whatever its actual origins, this was an extremely popular variety for many years at the gooseberry shows, largely for the size of its light crimson fruits, although its taste is excellent too, if one can forgive its rather hairy habit.

Golden Drop
before 1802

Not to be confused with the plum Coe's Golden Drop, which dates from around the same time, Golden Drop is a fine yellow gooseberry with semi-sweet, modestly sized fruit. Though its genesis is unknown, it was included among the varieties listed by the royal gardener William Forsyth (who gave his name to forsythia) in his *Treatise on the Culture and Management of Fruit Trees* of 1802, and it has been popular ever since. Jim Arbury, head of fruit at the Royal Horticultural Society, counts it as one of his own personal favourites.

Hero of the Nile
1799?

Nelson's victory over the Revolutionary French fleet in the Battle of the Nile on 2 August 1798 made him a national hero, if not exactly overnight – reliable news of the victory took a month to travel back to Britain, and at first it was believed that the French had won. He was showered with tributes, including a rather fetching diamond aigrette donated by the Sultan of Turkey, and before long everything from a kind of rose to a public house in Bognor was being christened Hero of the Nile in his honour, which suggests that this pale-green but heroically sized gooseberry was probably named around the same time too. According to the fruit historian Robert Hogg, it was raised by a Mr Moore, but more than that we do not know.

Howard's Lancer
1831

Among the best-flavoured of all cooking gooseberries, the greeny-yellow Howard's Lancer is recorded as having been grown by a Mr T. Howard of Blackley in Manchester and introduced in 1831. Unlike many varieties it does as well on light soils as on rich loam, and is a good choice for a north-facing wall – gooseberries actually prefer rather cool conditions, and slow-ripened berries usually taste the best. The size and vigour of the bush is matched by heavy crops of large, smooth, thin-skinned gooseberries, which can be harvested from mid- to late summer.

Leveller
1851

The yellow dessert gooseberry Leveller dates from 1851, and originated in the Lancashire town of Ashton-under-Lyne, where it was raised by a Mr Joseph Greenhalgh. What Mr Greenhalgh can't have known is that, over a century and a half later, his variety would still be going strong. And not just that: Leveller remains among the best-loved of all gooseberries, and it's often the first variety that's recommended to anyone who's keen to give gooseberry-growing a try. The reason? Well, despite its susceptibility to mildew, it offers an appealing combination of reliably heavy crops, large golden-green fruits and, most importantly of all, outstanding taste; in fact it's among the sweetest gooseberries of all, and come late summer its ripe, oval berries are as delicious eaten raw as cooked. In the years immediately following the Second World War when 'real' wine was still in short supply, the Merrydown cider company used Leveller to make an excellent gooseberry substitute. They obtained their supplies from farms around Chailey and Newick in East Sussex, where it's still grown on a modest commercial scale today on the light, sandy soils that suit it best. In 1993 Leveller won a rather belated Award of Garden Merit from the Royal Horticultural Society – just 142 years after it first appeared on the scene.

London
1831

Not many gooseberries have had songs written about them, but the lovely red London has, and once you know something of its history it's easy to see why. London comes not from London at all but from Cheshire, where it was originally raised by a Mr Wilcock of Acton, near Nantwich, and sold by John Banks Junior from the May Pole Inn in Acton from 1831 – the son, perhaps, of farmer John Bankes who was recorded in the 1851 census as then being sixty-two years old. Why John Banks decided to call it London is a mystery. Although it makes a fairly small, spreading bush, as long as it's well fed and mulched (or grown on rich soil) it will reward you with a big crop of large, heavy, ruby-coloured fruits, with smooth skins and an excellent taste. In the words of a song that dates from 1885, 'This London of renown was that famous Huntsman's son / Who was raised in a Cheshire village near the May-pole in Acton / While in bloom he was but small yet still so fast he grew / That everyone admired him, for his equals are but few.' It might not be great verse, but 'The Gooseberry Grower's Song' does commemorate an extraordinary fruit. London was the reigning champion on the gooseberry circuit for a remarkable thirty-six seasons, winning 333 prizes on the way. Its greatest triumph came in 1852, when a single berry tipped the scales at 37 pennyweights (almost two ounces or 57.54 grams), making it one of the heaviest gooseberries ever known. The old May Pole Inn still stands on Hill Top Road in Acton Bridge, although it no longer, sadly, sells prize gooseberries.

Lord Derby
before 1866

This wonderfully sweet dark-crimson dessert gooseberry has an obscure early history. Neither the date of its introduction nor the name of its begetter seems to be known (the earliest mention of it I have found so far dates from 1866), and its name offers fewer clues than one might hope. The Earls of Derby certainly had large landholdings in Lancashire, and many of them were Lord Lieutenants of the county, so it might well be a Lancastrian gooseberry; however, this doesn't solve the problem of which Lord Derby its name commemorates. The most famous of the clan was the fourteenth Earl of Derby, who served three times as Prime Minister between 1852 and 1868. One of his memorials is the Lord Derby apple, which dates from around 1862, but the gooseberry could equally well have been named after his father, the naturalist thirteenth Earl, or even his grandfather, the founder of the Derby horse-race, who died in 1834 when gooseberry fever was still at its height. For Kelvin Archer, who maintains an outstanding collection of old-fashioned gooseberries in his capacity as head gardener of Rode Hall in Cheshire, Lord Derby is the sweetest of all dessert varieties. 'Leave it to ripen fully,' he advises, 'to appreciate just how sweet it really is.' Whether it is 150 or 200 years old, Lord Derby continues to bear heavy crops, and is still a frequent winner in the Red Class section of gooseberry shows.

May Duke
1900

Although not as ancient or popular as some varieties, May Duke deserves to be more widely known, for its deep-red fruits are both delicious and versatile. It makes a shapely, upright bush, which bears downy-skinned, medium-sized berries as early as June. Picked when still green they give a wonderful flavour to jams, tarts and pies; they're excellent for bottling, too. If you can bear to leave them to ripen till July, when they flush to a rich dark red, they will be sweet and juicy enough to eat as a dessert. May Duke is a late Victorian variety, first sold in 1900 by George Pyne, a nurseryman from Topsham, on the Exe estuary south of Exeter. Soft-fruit cultivation was growing rapidly in Devon at the time, especially along the Tamar valley further south. May Duke was probably developed for this market, although as the London steam-boats landed at Topsham it would also have been easy (and cheap) to send it further afield, and before long it was widely grown. Why it's called May Duke is not entirely clear. It may, with typically Victorian optimism, be a reference to how early it comes into fruit, but May Duke also shares its name with what was then a well-known eighteenth-century cherry, perhaps because its ripe red berries bear a passing resemblance to cherries themselves.

Whinham's Industry
c. *1835*

Whinham's Industry is one of the sweetest red gooseberries and makes superlative jam, although in bad years it can be a martyr to mildew. It was bred by Robert Whinham (1778–1861) around 1835 at Allery Banks in Morpeth, Northumberland. Whinham was a keen plant breeder, but though he knew he had an outstanding variety on his hands he had little success in promoting it, and in 1858 he sold his stock to Matheson's nursery in nearby Oldgate Street, dying two years later in Morpeth workhouse. Matheson's succeeded where Whinham failed, and by the end of the century Whinham's was the most popular preserving gooseberry of all, with around 200 tons of fruit being sold from Morpeth every year; gooseberries still grow in the local hedgerows. Whinham's son, Robert Jr., became a travelling musician and composed the well-known *Whinham's Reel*, but tragically he died in Morpeth workhouse too.

Leeks

By this leek, I will most horribly revenge.
William Shakespeare, *Henry V* (1598–9)

Britain was famous for its leeks long before the Welsh got round to nationalising them. So ubiquitous were they in Anglo-Saxon times that a 'leek-garden' actually meant any kind of vegetable plot, and a gardener was, by extension, a 'leek-warder' – but then the Old English *leac* was something of a catch-all term that referred to almost any plant in what we'd now call the allium family. An Anglo-Saxon leek was a *por-leac*; a *yul-leac* was an onion. Although most of their names have now changed beyond all recognition, we still of course have garlic, whose Old English name was *gar-leac*, *gar* being the word for spear, presumably from the shape of garlic cloves.

Leeks gave their name to a number of British villages and towns, although not, irritatingly, to Leek in Staffordshire, which if nothing else serves as a warning to amateur toponymists. The first part of Leighton Buzzard, on the other hand, does mean leek-town (although where the Buzzard part comes from is still subject to heated debate), as does Laughton in South Yorkshire and the identically named villages of Leckhampstead in Berkshire and Buckinghamshire.

In a way the Welsh connection is a Saxon one as well. According to time-honoured legend, Welsh warriors beat off a Saxon onslaught after sticking leeks into their hats; it may be hard to see how this helped them win the battle, but it did at least distinguish them from the enemy. Welsh regiments of the British army still wear a sprig of leek in their caps on St David's Day, the first of March, to commemorate the patron saint of Wales, although as a national emblem the leek is slowly losing ground to the arguably prettier Welsh daffodil. Ironically there are more Scottish varieties of leeks than Welsh.

As with several other vegetables, the leek our ancestors were familiar with was rather different from the leek we know today. The fat modern leek, with its broad leaves neatly splayed on either side of the stem, is a relatively modern invention, and in all likelihood originated during the early eighteenth century. Before that, leeks were slimmer and less tidy and to our eyes would probably have looked more like spring onions. For some reason – perhaps because they are less inherently variable than some other crops – leeks never captured the imagination of Britain's nurserymen. Only two kinds of leek were available to the eighteenth-century gardener: the narrow-leaved French or Flanders leek and the newer, broad-leaved London or London Flag ('flag' referring to their shape, like flag irises). By the nineteenth century the narrow-leaved leeks had all but disappeared, and few new broad-leaved varieties were developed outside France. As late as 1852 the leading British seed company, Sutton's, was still only offering two varieties of leek, the Large Flag and the Musselburgh, compared with fifty-three varieties of pea and thirty-six kinds of broccoli. France remains the world's leading producer of leeks today.

Leeks have suffered over the years from being forced to grow to giant size by cloth-capped exhibitionists with little regard for culinary quality, but (as any sensible person knows) size isn't everything, and there is something to be said for using leeks when they are still fairly small; young leek tops, for example, make an excellent addition to stir-fried vegetables. Still, it has to be said that a giant leek is a wonder to behold.

Giant Carentan / Monstrueux de Carentan
c. 1874

Although not a British variety, Giant Carentan has been popular with British gardeners since it was introduced by the legendary (and still thriving) French nursery firm of Vilmorin in the late nineteenth century. Most probably a selected form of the older Large Rouen, it is a fast-growing, extremely hardy winter leek with a sturdy, dark-green stem, which does best on well-manured soil. Named after the town of Carentan in Normandy, it remains popular in France, and its delicate flavour makes it a good all-rounder for soups and stews – or when simply served on its own.

Lyon / Prize Taker
c. 1883

Its name suggests a French origin, but Lyon seems to have been introduced to this country in the early 1880s by Stuart and Mein, a firm of seedsmen from the Scottish border town of Kelso, which traded from the 1860s until 1900. Victorian nurserymen had a habit of making outrageous claims for their latest introductions; many of these might be most charitably described as over-optimistic, but when Stuart and Mein extolled Lyon's size and quality they were only telling the truth. Lyon's alternative name, Prize Taker, is an apt one, for a well-fed Lyon can grow to enormous size, and it has long been a highly esteemed show-bench variety. Despite its elephantine tendencies it is good for cooking too, being tender and mildly flavoured – in fact for many people it is the finest leek of all. Vigorous, easy to grow and ready to harvest by autumn, Lyon is hardy enough to stand through the winter.

Musselburgh
before 1834

Probably the oldest variety still grown, Musselburgh is named after the town on the Firth of Forth just east of Edinburgh. Leeks have been cultivated around Musselburgh for centuries, and it has been suggested that this variety was brought over by Dutch settlers in the fourteenth century, along with golf – although the latter claim is, perhaps understandably, regarded as slightly more contentious. The earliest references to the Musselburgh variety are from the 1830s, but it was probably developed during the eighteenth century, and may well have been the parent of the well-known London leek. Whatever its origins, Musselburgh is a handsome 'flag' leek (that is, with leaves like a flag iris, which gives this variety its alternative name of Scotch Flag) whose mild flavour belies its large size and its ability to withstand the hardest winters. It is, in fact, as tough as old boots, although given its Scottish antecedents perhaps that won't come as a big surprise.

Lettuces

It is said that the effect of eating too much lettuce is 'soporific'. I have never felt sleepy after eating lettuces; but then I am not a rabbit. They certainly had a soporific effect on the Flopsy Bunnies!

Beatrix Potter, *The Tale of the Flopsy Bunnies* (1909)

The world's favourite salad vegetable has been around since the days of Tutankhamun, when it was dedicated to the goddess Min, and its popularity has hardly waned since. Min was the goddess of fertility, and her association with lettuces had to do with one of their most striking characteristics: their white, milky, slightly sticky sap. This sap gives them their Latin name, *Lactuca sativa* (*sativa* meaning 'cultivated', as opposed to wild); in ancient varieties it also contained a mild narcotic, which explains why it was generally eaten at the end of a meal, although in later Roman times it was nibbled as a starter too.

Cultivated lettuces are related to an undistinguished-looking member of the daisy family, *Lactuca serriola*, found all round the Mediterranean and sometimes called the compass plant from the uncanny way it can align its upper leaves to north and south in full sun. Lettuce is thought to have originated as a cross between the compass plant and another species of *Lactuca* – possibly one that has since become extinct, although lettuces can still interbreed with compass plants and their surviving kin. Ancient Egyptian tombs contain depictions of tall lettuces with pointed leaves, but by the first century AD the Romans were growing various kinds, including purple, red and black, and it was the Romans who probably brought them to Britain in the first place.

Whatever the colour of their leaves or seeds, early lettuces seem mostly to have been of the tall romaine (literally Roman) type, with prominent midribs on the leaves. Cos, their other name, may indicate their ancient origins on the Greek island of Cos, although it has also been suggested that the name derives from an Arabic word for lettuce, which roughly transliterates as *xus*. Romaine lettuces continued to be the most widely grown kind right up to the eighteenth century; to keep the inner leaves pale and tender they were often tied gently together with string.

The rounder, 'hearting' lettuces we know today are a later innovation; they seem to have been introduced from Europe in the sixteenth century and were initially known as 'cabbage lettuce'. One of the best descriptions of this new type comes from the herbalist John Gerard, who noted in 1597 that 'Cabbage Lettuce hath many plain and smooth leaves at his first growing up, which for the most part lie flat still upon the ground: the next that do appear are those leaves in the midst, which turn themselves together, embracing each other so closely, that it is formed into that glove or round head, of which the simplest is not ignorant.' Hearting lettuces can be roughly divided into 'butterhead' and 'crisphead' types – butterheads having floppier leaves (but often more flavour) than modern crisphead cultivars like Iceberg. By the eighteenth century there were many varieties to choose from, including the loose-leaf or cut-and-come-again kinds, which can be harvested over a period of several weeks, not to mention the once well-known Tennis-Ball, whose tight little heads were sometimes pickled in brine. As with so many other varieties of fruit and vegetables, the largest number of nineteenth-century introductions came from France.

Lettuces are as popular today as they ever were, and a surprising number of old varieties survive, but their popularity has its downside. Research carried out in 2004 established that lettuce was the single most-wasted item in British households, with 61 per cent of people throwing away a bag of lettuce a week. What the goddess Min would have thought can only be imagined.

All the Year Round
before 1856

A selected form of the old black-seeded Tennis-Ball lettuce, All the Year Round was a popular market variety in nineteenth-century France, but it was also listed by several British seed companies by the 1850s. As its name suggests it can be sown from early spring (under glass) to late autumn, giving a continuous supply of medium-sized, butterhead lettuces from January to December. A hardy cultivar, it does best in cooler climates.

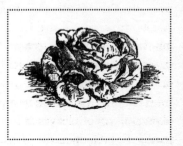

White-seeded All-the-Year-Round lettuce

Balloon
c. 1882

Another French variety, Balloon gets its name from its outsize leaves, which enclose the heart and give it a rather inflated look. It was first

Balloon Cos lettuce

listed by the French seedsmen Vilmorin in 1882, as Romaine Ballon de Bougival. Among the largest kinds of romaine or cos lettuce, it is less likely to bolt in warm conditions than many other varieties; it is also very hardy, and suitable for sowing right through the year. Bougival, birthplace of Georges Bizet and a favourite haunt of the Impressionists, lies west of Paris on the left bank of the Seine; in the eighteenth and nineteenth centuries it was noted for its market gardens.

Bloody Cos
before 1727

The strikingly named Bloody or Spotted Cos, whose dark-green leaves are splashed with red, is an old variety whose alternative name, Aleppo Lettuce, suggests that it may have been introduced from Syria. First noted by the English garden designer Stephen Switzer in his 1727 book, *The Practical Kitchen Gardiner*, it was popular in the eighteenth century for its highly decorative appearance. Although its leaves have prominent stems and it is generally considered a cos, it was often wrongly grouped with the 'cabbage' lettuces. It needs to be kept well watered in hot weather or it will tend to bolt.

Brown Goldring
before 1923

Originally known as Goldring's Bath Cos, the Brown Goldring lettuce has dark-green leaves with bronze-coloured tips. Hardy enough to be grown outside under cloches in winter, it has crisp heads and good disease resistance, and won an Award of Merit from the Royal Horticultural Society in 1923. Thomas Goldring and Sons was a pre-war company of seedsmen, fruiterers and florists based in Dodsley Lane, Easebourne, near the Sussex town of Midhurst.

Fat Lazy Blonde
before 1850

Better known in France as Grosse Blonde Paresseuse, Fat Lazy Blonde gets its politically incorrect name from its loose yellow-green leaves, which flop around for all the world as if it was falling-down drunk. In Britain it was sometimes called White Stone or Nonpareil; its alternative French name is Blonde d'été de St-Omer, which may be a clue to its origins, St Omer and the Pas de Calais having been a great centre of salad (and especially chicory) cultivation. An outsize butterhead variety, it has wrinkled outer leaves that enclose a loose but tender heart, and it holds up well in hot weather.

Lobjoit's Green
before 1856

Of all the cos varieties, none have a finer flavour than Lobjoit's Green, which once gloried in the alternative name of Vaux's Self-Folding Lettuce. (This wasn't a crazed Victorian invention along Heath Robinson lines: it was called self-folding because its leaves naturally enclose the heart, unlike most cos varieties of lettuce.) Its long, crisp leaves are pale green outside and almost white within, with a sweet, tender taste; to thrive it needs rich soil and liberal watering. Like so many nineteenth-century lettuces it seems to have originated in France, but it was evidently marketed by several British companies. The west London firm of W. J. Lobjoit and Son was founded in 1828 by the Rothschilds' head gardener, with market gardens first in Hammersmith and later in Barnes and Osterley Park; the Lobjoits descended from Huguenot refugees who settled in Kent during the early seventeenth century. The company was still trading in 1958.

Marvel of the Four Seasons
before 1880

Although not as well known as Fat Lazy Blonde, this large, lax butterhead lettuce also appears to have originated in France, where it was known as Merveille de Quatre Saisons. It has shiny dark-bronze outer leaves tipped with red and a crisp, creamy heart, and is suitable for sowing throughout the year, although to prevent it bolting it must be liberally watered in periods of hot weather.

Webb's Wonderful
1890

This crisphead lettuce has been popular for more than a century thanks to its excellent flavour and reliability. Within its loosely curled outer leaves it has a large, tightly folded, crisp white heart, and its growth is rarely inhibited by extremes of warm or wet weather. Webb's have been royal seedsmen to every monarch from Victoria to Elizabeth II. The company was founded in the mid-nineteenth century by Edward Webb, and was originally based in Wordsley, near Stourbridge in Worcestershire (now the West Midlands); by the twentieth century it was the biggest employer in town. In 1937 Webb's moved to Wychbold, south of Bromsgrove, and since 1971 it has been run by Edward Webb's great-grandson, Richard. The firm still sells Webb's Wonderful today.

Onions

I will not move my army without onions!
General Ulysses S. Grant, US President 1869–77

Some indication of onions' antiquity can be deduced from the fact that no wild equivalent of the cultivated onion, *Allium cepa*, has ever been found – which suggests that it was domesticated so many thousand years ago that either it has changed out of all recognition from its putative ancestor, or the original wild species has since become extinct. Either way, onions were already popular in ancient Egypt (so much so that when Rameses IV died in 1160 BC, onions were placed in the eye sockets of his mummified body) and worshipped as a symbol of eternal life. By the time of Hippocrates (around 460–370 BC) several types of onions were grown, including the red and white kinds we are familiar with today. The consensus seems to be that they were brought to Britain by the Romans, although onion seeds are so light and tiny that it seems likely they were traded around Europe even before then. Whatever the circumstances of their arrival, onions had become an important staple crop by the Middle Ages, along with beans and cabbages. They were also among the first European vegetable seeds to be introduced to the Americas: Christopher Columbus took onions to Haiti in 1494, and they were grown by the first British colonists at Jamestown in Virginia during the early 1600s.

Soft, mild-flavoured 'Spanish' onions have been known in Britain since at least the late sixteenth century, although they did not keep well; for storing, a long-lost variety called Strasburg was recommended instead. British gardeners seem to have been content to grow just a handful of varieties right through to the late eighteenth century – which is also the date of our oldest surviving cultivars – when enterprising landowners first began planting onions on a commercial scale, especially on the light soils around the aptly named Sandy in Bedfordshire. British onion cultivation had a relatively brief heyday, peaking around the 1860s, after the railways began to offer quick and easy access to the London markets but before cheap imports from Holland, Spain and Egypt began undercutting the British market. In 1860 a little over 300,000 bushels of onions were imported; by 1900 that figure had increased astronomically to more than seven million. This golden age stimulated the breeding of many new varieties, some for the market, but others (usually of giant size) for exhibition in the highly competitive fruit and vegetable shows that became so popular during the nineteenth century. By the end of the century so many cultivars were available that complete confusion set in, not helped by competing seed companies who often sold the same varieties under different names. As James Anderson wrote despairingly in 1875: 'The nomenclature of Onions, like most other vegetables in common use, appears to be in a state of great derangement.'

Onion production was highly labour intensive. Until relatively recently most plants were grown from seed, rather than from the young bulbs, or 'sets', that are generally sold today – sets apparently being an American innovation, dating back to the mid-nineteenth century. The seed beds had to be heavily manured (often using horse manure sent from London on the same trains that later transported the crop to market); planting, weeding, watering and harvesting were all done by hand. In Bedfordshire, where the bulk of British onions were raised, they were dried in large black-planked onion lofts after picking; each day the drying onions were shaken, and their seed collected in hessian sacking on the floor below. According to the Bedfordshire Architectural Heritage Trust, which launched a survey of Bedfordshire onion lofts in 2004, around fifty such lofts still exist around Sandy and Biggleswade. Onions are still grown commercially in Bedfordshire, but the United Kingdom is no longer a major onion producer – certainly not compared to China, which now supplies something like a third of the entire world onion market, followed by India, Russia and the USA.

Ailsa Craig
1887

One of the best-loved exhibition onions, the enormous Ailsa Craig originated in rather grand surroundings: a kitchen garden designed by the great eighteenth-century architect Robert Adam, at Culzean Castle, on the south-west coast of Scotland. It was raised in 1887 by David Murray, head gardener to Archibald Kennedy, third Marquess of Ailsa, and marketed nationally by John Sutton and Son from 1895. A cross between two popular onions of the day, Cranston's Excelsior and Danvers Yellow Globe, Ailsa Craig is a large, mild-flavoured onion with pale honey-coloured skin, good for both cooking and salads, although like most mild onions it does not keep for long. Its parents are interesting in themselves. Cranston's Excelsior, which was widely grown in Britain until the Second World War but since seems to have disappeared, probably originated at the renowned Cranston Nurseries in King's Acre, Hereford. Danvers Yellow Globe was an American variety, raised by a farmer called Daniel Buxton in Danvers, Massachusetts, some time before 1845 and introduced to Europe in the 1850s – a reminder of how international agricultural markets were even during the nineteenth century. David Murray was head gardener at Culzean from 1874 to 1910 and was renowned for his fruit and vegetables; his friendship with the third Marquess was such that the kitchen gardens were always amply provided for, despite the rackety state of the family's finances. According to Murray's successor, William Orr (head gardener from 1928 to 1963), Murray raised Ailsa Craig in the vegetable plots behind the walled garden.

Ailsa Craig gets its name from an uncanny-looking island off the Scottish coast, visible from Culzean, which the Kennedys acquired in 1560 and from which they took their title. The island rises to 340 metres (1,114 feet) sheer from the sea, with a domed top, and could, with a little imagination, be said to bear a passing resemblance to a submerged onion of titanic size. Apart from lending its name to an onion and a tomato and inspiring a second-rate sonnet by John Keats ('To Ailsa Rock', which begins 'Hearken, thou craggy ocean pyramid! / Give answer from thy voice, the sea-fowls' screams!' and does not get much better), the island is composed of a fine granite which provided the material for most of the world's curling stones. The fifth Marquess of Ailsa gave Culzean Castle to the National Trust for Scotland in 1945, but the family hung on to Ailsa Craig. Today it is home to 70,000 gannets.

Bedfordshire Champion
1869

Like Ailsa Craig this is a large, mild-tasting onion, which also seems to be related to Danvers Yellow Globe, although it has a similar shape to James' Longkeeping and pre-dates Ailsa Craig by twenty years. It was introduced by the same seed company, Sutton's of Reading, in 1869, and has been a popular variety ever since, thanks to its full-bodied flavour and generally good yields. Like so many popular varieties it became known by a bewildering array of alternative names over the years, including Sutton's Globe, Up to Date, Nutting's Golden Ball and Cambridge No. 10, as it was adopted by different seed merchants in various parts of the country. A few of these variants developed into what some would consider to be new varieties in their own right, showing better adaptation to local conditions or increased resistance to mildew, which the original variety lacked, but since the National Lists were imposed in 1980 all have had to be sold as Bedfordshire Champion again. Whether this is a triumph of clarity for consumers or a setback to genetic diversity continues to be a matter for heated debate. A century and a half on it is still sold by Sutton's – but as Bedfordshire Champion, of course, not as Sutton's Globe.

Giant Zittau
before 1876

Although it has been grown in Britain since the 1870s, Giant Zittau has German origins – Zittau being an ancient town on the very eastern edge of Germany, hard up against the Czech and Polish borders. The soil hereabouts is sandy and fertile and ideal for onion cultivation, and the Giant Zittau began life as a local variety, but its delicious, buttery flavour and remarkable keeping qualities gained it an ever-wider circle of admirers, and by the late nineteenth century it was well known in both Britain and France. It has the golden-brown skin and white flesh of a typical 'Spanish' onion, but unlike many outsize varieties it keeps well, and retains its buttery

Giant Zittau onion

James' Scarlet Intermediate carrots, which date from the early nineteenth century, are thought to have been named after a Mr James of Lambeth Marsh in London, whose market garden disappeared beneath Waterloo Station in 1848.

Cauliflowers were highly fashionable in the early eighteenth century, being expensive and rather difficult to grow, and they inspired Britain's first novelty teapots, like this one from the Fitzwilliam Museum in Cambridge, dated 1759–1766.

After his capture at the Battle of Blenheim, the French commander Marshall Tallard was exiled to Nottingham. He may not, as is sometimes claimed, have brought celery to Britain, but it seems possible that he introduced his British captors to the bizarre French custom of eating celery raw.

First mentioned in 1665, May Duke (top) is a one of the oldest cherries still grown.
Two other ancient varieties, the White Heart and the Black Heart, are shown below,
in a hand-coloured plate from George Brookshaw's magisterial *Pomona Britannica*,
first published in 1812.

Round and yellow rather than long and green,
the Lemon Apple cucumber – seen here in the kitchen
garden at Normanby Hall in Lincolnshire – looks nothing
like its modern counterparts. It has been grown in Britain
since the late nineteenth century, but may have begun
life in Australia.

John Tradescant the Elder (shown here
in a portrait attributed to Cornelius de
Neve) was one of the greatest plant
collectors of all time. He was almost
certainly the first person in Britain to
grow blackcurrants and runner beans,
in his famous London garden on
South Lambeth Road.

New Red Currant.
Laxton's No. 1.

Laxton's No. 1 redcurrant was
raised around 1914 by the famous
firm of Laxton Brothers, Bedford,
though it was still being described
as a new variety in their 1925 catalogue. Actually it should really be
called Laxton's No. 3.

This new variety is the best red
currant yet raised. It is a strong upright grower, carrying an enormous
crop of berries, a brilliant red in
colour. Price: 2/6 and 3/6 each.
(See page 23.)

Maintained by North
Lincolnshire Council,
the kitchen gardens at
Normanby Hall
contain one of the
best collections of
Victorian-era fruit
and vegetables in
the country.

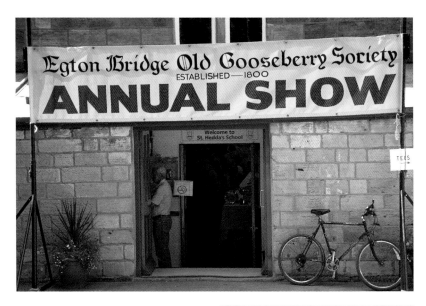

Gooseberry breeding became a fiercely competitive sport in the late eighteenth and early nineteenth century, and there were hundreds of gooseberry shows all over northern England at one time. Only a handful survive today. The oldest of all takes place at Egton Bridge, near Whitby.

The sweet red gooseberry, Whinham's Industry, dates back to around 1835, when it was bred by a Mr R. Whinham of Morpeth in Northumberland – possibly the same Robert Whinham who composed Whinham's Hornpipe and Whinham's Reel and died in Morpeth workhouse.

taste even after several months in storage. Its popularity also led to the development of several imitators, of which Ailsa Craig is sometimes reckoned to be one, and today there are so many variants of the original type that it is probably best to think of Giant Zittau as a family of broadly similar cultivars, rather than as a single variety. Zittau, incidentally, is one of the remaining strongholds of the Sorbs, a small indigenous ethnic minority of Slavic origin. They are famed for their decorated Easter eggs, which are often dyed using onion skins.

James' Longkeeping
c. 1793

Waterloo station might not seem the most likely place to find a historic onion, but until the late 1830s the ground beneath it was occupied by some of London's many market gardens, one of which was owned by Mr James. His onion, which was described in the Horticultural Society's journal in 1819 as a 'Well known sort raised by a market gardener of the name James several years ago', has robustly flavoured, medium-sized, pear-shaped bulbs which – as their name suggests – can be stored for months in good conditions. Although it is the oldest variety we have, James' Longkeeping was deleted from the National List as recently as 1993, but thankfully its seed has been preserved by Garden Organic in its Heritage Seed Library. It is very hardy, if rather slow to grow, which makes it best suited for winter harvesting.

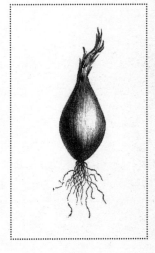

James' Longkeeping onion

Southport Red Globe
1880s

Southport Red Globe might sound like an archetypically British variety, but its name is misleading, for the Southport it refers to is not in Lancashire but in Connecticut, looking out over Long Island Sound. Today it is an affluent shore-front suburb, but in the mid-nineteenth century the area was known as the onion capital of America, and Southport Red Globe dates from those glory days, although surprisingly little seems to be known about its history. Like Ailsa Craig it probably derived from Danvers Yellow Globe, arguably the first major American onion variety. In common with most red onions Southport Red Globe has a strong, pungent taste, although only the outer skin is red (or rather reddish-purple): inside the flesh is white with a purplish tinge. It gives good crops, stores well and became extremely popular both in the States and in Britain, winning a First Class Certificate from the Royal Horticultural Society in 1888.

Parsnips

Fine words butter no parsnips.

Traditional saying

Compared to the exotic origins of many vegetables – potatoes from Lake Titicaca, say, or cucumbers from the Himalayas – the parsnip's ancestry is decidedly humble. So humble, in fact, that there is no need to travel halfway round the world to see them growing wild: the nearest stretch of railway line or landfill site would probably suffice, especially in the chalkier parts of Surrey, Hampshire and Kent. For the wild parsnip, *Pastinaca sativa*, is a common weed, found right across Europe into Turkey and Ukraine. Like most undomesticated vegetables it is a pretty tough customer, with thin, deep, stringy roots that no one in their right mind would want to cook; what it does have, though, is that distinctive, aromatic parsnip smell. The date of their domestication is not known, but the Romans seem to have liked them, although as they called both parsnips and carrots *pastinaca* it is hard to be sure which one their writers are referring to. According to Pliny, the famous early naturalist, a taste for German parsnips was among the less unmentionable peccadilloes of the emperor

Tiberius, and Germany has often been suggested as the area where larger parsnips were developed. Whether that is the case or not (and Italy has some claim as an alternative location) these early 'improved' varieties were almost certainly still far thinner and woodier than the parsnips we cook with now. But they were also more widely used, as a sweetener in the days before sugar was widely available, to make wine, and as an all-round alternative to potatoes, boiled and roasted as they are today.

Parsnips are happiest in cold conditions: their full flavour only really develops after frost, which converts the starch in the roots to sugar, giving them their characteristic sweet taste. For this reason they have always done best in northern climates, and they have long been popular in Germany, Britain and Russia, where wild parsnips were made into an early kind of borscht. (In Russian, parsnip is *pasternak*, which gives added savour to the name of Russia's Nobel Prize-winning poet Boris Pasternak.) Oddly, though, they never caught on in the United States, despite the fact that they were grown in the very first European settlement there: according to *A True Declaration of the estate of the Colonie in Virginia*, published in 1610, 'parsneps' were grown at Jamestown, along with 'cucumbers, muske melons, pompions [pumpkins], potatoes . . . carrets [and] turnups'. Their subsequent disappearance from American cuisine has been put down to their sweet flavour, which the unadventurous consider peculiar in a root vegetable; this also might explain why parsnips have never played such an important role in agricultural history as, say, turnips or potatoes. One symptom of parsnips' failure to engage the popular imagination is the fact that, right until the end of the eighteenth century, there appear to have been only two distinct varieties available (the 'common' parsnip and the faintly disturbing 'Swelling Parsnip'); and this at a time when there were at least fifteen different kinds of cabbage.

The nineteenth century brought new varieties, but it also brought duplicity and duplication, to parsnips as to so many other crops. As the Scottish-born garden writer Peter Henderson wrote in his 1867 best-seller *Gardening for Profit*: 'A number of varieties of Parsnips are enumerated in seed lists, but the distinctions, as far as I have seen, are hardly worth a difference in name, and I am inclined to think that the soil often determines peculiarities of variety.' That several nineteenth-century cultivars do survive is a testament to the dedication with which generation after generation of gardeners have conserved them, for parsnip seed is notoriously short-lived and unreliable, rarely remaining usable for more than a year; even when the seed is fresh germination rates are often low. On the other hand parsnips are among the easiest crops to store, and can be left in the ground right through the winter, developing their sweetest flavour by the following spring.

Cobham Improved Marrow
1940s?

Despite its intriguing name, very little has been recorded about this much-recommended variety, although it seems to have been introduced in the mid-twentieth century by the still-extant seed company Tozers of Cobham in Surrey. Tozers was established during the Second World War by A. L. Tozer and Dr Dermot Dawson as part of an effort to increase British vegetable-seed production, at a time when access to French-produced seed was difficult, not to say actively perilous. The Cobham Improved Marrow has smooth white skin, a chunky wedge-like shape and good resistance to that bane of the parsnip grower, canker, which causes infected roots to rot on the spot. Among its other advantages are fine flavour and one of the best rates of germination, which makes it a good variety to try for anyone who has not grown parsnips from seed before. It won an Award of Garden Merit from the Royal Horticultural Society in 1993, which was reconfirmed after further trials in 2001.

Hollow Crown
before 1825

Hollow Crown, which was already being referred to as a 'good old sort' in 1852, is probably the oldest parsnip still in cultivation. Its name refers to the way in which its 'shoulders', above ground, dip in slightly towards the central leaf-stems, rather than having the usual smoothly dome-shaped crown. It has been grown in Britain

since at least the 1820s, and was once the main variety grown in the Channel Islands for the early mainland market. Its fine white flesh has a sweet, mellow flavour, which gives credence to the claim that it makes a tasty marmalade, as well as the better-known (and allegedly delicious) parsnip wine. Like most parsnips it does best in deep, friable soil, where its roots can happily grow

Long Smooth Hollow-crown parsnip　　to a depth of 30–40cm (12–16in).

Tender and True
1897

A popular song by Sir Arthur Sullivan called 'Tender and True' was first published in 1874. It includes the memorable lines 'Oh! to call back the days that are not! / Mine eyes were blinded, your words were few, / Do you know the truth now, up in Heaven? / Douglas, Douglas, tender and true.' Quite why it should have inspired the name of a parsnip is not entirely clear, but it did, and the Tender and True parsnip is still regularly grown in the kitchen gardens at West Dean in Sussex and in Cornwall by the Lost Gardens of Heligan. It is noted for its refined quality, with smooth white flesh and long roots, which were much shown at horticultural exhibitions and won many prizes. Tender and True was still winning accolades a century later – including an Award of Garden Merit from the Royal Horticultural Society as recently as 1993.

The Student
1859

James Buckman was one of those remarkable Victorians whose scientific expertise straddled several fields, and who combined academic brilliance with an appealingly down-to-earth approach to scientific enquiry. Born in 1816, he became curator of the Birmingham Philosophical Institute in 1842, but it was during his tenure as professor of geology, natural history and botany at the Royal Agricultural College, Cirencester, from 1847 to 1863 that he really made his mark. Buckman gained a reputation as one of the country's leading plant breeders, but he also found time to conduct archaeological surveys and photograph his fossil collection, not to mention keeping up a lively correspondence with other scientists, including Charles Darwin, with whom he exchanged notes on everything from pigeons to kidney beans. It appears that he bred The Student largely as an experiment, using the seed of wild parsnips to demonstrate how quickly wild plants could be 'improved' (or 'ennobled' in the terminology of the day) and re-domesticated under favourable conditions. 'Our ennobled examples of these were considered so perfect,' Buckman wrote afterwards, in the

The Student parsnip

college's annual report of 1860, 'that it was thought advisable to consign the whole of the seed of 1859 to Messrs. Sutton of Reading, as new varieties of any cultivated crop plant are always desirable, and more especially when, as in the present case, the new form has been directly derived, not from a variety, but from original wild stock.' Getting Sutton's, the leading seed merchants of the day, to market The Student was a shrewd move on Buckman's part, although it is not clear whether he, or the Royal Agricultural College, earned anything for their toil. It seems quite possible that he was motivated by a spirit of philanthropy rather than an interest in profit, especially given the fact that he named the parsnip not after himself but after his students, which surely suggests a scientist of unusual professional modesty. (Then again, how many people would wish their name to be immortalised in a parsnip?)

Whatever financial arrangements were arrived at, Sutton's considered The Student to be a huge step forward in parsnip cultivation. They introduced it to the commercial market in 1861, and by the end of the century it was among the most widely planted varieties in the country. It has long, smooth roots, which will grow up to 91cm (36in) long given deep enough soil, but which rarely become coarse in texture, remaining fine and sweet, with a mild and pleasant flavour. In some ways The Student could be deemed Professor Buckman's swan-song, for he is said to have lost his post at Cirencester in 1863 because he supported Darwin's theory of evolution. (Charles Darwin was certainly among the subscribers to Buckman's retirement testimonial, sending a cheque for £2 2s.) Buckman retired to Bradford Abbas, near Sherborne in Dorset, where he helped found the Dorset Natural History and Antiquarian Field Club, collected fossils and farmed 'on scientific principles' until his death in 1884; he is buried in the village churchyard there.

Pears

Oh Sir! Whatever happens, let me gain
One of those pears up there that I can see,
Or I shall die! I long so terribly
To eat a little pear, it looks so green.
Geoffrey Chaucer, *The Merchant's Tale* (*c.* 1390)

Apples and pears have a fascinating relationship. Their similarities are obvious – to the extent that many people find it difficult to distinguish between pear and apple trees when they're not actually laden with fruit. (If you do want to distinguish them, here are some rule-of-thumb suggestions: if they're flowering, have a sniff – apple blossom, which is often tinged with pink, is faintly sweet-smelling, but pear flowers, which are generally ivory white, have a sour scent; pear leaves are often more shiny and pointed than apple leaves, which tend to be rougher, downy and more rounded in shape; and apples are generally fairly wide-spreading trees, whereas pears tend to be more upright and twiggy, often with rather craggy bark.) Pears, however, have never had the mass-market appeal of apples, an oddity that's graphically illustrated by the fact that while the National Fruit Collection in Kent includes

1,867 varieties of apple, it has just 469 varieties of pear. Why? Well, for one thing, dessert (or eating) pears have a much shorter history than dessert apples. For those of us who are accustomed to the super-sweet, melt-in-the-mouth taste of today's Comice and Conference, it might come as a surprise to learn that, at least until the seventeenth century, the idea of eating pears raw would have been considered pretty barmy. Pears are more difficult to harvest than apples, too. Unlike apples they need to be picked before they're ripe, and once picked they're easily bruised, which makes them hard to transport successfully over long distances – part of the reason we see so few pear varieties in the shops, and why so many of them are like lumps of wood when they arrive.

Our ancestors regarded pears rather like we regard quinces now: that is, as a cooking ingredient, not as something that dribbles down your chin. And this wasn't just a matter of taste, or (more practically) in obscure recognition of the fact that eating anything raw in those days was a bit of a risk, but because most pear varieties of the time were hard as rocks, gritty as sand and altogether pretty unpalatable until they had been boiled or baked for several hours. Which is not to say that pears were not esteemed. On the contrary, some varieties were held in high regard. None more so than the so-called warden pears, of which the Black Worcester is the most distinguished survivor. The reputation of these cooking pears was so high, in fact, that for centuries they were regarded as a distinct species in their own right. Just as Lady Mary Wortley Montagu divided the human world into 'men, women and Herveys' – in reference to the exasperatingly effete John, Lord Hervey (1696–1743) – so this branch of the fruit family was formerly divided into apples, pears and wardens.

Their name is believed to have derived from Warden Abbey, at Old Warden in Bedfordshire, a Cistercian monastery that was founded in 1135. All sorts of fruit and vegetables were first cultivated in Britain in monastery gardens, although many of them may originally have been introduced by the Romans, only to be forgotten again during the upheavals of the Dark Ages. The abbey itself has long since disappeared, but a grand Elizabethan house was built on the site by the Gostwick family, and a fragment of this survives. By happy chance it is now leased by the Landmark Trust, thus offering the opportunity to reside on the spot where this most ancient of pears originated.

Although there were a fair number of native cultivars by the end of the sixteenth century, including a rare dessert variety called the Butter pear, it was the French and their near-neighbours the Belgians (or rather, Belgians-to-be, since their country wasn't named Belgium until 1831) who took the initiative in pear-breeding from the seventeenth century on – which is why so many pears, like roses, have French names. In some ways this was a quirk of history, but there's another reason that British pear cultivation has always played second fiddle to apples and the French. Pears are less hardy than apples, and they thrive best in warmer conditions than are generally found over here. That's not to say they can't be grown successfully even in the north of Britain, as long as local conditions are favourable: pears were once widely planted in south-east Scotland, and the walled garden at Cannon Hall in Barnsley has a fine collection of historic varieties. In the nineteenth century the Worcestershire town of Pershore became so famous for its pear orchards that it was nicknamed 'Pearshore', and perry pears (those small, inedible pears used for pear cider) are still grown in parts of Gloucestershire and Somerset. (Sadly the hundreds of varieties of perry pears and cider apples go beyond the scope of this book, which is concerned with culinary fruit and vegetables.) Commercial orchards of all kinds have suffered a dramatic decline in the last fifty years, and pears have been as hard hit as any other crop: 50 per cent of British pear orchards were lost between 1970 and 1998, and their decline has continued steadily since. Luckily pears are the longest-lived of all fruit trees, and individual trees can survive for around 300 years, so there may well be many ancient varieties still waiting to be discovered. No wonder the old saying went: 'Plant pears for your heirs.'

Despite the climatic disadvantages they face, British growers can take the credit for two world-famous pears: Williams' Bon Chrétien, also known by its American name of Bartlett, which was found in the Berkshire village of Aldermaston around 1770, and Conference, which was raised in Hertfordshire around 1885. From humble beginnings, these two varieties have come to dominate international pear production, their primacy challenged only by the great Doyen du Comice from France.

Black Worcester
before 1575?

One of the ancient race of 'wardens', Black Worcester is probably the oldest variety of pear to survive in cultivation. This large, rough-skinned, chestnut-brown cooking pear has been associated with the city of Worcester for centuries, and (most unusually) features on the Worcester coat of arms. Like many tall, vigorous pear trees they were often planted as windbreaks, and turn up in hedgerows all over Worcestershire; in average-sized gardens they are best grown on a dwarfing rootstock such as quince. Black Worcesters are robust, disease-resistant trees, and if picked between late October and early November the rock-hard fruit will keep till April – a useful quality in the days when there were few sweet things to eat at that time of year. Warden pies are mentioned by Shakespeare in *The Winter's Tale* (1609), and in 1660 Robert May offered this recipe in *The Accomplisht Cook* (republished in facsimile by Prospect Books, 2000):

To make a Warden or a Pear Tart quartered. Take twenty good wardens, pare them, and cut them in a tart, and put to them two pound of refined sugar, twenty whole cloves, a quarter of an ounce of cinnamon broke into little bits, and three races of ginger pared and slic't thin; then close up the tart and bake it, it will ask five hours baking, then ice it with a quarter of a pound of double refined sugar, rose water, and butter.

Conference
1885

One of those rare old varieties that is as popular today as it has ever been, Conference was 'scientifically' (that is, intentionally rather than inadvertently) bred by Thomas Francis Rivers at his once-legendary family nursery in Sawbridgeworth, just north of Harlow in Hertfordshire. Its name commemorates the national Pear Congress, which took place at the Royal Horticultural Society's show grounds at Chiswick in October 1885 (perhaps Rivers called his new pear 'Conference' because he felt that the name 'Congress' would be too suggestive for his time; or – more likely, to my mind – he named his seedling in the months before the Pear Congress received its official title, when the *Gardeners' Chronicle*, for example, was advertising it as a 'conference'). The Congress itself was a bit of a damp squib. As the *Gardeners' Chronicle* recorded a couple of weeks later: 'It has been a matter for regret that quite one half the days the show of Pears was open were wet ones, thus seriously affecting the attendance of the public; still further, it is evident that Pears have entirely failed to create the interest which attached to the Apples two years since.' Still, the *Chronicle* went on to note that 'The only bona fide seedling kind to which a First-class Certificate was granted was Mr Rivers' Conference, a long tapering kind, of delicious flavour and soft luscious flesh, somewhat tinted with pink, and ripe in November' – a description that still holds true today. Conference quickly became Britain's best-selling pear. Its commercial success may have something to do with how heavily it crops and how well it keeps in refrigerated storage, but what has really guaranteed its popularity is its sweet, juicy flavour; its all-round quality was reconfirmed by the Royal Horticultural Society in 1993 when it was given an Award of Garden Merit.

Conference does have some failings: its flesh can be rather coarse and gritty, and its flower buds are said to be especially tempting to those airborne vandals, bullfinches. Yet well over a century after its birth it still leads the field: in 2004, some 1,383 hectares (3,417 acres) of orchards in England and Wales were planted with Conference, compared with just 177 hectares (437 acres) of Comice.

Green Pear of Yair
before 1814

Scotland may not seem like prime pear territory, but the Green Pear of Yair is a rare old Scottish dessert variety, which is still grown at Kellie Castle, near Pittenweem in Fife, and can occasionally be found for sale. Large and speckled with russet marks, it ripens in early August and probably comes from the Border country, as its name suggests: Yair House, formerly owned by the Pringle family, overlooks the River Tweed a few miles east of Galashiels and not far from Sir Walter Scott's house at Abbotsford. The Green Pear of Yair was noted by John Sinclair in 1814, but more fully described by the garden writer Charles McIntosh in 1828, who noted that it was 'Said to be indigenous to a beautiful seat on the river Tweed, about thirty miles from Edinburgh. Colour green; size small; sweet and juicy. Should be eaten off the tree; does not keep many days; is a great bearer, and free grower.' In the early nineteenth century there were extensive orchards in the area, and pears from nearby Jedburgh are said to have been sold as far away as London. You can still see their descendants in the town, in the gardens of Queen Mary's House on Queen Street.

Hessle
before 1827

Few pears are hardier or earlier to ripen than Hessle, a rounded yellowish pear which has a long history of cultivation in Scotland and the north of England. Its full story is unknown, but its name connects it with the Yorkshire town of Hessle (pronounced 'Hezzle'), now a suburb of Hull near the north end of the Humber Bridge. It is probably best regarded as a cooking rather than as a dessert pear, as its hardiness is not matched by its flavour, which though juicy and sweet is best described as bland. Hessle can be picked in early September and used soon afterwards.

Pitmaston Duchess
1841

In the early nineteenth century the village of St John's, just across the River Severn from the centre of Worcester, became famous for its nurseries and market gardens: the St John's Nurseries, which occupied almost 160 acres by the late 1800s, was one of the largest nurseries in the world. St John's sunny, west-facing position and light, sandy soil on a natural terrace above the river made it perfect for growing fruit, and several renowned varieties were raised there, including the Pitmaston Pine and the Worcester Pearmain apples and the Pitmaston Duchess pear. Both the Pitmaston Pine Apple and the Pitmaston Duchess pear were introduced by John Williams, a local landowner who lived next door to the St John's Nurseries in the rather grand Pitmaston House. Williams was a keen horticulturalist and a corresponding member of the Horticultural Society of London (later to become the Royal Horticultural Society), whose other passions were strawberries and roses; in 1828 he raised *Rosa* 'Williams' Double Yellow', which is still popular today.

Pitmaston Duchess was raised as a cross between the Belgian pear Glou Morceau and the French Duchesse d'Angoulême (named after the first daughter of Marie-Antoinette and Louis XVI). Until 1870 it was known as the Pitmaston. Duchesse d'Angoulême, which explains why the French spelling is still sometimes used for its name. One of the best and largest dual-purpose garden pears, Pitmaston Duchess makes a big, fast-growing tree, which often has a spectacular show of flowers in spring. The fruit is large, light green and slightly rough, turning pale yellow and sometimes flushing red as it ripens; it can be picked from mid-September, and is at its best the following month both for cooking and as a meltingly juicy dessert. John Williams died in 1885 and his estate was inherited by his son, who died childless in 1892, leaving Pitmaston House to his nephew, the preposterously named Francis Wigley Greswolde Greswolde-Williams; the gardens have since largely been built over, but Pitmaston House still stands on Malvern Road, under the occupation of Worcestershire County Council.

Williams' Bon Chrétien / Bartlett
1770

Open a tin of pears and this is the variety you are almost certain to find inside: Williams' – or Bartlett as it's known in the United States – is the world's most popular pear, and millions are canned every year in California, Australia and South Africa. Williams' Bon Chrétien (literally 'Williams' Good Christian') comes from the Berkshire village of Aldermaston, better known these days for its Atomic Weapons Establishment than its important role in pomological history. Despite its name, Williams' Bon Chrétien has nothing to do with John Williams (see Pitmaston Duchess, above), although it is occasionally credited to him by mistake. It was found around 1770 as a seedling in the garden of a schoolmaster called Wheeler, whose successor to both school and garden, John Stair, took grafts which somehow ended up at a nursery in Turnham Green, on the western edge of London. The nursery was run by Richard Williams, and the seedlings presumably resembled the ancient variety Bon Chrétien: thus Williams' Bon Chrétien. This complicated saga continued across the Atlantic, for grafts were sent to a Boston nursery around 1797, some of which were subsequently planted by a ship's-captain-cum-farmer called Thomas Brewer in Roxbury, Massachusetts. In 1817 Brewer's orchard, farm or (in some accounts) estate was bought by Enoch Bartlett, a local merchant, who also had an interest in horticulture. Impressed by the pear trees he had inherited but not knowing what they were called (labelling was evidently as hit-and-miss an affair in the early nineteenth century as it is now), he began selling them under his own name, and they quickly caught on. It was only when further imports of Williams' Bon Chrétien arrived in America a decade or so later that growers realised they were dealing with the same variety, but by then Bartlett's name had stuck, and that is how it has been known in the States ever since. Its success can be partly assigned to its reliability, and also to its useful habit of being at least partly self-fertile – most pears need to be cross-pollinated with pollen from a different variety in order to set any fruit. A pale-green pear which helpfully turns golden yellow when ripe, Williams' has a slightly musky flavour; as a tree it crops well, but is unsuitable for damper climates, in which it suffers badly from scab.

Williams' Bon Chrétien pear

Peas

Pease porridge hot,
Pease porridge cold,
Pease porridge in the pot
Nine days old.

Nursery rhyme, *c.* 1797

Modern peas share the industrial advantages of many other popular crops: their pods all ripen at precisely the same time on dwarf-sized plants that can be harvested easily by machine, so avoiding the necessity for labour-intensive supports. The result? Cheap and tasty frozen peas: uniform in size and dependable in flavour but, dare one say it, bland. Yet peas come in all shapes and sizes, and they may well be the oldest vegetable growing in our gardens. Archaeological evidence suggests that peas were among the earliest cultivated crops, and they were certainly widely used in the ancient world: there are nine recipes for pea dishes in the *Apicius*, a fifth-century Roman cookery book. Today we tend to think of peas as a fresh vegetable, but until surprisingly recently they were treated more like chickpeas or lentils, almost always being cooked in soups and stews. Dried peas, like their frozen descendants today, were plentiful and easy to transport. They were also nutritous and cheap, qualities that were much appreciated by the poor, who boiled them up to make pea porridge (or 'pease pottage'), a dreary dish whose memory lives on in the nursery rhyme and also, interestingly, in the form of mushy peas, whose lowly gastronomic standing offers a remarkable example of how social associations can outlive their origins, sometimes by several centuries.

The taste for fresh or garden peas, those sweet little morsels that are so delicious straight from the pod, seems to have developed first in Italy in the late 1300s, where they were known as *piselli novelli*. So why are we more familiar with their French name, *petit pois*? And why did so many old varieties of garden peas come from France? The answer might have something to do with that most scheming of French queens, the Italian-born Catherine de Medici, who married Henri II in 1533 and is said to have brought her favourite foods with her from Italy, including *piselli novelli*. (Her greatest passion, apparently, was artichokes, although her obsessive consumption of them gave her appalling indigestion.) Whatever the truth of the stories about Catherine de Medici – and documentary evidence is admittedly thin to non-existent – court and aristocratic patronage undoubtedly turned *piselli novelli* into a high-fashion food, and dried peas began to decline in status. The introduction of garden peas to Britain may also have a royal connection. During his long exile in France, Charles II would have become familiar with *petit pois*, and their popularity seems to post-date his Restoration in 1660, as John Worlidge implied in his *Systema Horticulturae* of 1677, when he wrote that 'the meaner sort of [peas] have been long acquainted . . . but the sweet and delicate sorts of them have been introduced to our gardens only in this latter age.'

Of course dried peas never went away; they were simply joined by garden peas and, later still, by sugar peas, or mange tout, with their edible pods – another French innovation. In many ways the nineteenth century was the golden age of peas, as for so many other vegetables: gardeners had hundreds of varieties to choose from, a state of affairs that had a revolutionary knock-on effect on nineteenth-century science. Both Mendel and Darwin used peas in their experiments into heredity and genetics, so they helped shape evolutionary theory, which is more than you can say for turnips. Sadly, many old varieties have since been lost, including the ancient Hastings and the legendary Hotspur, but there have been some remarkable survivals too. Appropriately enough, one of the best places to see old kinds of peas today is at Down House in Kent, Darwin's former home, where head gardener Toby Beasley has been assiduously collecting many of the varieties that Darwin mentioned in his work.

Alderman
1891

Once upon a time peas were tall, rangy creatures, quite unlike the short varieties we're accustomed to today. Alderman is a rare survivor of this giant race, easily hurtling up to two metres (six and a half feet) and beyond. But height is far from being its only quality: its flavour is fantastic. A late or main-crop variety for shelling or simply eating straight from the pod, Alderman has large white flowers, followed by long, dark-green pods bursting with nine or ten fat, exceptionally sweet peas. An offspring of Duke of Albany (see below), it was selected by the renowned Laxton Brothers nursery of Bedford and went on sale for the first time in 1891.

Tall peas need solid support and are best treated more like runner beans, but their advantage is that they take up relatively little space, and they're less back-breaking to pick than dwarf varieties. Given a strong frame and regular watering (it has little tolerance of drought), Alderman is a long and prolific cropper, whose peas remain delectably sweet even when they reach the size of small marbles.

Carlin
before 1562

Pigeons and religion may sound like strange bedfellows, but the Carlin pea is where they meet. In the north-east of England, Carlin peas have long been used as pigeon food, but they also have a long association with Lent, and more specifically with Care or Carlin Sunday, a festival that was once widely celebrated on the Sunday before Palm Sunday. Its association with Lent was both practical and symbolic. Carlin peas are very high in protein but they're also a rather unappealing shade of ashen grey, so they would have been a very welcome and appropriate addition to a Lenten diet. The dried peas are soaked in salted water overnight, then boiled and served with salt and vinegar, or doused in mint sauce, beer or even rum. A sardonic depiction of this feast appears in an 1824 engraving by Thomas Bewick. Entitled *Carling Sunday*, it shows a jug decorated with the punning motto 'Pease & Plenty' and a dish of Carlin peas about to be gobbled up by some naughty-looking mice. Their connection to the north-east, and to Lent, is explained in several local legends. One story goes that a shipload of peas saved the citizens of Newcastle from starvation during the Civil War siege of the town in 1644. Others claim that once, when food was painfully short (perhaps during Lent), a ship carrying a cargo of dried peas was shipwrecked somewhere on the north-east coast. Local people salvaged the peas, which by that time were swollen with brine, and liked the taste of them. Several towns along the coast claim that the peas first came ashore there, and

Carling Sunday – engraving
by Thomas Bewick

in one version of the story, the name of the ship's captain was Karlin or Carling.

Of all the domestic varieties of pea, the Carlin has a good claim to be the oldest in existence: the *Oxford English Dictionary* has a reference to 'Carling' peas from 1562. Carlins are tough and tolerant of cold weather, although their thick stems have a tendency to snap in the wind unless they are given adequate support. The plants grow up to two metres (six and a half feet) tall, and have sweetly scented purple-and-lilac flowers. Its seeds, like those of most cold-tolerant varieties, remain round when dried rather than wrinkled, and apart from their use in soups and pigeon lofts, they also serve as excellent ammunition for pea-shooters.

Champion of England
1843

During the mid-nineteenth century William and Julius Fairbeard ran a nursery in the village of Teynham, midway between Faversham and Sittingbourne in Kent. In the early 1840s William raised two new varieties of peas from a single pod of an older

Champion of England pea

marrowfat pea called Knight's White Dwarf. One of them he called Early Surprise. The other, which he started selling in 1843, was originally known as Fairbeard's Champion of England (often mistakenly called Fairford's Champion), but soon became universally known simply as Champion of England. Charles Darwin was so interested in the Fairbeards' work in plant-breeding that he corresponded with them, and he grew Champion of England in his garden at Down House in Kent; it even gets a mention in his 1868 book, *The Variation of Animals and Plants Under Domestication.*

Champion of England was quickly recognised for its outstanding vigour and the tender sweetness of its peas. In 1876 the *Journal of Horticulture* judged it to be the best variety of garden pea on the market, and its fame spread rapidly as far as Canada and the United States, where its dried seeds sold for five dollars a quart.

Although not as tall as some Victorian varieties, Champion of England needs staking, and can grow up to two metres (six and a half feet) in the two and a half months it takes to reach maturity. Like most varieties with wrinkled seeds it is classed as an 'early' pea, and begins producing a huge number of short, fat pods on numerous side-stems once it grows above 50cm (20in) tall. Unlike many peas it crops well whether the growing conditions are damp or baking hot. One odd feature is that the higher, later pods often contain twice as many peas as the first pods lower down.

Duke of Albany
1881?

Like Alderman (see above), Duke of Albany is a giant pea – but then it's hardly surprising that they look quite similar, since Alderman was one of its offspring. Although rarely seen in catalogues these days, Duke of Albany (also known as Boston Hero in the USA) was still commercially available in 1954, when it was being sold by the London company Carter's for its striking dark-green pods. Unlike some old vegetables, Duke of Albany is well worth growing for its taste alone: its peas are so sweet and tender that they can happily be eaten raw; they need the minimum of cooking, and they also freeze well. Its only drawbacks are its height (getting on for three metres, or nearly ten feet), a tendency to wilt in very hot or dry conditions, and an unfortunate susceptibility to powdery mildew. But its productivity easily outweighs any disadvantages: it often has ten peas to the pod. Like other tall peas its height makes for ease of harvesting, and means that it easily outgrows any surrounding weeds.

Duke of Albany seems to have been introduced by Carter's as a selected form of the well-known hybrid Telegraph; its name suggests that it was introduced around 1881, when Queen Victoria's fourth son Leopold was created Duke of Albany. Carter's bought the seed from William Culverwell, gardener to Sir Frederick Milbank of Thorp Perrow, near Bedale in North Yorkshire, who had introduced Telegraph in 1876. Telegraph proved such a variable hybrid that Carter's were able to raise three other varieties from it, namely Stratagem, Pride of the Market and the equally successful Telephone.

Kelvedon Wonder
1925

This prolific dwarf marrowfat variety was most probably introduced in 1925 by Hurst and Son, wholesale seedsmen, whose office was at Houndsditch in the City of London but who owned trial grounds in the village of Feering, just outside Kelvedon in Essex. The Sherwoods, who owned the company, lived at Prested Hall nearby, and hosted staff cricket matches on the lawn; in 1895 they defeated a team from Sutton's Seeds. The hall was requisitioned by the army during the Second World War, but today it is a hotel.

Kelvedon Wonder's small size combined with high productivity made it ideal for smaller gardens, and it remains a popular home-growing variety, winning an Award of Garden Merit from the Royal Horticultural Society in 1993.

Prince Albert
c. 1842

One of the many kinds of fruit and vegetables named after the Prince Consort, the Prince Albert pea made its first public appearance in 1842, when it was advertised by the London firm of Cormack and Oliver, seedsmen and nurserymen of New Cross and Covent Garden. One of the fastest-growing and earliest-harvesting of all peas, it was put through its paces in 1844 by *The British Cultivator and Agricultural Review* magazine. After sowing them on 4 January, their correspondent reported that they 'were up on the 14th; in bloom on the 1st April; and were gathered entirely on May 14th. I could have gathered a small dish on the 10th of May from them. This a very prolific and fine-flavoured Pea.' It still is. At Down House in Kent, home of Charles Darwin between 1842 and his death in 1882, head gardener Toby Beasley raises many of the old varieties of peas that Darwin himself grew as part of his experiments into heredity. 'From a taste point of view almost all the old pea varieties are great straight from the pod,' says Toby, 'but if I had to plump for one I would go for Prince Albert. It's an early variety so it's nearly always the first to crop, it tastes good and it is one Darwin used. Their taste seems quite dependent on regular watering, so plants sown for early cropping often seem to taste better to me. Once the heat of the summer dries the soil out it reflects in the quality of taste in the peas.'

Prince Albert was introduced to the United States in 1845 – an example of the remarkable speed

Prince Albert pea

of communication, even then, between Britain and America – and became equally popular across the Atlantic, although one commentator suggested it was remarkably similar to an older variety called Early Flame, which Thomas Jefferson used to grow at Monticello. Although it is unlikely that we will ever know whether Cormack and Oliver raised Prince Albert themselves or simply renamed Early Flame in honour of the new Prince Consort (who married Queen Victoria in 1840), we do at least know something about the company, which was founded around 1780. Close examination of George Crutchley's 1833 map of Deptford appears to include the legend 'Cormack's Nursery' alongside the short-lived Croydon canal, filled in to create the Deptford-to-Croydon railway in 1836. (Today the site of the nursery is occupied by Auburn Close, immediately behind New Cross Gate station off Goodwood Road.) Their central London showroom has suffered a happier fate. As the *Architectural Magazine* noted in 1838, Cormack and Oliver were the first tenants of the splendid conservatory that stood on the first floor of the newly built Covent Garden Market. Although Covent Garden's nurserymen and seed merchants have all long gone, Cormack and Oliver's conservatory, though much refurbished, still exists, and now plays host to a restaurant.

Tutankhamun
c. 1324 BC or c. 1922

It's tempting to say that the legend of peas germinating from ancient Egyptian tombs is as old as the pyramids, but as myths go it is striking for its tenacity. The Heritage Seed Library, maintained by Garden Organic, preserves a variety known as Prew's Special, which originated, according to its donor, in Egypt. Further research revealed that the peas were originally grown by a gardener on Lord Portman's estate in Dorset during the 1920s. According to the story, Portman's son was a friend of Lord Carnarvon, whose main claim to fame was, of course, that he was with the archaeologist Howard Carter when he excavated Tutankhamun's tomb in 1922. Carter certainly found carbonised peas (among thousands of other things) in the tomb, so the inference is that Carnarvon gave some of them of to his friend Portman, in whose garden the seeds sprang back to life (possibly Arthur Portman, who became a trustee of Carnarvon's estate when he died, allegedly under mysterious circumstances, in 1923). A variant of this account, quoted in a history of Sutton's Seeds, records that the donor of the peas claimed they came from Carnarvon's own estate at Highclere, Berkshire.

It's a romantic story, but what's most fascinating about it is not its veracity (or otherwise), but the fact that it so closely echoes a number of similar stories, some of which date back to the early nineteenth century. In 1848, for example, *The Annals of Horticulture* carried the following report:

A vase found by Sir Gardener Wilkinson in a mummy pit, with an Egyptian sarcophagus, 2,845 years old, was presented to the British Museum. On examining the vase, which was supposed to have contained valuable relics, only a few grains of wheat, vetches, and peas were discovered. Three of these peas were presented by T. J. Pettigrew, Esq, to Mr Grimstone, of the Herbary, Highgate. On the 4th of June, 1844, these were planted in compost, resembling as nearly as possible the alluvial soil of the Nile, and they were placed in a forcing frame. In thirty-five days, one of the seeds germinated, and in that year produced nineteen pods, from which fifty fine peas were preserved. In 1845, they were sown in the open air, and made luxurious growth . . . Through the long drought of 1846, when almost everyone's peas were destroyed, these Egyptian peas – without water – continued green and flourishing, and bearing from 70 to 120 pods on each stem. The original seeds were very small, but by cultivation they have now acquired the size of our marrowfats.

With admirable journalistic impartiality, the *Annals*' correspondent concluded his report by noting that 'It is proper to state, that we have not ourselves seen these peas, nevertheless they are doubtless worthy the notice of the curious.'

For all their interest, these tales of so-called 'mummy peas' all fall into the category of what, in other contexts, would usually be described as urban myths. It would be lovely to believe that peas could survive for 3,000 years and still germinate, but the light of scientific reason reveals the notion as a piece of wishful thinking. Dr Mark Nesbitt, honorary research fellow at the Royal Botanic Gardens, Kew, finds the stories fascinating, but cites several circumstances that make them (to say the least) unlikely, however appealing they might be. To begin with, no single scientifically conducted germination test on authenticated seeds from Egyptian archaeological sites has ever been successful. To anyone who has much experience with old packets of seed this will not come as a surprise: few vegetable seeds remain viable for more than a decade or so, but even allowing for exceptions, modelling conducted by the seed scientist John Dickie at Wakehurst Place suggests that a few hundred years under Egyptian tomb conditions (hardly in themselves ideal) would outsee the viability of most crop seeds. The oldest scientifically dated seeds to have germinated are of a date palm, and date back around 2,000 years – remarkable in itself, but still 1,300 years younger than Tutankhamun's peas. As Dr Nesbitt points out, 'All claims of older material are dubious because the material has not been directly dated by radiocarbon-dating part of an actual germinated seed.' A shame, but then perhaps Tutankhamun peas are best left to mummies.

Plums

To market, to market,
To buy a plum bun:
Home again, home again,
Market is done.

John Florio, *Worlde of Wordes* (1611)

There is something rather bewildering about plums. Few British crops have a more complex ancestry or a more convoluted history, but the real nightmare lies in the names for this fruit. Apples are always called apples, after all, although they come in many different forms. A plum, by contrast, can certainly be a plum, but it can also be a damson, a bullace, a greengage or a mirabelle – not to mention a cherry plum or a prune. It's all most confusing, but bear with me while I try to explain.

Bullaces and cherry plums (the latter being so called because their fruits are cherry-shaped, with a similar range of colours) are both thought to derive directly from wild species: the Caucasian *Prunus cerasifera* in the case of cherry plums, and the widely spread *Prunus institia* in the case of bullaces. Bullaces, with their small, acid fruit, are thought to be the ancestors of both the damson (used mainly for cooking and drying) and the sweet mirabelle of north-eastern France. Most of the larger, sweet 'European' plums – generally referred to as *Prunus domestica* – have long been thought to have originated from hybrids between cherry plums and yet another wild species, *Prunus spinosa*, better known to most of us as the blackthorn or the sloe, whose pea-sized, fiercely sour black fruits give sloe gin its distinctly almondy taste. Both blackthorn and cherry plums grow wild between the Caspian and the Black Sea, and natural hybrids between the two occur in the ancient forests south of Maykop, capital of the Russian republic of Adygea, in the foothills of the Caucasus. Some recent genetic research, however, has challenged this, and suggests that the cherry plum (sometimes called the myrobalan) was the sole parent of *Prunus domestica*, the sweet European plum. Confused? Join the club. (Prunes and greengages, incidentally, are simply selected varieties of the European plum: greengages are characterised by their sweet green flesh, while prunes have been bred for their high sugar content, which makes them more suitable for drying.)

Although neither cherry plums or sweet European plums are native to the British Isles, they were almost certainly among the many other kinds of fruit and vegetables, from figs to lettuces, that were introduced to Britain by the Romans. There is even some evidence that they (or at least their dried fruits) were known before then, judging from the sweet-plum stones found during archaeo-logical excavations at the famous Iron Age hill fort of Maiden Castle in Dorset. By the Middle Ages plums were cultivated as far north as Scotland, at least in monastery gardens, although there seem to have been very few varieties to choose from. The most popular was the damson, whose name, like silk damask, comes from the Syrian city of Damascus, its most likely place of origin. In the past most plums appear to have been cooked or preserved like prunes instead of eaten raw, a tradition that continued well into the seventeenth century; in England the recommended preserving methods included drying them on a sunny roof or spreading them in a bread oven. French prunes were at least as popular as they are today, and back then were imported in barrels – something which gives the story of the Dittisham plum, below, added plausibility.

Interest in fruit cultivation of all kinds revived under the enlightened direction of Henry VIII (in the introduction to his *Pomona* of 1662, John Evelyn claimed that 'It was through the plain industry of one Harris, a fruiterer to Henry VIII, that the fields and environs of about thirty towns in Kent only, were planted with fruit from Flanders, to the universal benefit and general improvement of the county'), and the following century saw many new varieties, shapes and sizes of plum introduced, not just from France, Germany and Spain but from as far away as Hungary and the Balkans. What we now call the Green Gage and the French call the Reine-Claude first arrived around this time, recorded by the botanist John Parkinson in 1629 – although in his day it was known as Verdoch. Curiously, very few British plum varieties date from this time (perhaps because there were so many alternatives available from abroad), with the exception of Fotheringham, first mentioned in 1665 and still grown today. Yet all this activity proved to be relatively short-lived, and there were few further developments in the next 150 years. In fact it was not until the early nineteenth century that landowners and nurserymen began taking plum-breeding seriously again, led by the newly formed Horticultural Society of London.

Foremost among them was Thomas Rivers, from whose nursery at Sawbridgeworth in Hertfordshire came many of the finest fruit varieties of the Victorian age, including thirty-one kinds of peach and more than twenty varieties of plum; some of them are still well known today. Rivers' lead was followed by another outstanding nurseryman, Thomas Laxton of Bedford, whose sons carried on his work into the next century. Given the care Rivers and Laxton took to develop new varieties, it seems ironic that the most famous plum of the nineteenth century, the Victoria, may have come from a chance seedling found in a village garden. But then plums have a habit of producing varied offspring, some of which are peculiarly well adapted to local conditions: among them are the Shropshire and Westmorland damsons, whose fortunes have been enjoying something of a revival on the back of the huge renaissance of interest in old varieties of apples. It's an encouraging development, although there are still plenty of other fine plums waiting to be rediscovered among the 300-odd varieties in the National Fruit Collection.

Bryanston Gage
c. 1800

This old Dorset variety seems to have been a chance cross between the original Green Gage and Coe's Golden Drop (see below). The fruit combines characteristics of both, starting off leaf green like the Green Gage but turning pale yellow as it ripens, like a larger, rounder version of Coe's Golden Drop, although the Bryanston

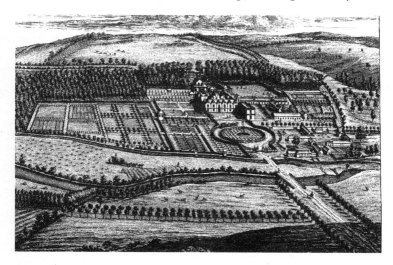

Bryanston and its gardens

On the first of March each year, St David's Day, the Welsh Guards bedeck themselves with ceremonial leeks in honour of their country's patron saint. Leeks have been associated with Wales since ancient times, when Welsh warriors distinguished themselves from their enemies by sticking sprigs of leek in their hats.

The uncannily shaped Ailsa Craig is possibly the only island to have inspired both a poem (written by John Keats) and an onion, raised in 1887 by David Murray, head gardener to the Marquess of Ailsa at nearby Culzean Castle.

Charles Darwin lived at Down House in Kent from 1842 until his death forty years later. He corresponded with many of the leading fruit and vegetable breeders of his day and conducted many of his own experiments there. He was particularly interested in peas, and many of the varieties Darwin grew have recently been replanted in his garden.

The first Williams' Bon Chrétien pear was found in 1770 at Aldermaston, Berkshire, growing in a schoolmaster's garden. It was named by the London nurseryman Richard Williams for its resemblance to the older Bon Chrétien, but it was inadvertently renamed Bartlett when it was introduced to the United States. Today it is the most widely planted pear in the world.

The Pershore Yellow Egg plum was discovered around 1833, growing wild in Tiddesley Wood, near the Worcestershire town of Pershore. Tiddesley Wood survives today, and ancient Yellow Egg plums can still be found there, growing alongside new young trees planted by the Worcestershire Wildlife Trust.

The picturesque Devon village of Dittisham, on the steep banks of the River Dart, was once famous for its orchards, and it even has its own unique plum, the Dittisham Ploughman, which has happily been rescued from extinction.

Among the best-tasting potatoes of all, Duke of York (seen here in flower and at harvest) was raised in Scotland by William Sim of Fyvie, Aberdeenshire, and first came on the market in 1891. Sim made so little money from his potatoes that he emigrated to the United States, where he became the country's leading grower of carnations.

Yes, those are potatoes, and their placement is not some bizarre act of random homage: Antoine-Augustin Parmentier, whose tomb can be seen in the Paris cemetery of Père Lachaise, fought the French prejudice against potatoes and persuaded Marie Antoinette to wear their flowers in her hair.

Gage is more attractive in appearance than either of its parents. It was discovered around 1800 in the gardens at Bryanston, Lord Portman's country house near Blandford Forum, and first listed by the Horticultural Society of London in 1831. Like the majority of cultivated plums it needs to be planted with another variety for successful pollination, and this, along with its large size and spreading shape, makes it unsuitable for small gardens unless it is grafted on to a dwarfing rootstock. Being later than some cultivars, its flowers are slightly less likely to be damaged by frost; it crops well, and the fruit is generally ready to pick by mid-September. Lord Portman's vast kitchen gardens have stood largely empty since the house became a school in 1928, but it would be nice to think that a venerable Bryanston Gage still survives in an odd corner of the estate. Fortunately for us its excellent, sweet flavour, although not as distinctive as the Green Gage, ensured its popularity, and it is still available from specialist nurseries.

Cambridge Gage
1800s

There is no sweeter plum than the Cambridge Gage: plucked in late August when really ripe it virtually melts in the mouth. Its crops may vary in size from year to year, but that is a small price to pay for such delectable fruit, and on most other counts it is considered the most reliable of the many varieties of gage. In size and colour the Cambridge Gage is almost identical to the Green Gage, that is until it is completely ripe, when it flushes to pale yellow; at this point its fine skin is too delicate for it to be stored or picked on a commercial scale, although the Essex firm of Wilkin & Son still grow it for their Tiptree greengage jam. It won a coveted Award of Garden Merit from the Royal Horticultural Society in 1998, whose judges noted its 'honey sweet' flavour.

Coe's Golden Drop
before 1800

Writing in 1831, George Lindley recorded that Golden Drop 'was raised by the late Jervaise Coe, a market gardener at Bury St Edmund's, in Suffolk, more than thirty years ago. He informed me it was from the stone of a Green Gage, the blossom of which, he supposed, had been fertilised by the White Magnum Bonum, the two trees of which grew nearly in contact with each other in his garden.' Coe raised several varieties of plum from seedlings of the Green Gage – quite possibly from some of the first Green Gages to be grown in Britain, just a couple of miles up the road at Hengrave Hall – but the beautifully named Coe's Golden Drop is the only one of his introductions that seems to have survived. Deservedly so, for it is widely considered to be the most lusciously flavoured plum of all: juicy and sweet, with a stone that comes easily away from its tender, golden flesh. Its one failing is its waywardness: in some years it will bear a heavy crop of large, oval, yellow plums, in others hardly any. As a result it has never been grown on a commercial scale, but its taste is so outstanding that it has always been a favourite for growing in gardens, where its unreliability is more

Coe's Golden Drop plum

likely to be tolerated. It was first sold around 1800, and was followed in the nineteenth century by two off-spring of its own: Coe's Crimson Drop, with dark-red fruits, and Coe's Violet, distinguished from its parent by a delicate violet line from top to bottom. A rather late-ripening plum with a distinctively pear-like shape, Coe's Golden Drop is ready to pick towards the end of September. According to George

Lindley: 'It requires an east or a west wall; on the former the fruit attains its greatest perfection.'

Czar
1874

One of the last fruit cultivars to be developed by the great nurseryman Thomas Rivers (1791–1877), Czar was a cross between the once-popular Prince Engelbert and his own redoubtable Early Prolific, which he had introduced as a young man fifty years before.

Thomas Rivers (1791–1877)

It has large purple fruit with greenish flesh, and a sharp but pleasant flavour, best suited to cooking and making jam. Although not a particularly fine dessert variety, Czar's other qualities made it very popular: it is a heavy-cropping, reliable tree of medium size, with some resistance to frost. It first fruited in 1874, which is a clue to how it got its otherwise mysterious name, for that was the year Tsar Alexander II made a highly publicised (and rather shambolic) visit to Britain to see his daughter, who had recently married Queen Victoria's son Alfred. Alexander's seventy-person entourage was due to land at Gravesend on 13 May that year, but the imperial yacht ran aground on a sandbank off the coast of Holland. Eventually it was refloated, but instead of proceeding to Gravesend (where thousands of excited Londoners had been waiting all day), it docked at Dover instead. The Tsar and his party finally arrived at Windsor station nine hours late, before proceeding to what was supposed to be lunch with Queen Victoria, which began around 11 p.m. 'What a contretemps!' Victoria recorded in her diary that night. As it turned out this would be the last time a Russian head of state would visit this country for almost 130 years. The Tsar was assassinated seven years later. The next Russian leader to step on to British soil was Vladimir Putin in June 2003.

Dittisham Ploughman
1700s?

The Ploughman is a fascinating survival, and where it came from is something of a puzzle. Confined to the parish of Dittisham (or 'Ditsum') in Devon, on the opposite bank of the River Dart to Agatha Christie's grand house, the red, medium-sized Dittisham Ploughman resembles a rounded Victoria plum, although the plum expert H. V. Taylor believed it was most closely related to a German variety he called Fluegel (a variety I have been unable to trace). Despite its rarity it deserves to be far more widely grown, for few plums make jam that looks plummier, sets more reliably or tastes as good. Its stones are easy to extract as well.

The village was once surrounded by small, individually owned orchards, but they probably never covered more than about twenty acres and today there are only a few of the old plum trees left. That the Dittisham Ploughman has not died out altogether is mainly thanks to the Ditsum Plum Project, which was set up in 2003 and culminated in *The Plum Project Book*, published in June 2006. In the late nineteenth and early twentieth centuries, when the lush, steep-sided valley of the River Dart was famous for its fruit- and flower-growing, the plum harvest brought some useful extra income each August, and everything else came to a standstill while all hands helped with the harvest. The stories of how this unusual plum ended up in a tiny village in south Devon are colourful enough, but one of them could well be true. In one version, barrels of prunes were washed up after a shipwreck and salvaged by the villagers, who either planted the stones or – perhaps finding the salty prunes inedible – simply chucked them over a hedge, only later to discover that some of them had taken root. In another, less romantic version, the plums were simply bought from one of the foreign merchants who landed in nearby Dartmouth.

Green Gage
c. 1724

If any variety illustrates the complicated history of plums better than any other it is surely the Green Gage. It is the most famous example of a whole family of sweet, green-skinned plums – collectively known as the gages – which are thought to have originated in Armenia. Long esteemed for their wonderful flavour and unusual colour, they appear to have spread across Europe via

Green Gage plum

Greece and Italy. The variety seems to have entered Britain from France in the early 1700s, although it was known here at least a century before that, called Verdoch, a corruption of its Italian name, Verdocchia. To the French, however, it was (and still is) known as Reine-Claude, after Queen Claude (1499–1524), first wife of François I, during whose reign it was first grown in France. That we now call it the Green Gage and not Verdoch or Reine-Claude is thanks to an all-too-common gardening accident. The story goes that around 1724, an English Catholic priest called John Gage, studying at a seminary near Paris, sent some young gage trees to his brother, Sir William Gage of Hengrave Hall, a handsome Tudor manor house which still stands near Bury St Edmunds in Suffolk. En route the saplings lost their labels, so Sir William's gardener is said to have named them 'Green Gages' after his boss. Not much else seems to be known about John Gage, although a Jesuit priest with the same name is recorded as having built himself a house and chapel in Westgate Street, Bury St Edmunds, in 1760. It would be nice to think it was the same John Gage, and that he grew Green Gages there.

Kirke's Blue
1820s

From the late seventeenth century until the early 1850s, the area of London between Hyde Park and the village of Brompton was famous for its nurseries and market gardens. Greatest of them all was the Brompton Park Nursery, described in 1715 as 'the noblest

Nursery of the World', which supplied many of the great houses of Britain and eventually extended over the best part of a hundred acres. Less well known was the Brompton Road nursery run by Joseph Kirke, who began selling Kirke's Blue in the 1820s. Apparently he did not raise the variety himself, but where he obtained it from remains unclear: some say it originated in Norfolk, others that it came from the Poupart family nursery nearby. (The firm of Poupart still exists, supplying fruit and vegetables to British supermarkets.) It was evidently still quite new in 1831, for in his *Guide to the Orchard and Kitchen Garden* of that year, George Lindley recorded: 'It was brought into use a few years ago by Mr Kirke, of Brompton, and is believed to be of foreign origin.'

Kirke's Blue is a naturally small, bushy tree, which makes it perfect for growing in the garden. Its round, dark-purple fruits have a blueish bloom, and are among the best-flavoured dark dessert plums, with juicy flesh and a free stone. As for Joseph Kirke's nursery, it probably disappeared, like the great Brompton Park Nursery itself, beneath the Victoria and Albert Museum. Spare a thought for him, and Kirke's Blue, next time you are there.

Pershore Yellow Egg
c. 1833

Excellent for cooking and jam, if too dry to be pleasant eaten raw, the Pershore Yellow Egg has a fascinating history. It was discovered around 1833 growing wild in Tiddesley Wood, just outside Pershore in Worcestershire, by a local man called George Crook (or Crooke). Like many plums it sends up suckers from its roots, and some of these were transplanted to Gigbridge Lane in the town. In the days when Pershore was nicknamed 'Pearshore' for the number of fruit orchards around it, the Yellow Egg's outstanding culinary qualities would quickly have been recognised, and by the end of the nineteenth century it was so well known that it was often referred to simply as the Pershore Plum. As its name suggests it is bright yellow and egg-shaped, and although it is almost tasteless when raw, during cooking it develops a fine flavour. For many years it was the main variety used in jams and canning, and even today it makes an excellent garden tree, being self-fertile, prolific and resistant to many of the diseases that plums are heir to. By happy chance not only does Tiddesley Wood survive, but you can still see Yellow Egg plums growing there, in an old orchard that along with the rest of the wood is today looked after by the Worcestershire Wildlife Trust.

Victoria
before 1838

The best-known of all plums also turns out to be one of the most mysterious. Pick up any other book on the subject and you'll read pretty much the same account: that it was found in a cottage garden in the Sussex village of Alderton. It's certainly a romantic tale, which is probably why every authority has blithely repeated it since the claim was first made. But as a historical record it has a fatal flaw. For it takes only a quick look through the maps to reveal that there is no such place as Alderton, at least not in Sussex. (Some old place-names, admittedly, disappear, but William Cobbett's *Geographical Dictionary of England and Wales*, published in 1832, lists no Sussex Alderton either.) There are Aldertons aplenty outside Sussex – in Gloucestershire, Shropshire, Northamptonshire, Wiltshire and Suffolk – but it has always been said that Victoria was a Sussex plum. Did everyone simply repeat a bit of dodgy information? Quite possibly, since the Victorians seem to have been as lazy at checking facts as anyone else. Yet if the Victoria did not come from Alderton, why was Alderton still being given as one of its alternative names as late as the 1870s? It all seems terribly confusing, but here are a few possible solutions.

To begin with, while Alderton may never have been a Sussex village, it is a common Sussex surname. Could the 'Alderton' plum have been named after the person who found it, rather than the village it was found in? Plenty of other varieties of both fruit and vegetable, after all, bear the names of their breeders, or the name of the nurseryman who first sold them, and in fact the Victoria was also known, in its early days, as both Sharpe's Emperor and Denyer's Victoria. There again, it could be as simple as a spelling mistake, made once then lazily perpetuated. There may be no Alderton in Sussex, but intriguingly there is a pretty and still rather remote little village called Walderton that sits in a fold of the Downs between Chichester and Emsworth. Could Walderton be Alderton? If it is, it raises the exciting possibility that the original Victoria plum tree might still be found in one of its cottage gardens. (A less attractive option is that it long ago disappeared under the urban sprawl of Hove, in what was the hamlet of Aldrington: in the distant past its name was occasionally spelled as Aldington or Aldertone.)

The first documentary record of the Victoria plum that I have so far found dates from 1838, when the American *Magazine of Horticulture, Botany, and All Useful Discoveries and Improvements in Rural Affairs* announced:

Denyer's new Victoria plum. A new variety under this name has been raised in England by Mr Denyer, nurseryman. It is of a large size and delicious flavor. It is a sure and free bearer against a wall in any aspect. It is also more prolific as a standard than any other. Mr Thompson commends it to the notice of all cultivators. We hope it will be soon introduced.

Who Mr Thompson was I do not know, but Edward Denyer (who ran a nursery in Brixton) was evidently claiming the plum as his own.

Yet there is another version of events, less well known but equally plausible. In his 1859 *Catalogue of Fruits*, preserved in the Lindley

Library in London, the great horticulturalist and fruit expert Thomas Rivers claimed that the 'Victoria, or Alderton of Sussex' was simply 'an old variety with a new name', and appended this note at the bottom of the page: 'This plum has been well known in the neighbourhood of Ticehurst, Sussex, for more than fifty years, as the Royal Dauphin or Dolphin, and [is] reported to have been brought from France. At Gloucester I found it under the name of Dauphin, and [it was] also said to have been brought from France by the captain of a trading vessel.' Could the greatest British plum actually have been French?

Whatever its origins, Victoria went on to become the single most popular plum in Britain, a fact which puzzles many people who have eaten it raw, since its flavour is not that remarkable. What this tells us about national tastes is not that the Victorians were less discriminating than we are, but rather that we have grown accustomed to assuming that every fruit variety is designed to be eaten uncooked. Our ancestors made no such assumptions. In fact, in the nineteenth century you were more likely to eat plums cooked than raw, especially if you were poor. Plum jam was the cheapest and most popular conserve on the market, and by 1900 the jam industry alone was using over 40,000 tons of plums every year. Although it was by no means the only variety used, Victoria is perfect for jam, tarts and bottling, since it develops an excellent flavour when cooked and retains its rich rose colour – something that cannot be said for many other varieties. Unusually among plums it is self-fertile, and produces a reliably good crop of fruit, although of all varieties it is the most susceptible to the crippling silver-leaf disease, which spreads via fungal spores and can eventually kill the tree. Despite this it remains Britain's most important commercial plum, with around 530 hectares (1,300 acres) devoted to its cultivation.

Warwickshire Drooper
before 1900

It might sound more like an unfortunate condition than a type of fruit, but this gloriously titled plum is actually named after the way its branches droop from the tree, almost giving it the look of a weeping willow. Odd growth habits aside, its rather handsome yellow, egg-shaped fruits are excellent for cooking and preserving, and at their best they make a decent dessert plum. It was once a popular variety, widely planted in the Midlands and sent to the London markets, but today it is rather rare, and well worth cultivating. In its county of origin the fruit was sometimes fermented to make an alcoholic drink known as Plum Jerkum, which was reputed to 'leave the head clear while paralysing the legs' and whose exciting effects surely deserve to be rediscovered.

Westmorland Damson
before 1800

In his classic book *The Plums of England* (1949), H. V. Taylor lamented that 'The plum holds a more lowly place in the order of things in England than either the apple or the pear, and this is reflected in the position given to the trees.' While cherries, pears and apples were generally planted in orchards, plums were often consigned to the edges of fields, or planted as windbreaks for more valuable trees. Yet their humble status may have been some old varieties' salvation. Since Taylor's book was published, many thousands of acres of apple, pear and cherry orchards have been grubbed up, but in the counties where plums were traditionally grown in hedgerows and around the edges of fields (namely Cheshire, Lancashire, Shropshire and the former county of Westmorland, since subsumed within Cumbria) it was rarely considered to be worth the effort of grubbing them up – with the paradoxical result that old plums have often survived where more highly valued fruit trees have been destroyed. Nowhere is this phenomenon more striking than in the Lyth and Winster valleys, south-west of Kendal in Cumbria, which are the heartlands of the Westmorland or Prune Damson. This ancient local variety was probably cultivated from a chance seedling (possibly from a Shropshire variety called the Blue Violet) and has been grown in the area since at least the eighteenth century. Like all damsons it is too sour to enjoy raw, but for jam, cooking, bottling and canning it has no equal. The plums were also used for dyeing cloth by textile manufacturers.

Until the Second World War the Westmorland Damson was an important local crop, and on Damson Saturday every September hundreds of tons were sold at Kendal market, then taken by train to the jam factories of Lancashire. Some were processed more locally, at least briefly: in a masterpiece of bad timing the Westmorland Damson Growers Association was formed in 1938, and a small canning plant and jam factory was built. In the innocent, nature-loving days when Britain's orchards were a tourist attraction in their own right, they also drew thousands of tourists to the area each April on what became known as Damson Sunday, to admire the heart-lifting sight of the trees in full bloom. The war destroyed the damson trade – lack of manpower was one factor; the shortage of sugar was another – and after the war there were more exotic destinations on offer for the average tourist, but the plum trees survived, many of them growing on fields too steep and stony to be of much use for anything else. They can still be seen today, and although inevitably the trees have suffered from half a century of neglect, Westmorland Damsons can still be bought from local shops and roadside stalls each September. In 1996 a new Westmorland Damson Association was formed, whose aims are to restore the orchards as far as possible and to

find new markets for the plums; they also host an annual Damson
Day in late April. Several enterprising local businesses now use
Westmorland Damsons in products ranging from damson gin to
damson beer.

Potatoes

What can the world do without potatoes? Almost as well might we now ask, what would the world be without inhabitants?

Samuel Cole, *The New England Farmer* (1852)

L
ike many of our commonest vegetables, potatoes are more exotic than they look. There are around 200 species of wild potato in South America, but the most likely ancestors of the domesticated kind we grow (known to botanists as *Solanum tuberosum*) originated on the high Andean plateau around La Paz and Lake Titicaca in Peru. They were cultivated by the Incas, first noted by the Spanish around 1537, and seem to have arrived in Europe towards the end of the 1560s in the holds of Spanish ships. The first documentary evidence for their arrival comes from 1573, when potatoes were ordered for a hospital in Seville. Within twenty years they had spread to England, France, the Netherlands, Italy and Ireland, where they were to have their biggest impact, both for good and ill. Sir Walter Raleigh has been credited with their introduction so often that it seems almost churlish to cast doubt on the story, but while there is no hard evidence either way, it does

appear possible that he was among the first to grow them in Ireland, on the vast estate he was granted after helping in the bloody suppression of the second Desmond rebellion in the early 1580s; hardly what one would call a happy start.

Whether they were brought to Ireland by Raleigh or, as is sometimes claimed, washed up with the wrecks of the Spanish Armada a few years later, potatoes were adopted by the starving Irish peasantry with an alacrity unmatched elsewhere. It might seem strange today, but until comparatively recently potatoes were regarded with the same kind of suspicion as the tomato (that other great Peruvian import), and for precisely the same reason: the flowers of both plants bear a close resemblance to mandrakes and deadly nightshade, whose toxic effects were already well known – and indeed they belong to the same botanical family, the *Solanaceae*. Given that all parts of the potato are toxic apart from the tubers, and even these are poisonous when green, perhaps we shouldn't be so surprised that they were treated with caution, at least initially. What is more surprising is how long it took for those fears to be overcome. Outside Ireland and parts of Germany there was little large-scale potato cultivation until the late eighteenth century; in some places they were grown as a fodder crop, but they were barely thought fit for human consumption – in France they were actually banned in 1748 as a threat to the nation's health.

Their wilderness years might have been even longer had it not been for the enlightened advocacy of one man: Antoine-Augustin Parmentier, a French chemist whose name has been immortalised in dishes such as *hachis parmentier*, the French equivalent of cottage pie. Forced to eat vast quantities of potatoes by his fiendish Prussian captors during the Seven Years War, Parmentier developed a lifelong affection for them (potatoes, that is, not Prussians). Back in France he became an ardent potato promoter, ultimately gaining the royal seal of approval when he persuaded Marie Antoinette to wear potato flowers in her hair. Although this did little for Marie

Antoinette in the longer run, it did wonders for potatoes, and the decree against their cultivation was finally lifted in 1772. They even played their part during the Revolution, when the royal gardens of the Tuileries were grubbed up and replanted with potatoes. Parmentier fared better than Marie Antoinette during the tumbril years, surviving to be appointed Inspector General of the French health service by Napoleon, a post he held from 1805 until his death in 1813. The decoration of his tomb, which can still be seen in the cemetery of Père Lachaise in Paris, includes a bas-relief basket of potatoes.

The nineteenth century was the golden age of potatoes, but it also saw their nadir. In Ireland, where potatoes provided pretty much the only food for a poor and downtrodden population, a whole series of major crop failures reached their devastating climax in the Great Hunger of 1845–9, in which an estimated one million people died. The famine was precipitated by a wind-borne oomycete, or water mould, *Phytophthora infestans*, better known as potato blight, which seems to have entered Europe during the 1830s, most probably in a cargo of infested potatoes from America or Mexico. The disease – which causes plants to wilt and rot and quickly turns potatoes into a foul-smelling mush – swept across the whole of northern Europe, causing devastation wherever it went. It arrived in Britain in August 1845, blown across the Channel to the Isle of Wight. From there it spread west, reaching Ireland by September. What followed was a disaster, its impact magnified by the fact that the Irish poor had come to rely almost entirely on a single variety of potato, the infamous Lumper. Scottish in origin, the aptly named Lumper owed its popularity to neither its taste (unexceptional) nor its appearance (lumpy), but its productivity: in good years Lumpers yield a heavy crop, and they were about the only thing capable of sustaining an entire family on a small plot of land through the winter. But they had one crucial failing: they lacked the slightest resistance to blight, so the disease was able to race across the entire country, destroying every potato in its path, on the surface or underground. Different varieties of potato have varying degrees of blight resistance, so had the Lumper not been the only kind grown, other varieties might have survived, and fewer people might have endured a miserable end as a result. By the end of the Great Hunger around a million people had died, and the following few years saw another one and a half million flee the country for what could only be a better life abroad.

The tragic irony was that there were plenty of alternatives to Lumpers even then. As Jenny Uglow points out in her delightful *Little History of British Gardening*: 'In 1847, the worst year of the Irish potato famine, *The Annals of Horticulture* listed forty-nine varieties of potatoes: sixteen early, twenty-seven late and five rare varieties, grown in the Horticultural Society's garden, including "Golden Potato of Peru, Pied Golden Potato, Mouse Potato, Pine Apple or Cone Potato, Spanish Dwarf Potato".' The Irish famine might have been a blot on history, but it did have one positive outcome, for it spurred the development of new (and potentially more disease-resistant) varieties of potato. It could also be said to have given people the first inklings of two things we take almost for granted today: the dangers of monocultures, and the concomitant importance of biodiversity. For all the apparent diversity of the Horticultural Society's collection, the vast majority of pre-famine potatoes descended from the same small ancestral gene pool, mainly from the first potatoes to be brought across the Atlantic in Elizabethan times. Growers had already noted how old varieties in their own time, which then as now were generally propagated from leftover tubers rather than from seed, became less vigorous and more prone to disease over the years. The reason, as we now know, is because if plants are propagated vegetatively (that is, by cuttings, grafts or, like potatoes, from tubers) rather than from seed, they are gradually crippled by viral infections, whose deleterious effects build up in their cell tissue over time. Victorian growers saw that plants raised from seed were generally healthier, although the genetic shuffling that takes place during sexual reproduction meant that they were far more variable than plants grown from grafts and cuttings, which are identical clones of their parents – with all their parents' good points, but all of their bad points too.

Haunted by the spectre of blight, the 1850s and 1860s saw a concerted effort to improve potato stocks. Apart from their susceptibility to disease, all potatoes grown before then shared the same shortcoming, in that they were rarely ready to harvest before the autumn. The Horticultural Society might have listed sixteen 'earlies', but all that meant was that they could be harvested in August, not June like the earlies we have today. The work of late Victorian breeders in Scotland and the north of England began to extend their season, as well as increasing their disease resistance. Arguably the best of these new varieties was Paterson's Victoria, developed around 1860 by William Paterson of Dundee, who spent thousands of pounds importing fresh kinds of potato from as far afield as Chile. Victoria went on to father more hybrid varieties of potato than any other before or since, but it has shared the same fate as all too many once-famous cultivars, and can no longer be found in British collections – although it may still survive in eastern Europe: the European Cultivated Potato Database holds records of Victoria from Poland, Germany, Austria, Russia and the Czech Republic.

By the end of the nineteenth century the focus had shifted to America, along with millions of European immigrants (those one and a half million survivors of the Irish potato famine among them), many of whom, it has been claimed, packed their native potatoes in their luggage. It sounds an unlikely story, but given that Scottish and American growers apparently had no trouble posting new kinds of potatoes to each other at the time, perhaps there is more truth in it than one may suppose. Among the new varieties to emerge from this fecund period was the Burbank Russet, whose prototype was introduced in 1874 by the legendary American horticulturalist Luther Burbank; it is still the single most widely grown variety in the United States, accounting for something like 40 per cent of the market. Its British rival, King Edward, entered the fray in 1902. Like so many varieties in this book no one thought to record its exact origins, but it is believed to have begun life in Northumberland, where it was first known as Fellside Hero.

Scotland has led the British market since the late nineteenth century, partly thanks to Scottish entrepreneurship but also because potatoes – coming from a land of cold nights and high altitudes – do well in the cool, clean Scottish climate, and suffer less from blight, which is most prevalent in warm, damp conditions. Several of the most successful varieties of the early twentieth century were bred by Archibald Findlay in Auchtermuchty, among them the international best-seller Up to Date, British Queen and the hugely popular Majestic, all of which are still available, if no longer so widely grown.

Arran Victory
1918

This striking purple-skinned potato comes, as its name suggests, from the Isle of Arran, off the west coast of Scotland. It was raised by Donald Mackelvie, a prosperous grocer from the small town of Lamlash, who is one of the few potato breeders to have had a poem written about them. Published in James Nicol's *Book of Arran Verse* (1930), it reads: 'Health to McKelvie! / Long shall we praise his name / Whilst Arranmen delve ye. / Arran Chief, Arran Rose, / Comrade and Ally, / Yea where the Consul grows – / Health to McKelvie!' (Potatoes are still waiting for their Shakespeare.) Born in 1867, he began experimenting with potatoes around 1901 and launched his first commercial variety, Arran Chief, ten years later. Mackelvie went on to develop a whole series of 'Arran' potatoes, which eventually brought him fame and an OBE, if not much of a fortune: in the days before plant breeders' rights, raising new varieties was best done for love, not money. Three of his other introductions are worth noting, and are still available. Arran Consul (1925) became known as 'the potato that won the war' in testament to its productivity and legendary storage qualities during the Second World War; Arran Pilot (1930) remains the first choice for home gardeners, despite the wildly variable size of its tubers; while Arran Comet (1957), released a decade after Mackelvie's death, has such excellent flavour, productivity and disease resistance that it deserves to be better known. Arran Victory, the oldest of Mackelvie's introductions to have survived, is one of the tastiest of all mashing potatoes, with creamy white flesh under a dark-purple skin.

British Queen
1894

From the 'tulipomania' of the seventeenth century to the dotcom boom of the early twenty-first, speculative bubbles have a long and inglorious history, but relatively few economists are likely to be familiar with the Scottish Potato Bubble of 1900–4. Documented by Alan Romans in his fascinating *Potato Book*, it was responsible for the fame of Archibald Findlay, who raised a whole string of outstanding potatoes, including British Queen – but it almost ruined him too. Findlay was the most talented potato grower of the late Victorian era. He built a name for himself by a combination of careful breeding and skilful marketing, entertaining major buyers on his farm in Fife and promoting his potatoes around the country. After the international success of Up to Date, which was launched in the same year as British Queen, demand for his varieties began to outstrip supply, and their prices rocketed as a result, especially after a series of bad harvests at the start of the twentieth century. By naming his next releases Millionmaker and Eldorado, as Alan Romans points out, Findlay can hardly be said to have discouraged people from irrational speculation, but almost inevitably the whole speculative bubble ended in tears. After buying a large farm in Lincolnshire against the expectations of future profits the bubble burst, and Findlay retired to Auchtermuchty with a ruined reputation. Fortunately a number of his finest varieties survive, including Up to Date and British Queen, which is still highly regarded: as recently as 1998 it won an Award of Garden Merit from the Royal Horticultural Society in recognition of its excellent flavour and heavy yields. It makes wonderful mash.

Duke of York
1891

Still popular over a century after its introduction, Duke of York has long been regarded as one of the best potatoes for taste. Like many of our finest varieties it was raised in Scotland, by William Sim of Fyvie in Aberdeenshire. Born in 1869, Sim developed an interest in breeding – not just potatoes, but also cows and carnations. Duke of York was first sold in 1891, and its excellence was quickly recognised, but by the time its popularity had become assured Sim had, like so many of his countrymen, already emigrated to the United States. He opened a nursery outside Boston, where he bred snapdragons and African violets, before applying his talents to carnations. Over the next forty years Sim carnations became known across the United States, but sadly William Sim missed out on the success of his second great introduction by dying in 1940, just a few years before the brilliant red carnation that bears his name became the best-selling variety in America.

Epicure
1897

So many British potato varieties began life in Scotland that it comes as a surprise to find one that originated in Hampshire – although these days it is more likely to be found in Scotland than in its native land. Epicure was first grown in Christchurch, where the rivers Stour and Avon meet. The rich alluvial soils here are ideal for potato cultivation, and in the late nineteenth century a highly regarded nurseryman called James Clark bred a number of fine new varieties including Magnum Bonum, Maincrop (sometimes called Langworthy) and Epicure, which were sold nationwide by Sutton's Seeds. Epicure is the only one still readily available, a testament to its outstanding flavour and floury texture, as well as to its ability to survive hard frosts – something that recommended it to Scottish growers in particular.

Golden Wonder
1906

I had always assumed Golden Wonder crisps were given their name as a result of years of marketing analysis and focus groups, but no: they were named, quite casually, after a potato. Golden Wonder was a chance mutation, discovered in 1906 by John Brown in a field of the once-popular Maincrop variety (see above), near the Scottish town of Arbroath. It differs from Maincrop in having a russet-brown skin, and being one of the driest of all potatoes – which makes it excellent for crisps. According to potato guru Alan Romans it grows best north of Aberdeen, and its full flavour takes a while to develop, so it should ideally be stored until January. It is excellent for growing in containers. Golden Wonder crisps were first made in 1947 by William Alexander, an Edinburgh bakery owner, who used the spare capacity of his bakery for cooking crisps after he had finished making bread for the day. They were the first ready-salted crisps, and by 1966 they were the most popular brand in Britain. Ironically, Golden Wonder crisps are no longer made with Golden Wonder potatoes, but with Lady Rosetta, a modern Dutch variety.

Home Guard
1942

A real *Dad's Army* potato, Home Guard was launched in 1942 by a Scottish company, McGill and Smith of Ayr (which still exists), and members of the Home Guard were roped in to help promote it – doubtless with the help of the wartime cartoon character Potato Pete. A productive, early variety which is resistant to scab, Home Guard sold well from the start; it was widely planted in Pembrokeshire, and remains popular in Ireland. Although it is a good potato for boiling or steaming, it is not recommended for chips.

Kerr's Pink
1907

If William Sim was unfortunate in leaving Scotland before his Duke of York potato became a popular success, spare a thought for poor James Henry. Henry farmed in the Scottish village of Cornhill, a few miles inland from Banff, and in 1907 he raised a new variety of potato that was originally known as Henry's Seedling. In 1916 it won the Lord Derby Gold Medal at the long-running agricultural field trials in Ormskirk, but by this time James Henry seems to have emigrated to Canada, and his seedling potatoes were bought by a merchant called Mr Kerr, who gave them his own name in 1917 and, it is said, sold them for a small fortune. It sounds unfortunate, but in fact it was simply unjust, for even if Henry had remained in Britain it is unlikely he would have made as much money from his potatoes than the merchant: in the days before plant breeders' rights there was no way for the person who developed a new variety to ensure they received any kind of profit or royalty. The best a plant breeder could hope for was to sell their first stock of plants for the highest price they could, since after that it was a free-for-all. Not until 1964, when the first Plant Varieties and Seeds Act was introduced, did growers begin to enjoy any legal protection – rather too late for James Henry.

Kerr's Pink is an attractive late-harvesting potato, still very popular in Scotland and Ireland; it has pale-pink skin and creamy white flesh, whose floury texture makes it good for roasting, and it is considered almost equal to British Queen and Arran Pilot when it comes to making perfect mash.

Lumper
before 1810

The idea of growing something that was responsible – albeit indirectly – for the deaths of a million people may seem faintly distasteful, but the Lumper potato has such an extraordinary history it surely deserves to be preserved. Lumpers are believed to have originated in Scotland, but by the early nineteenth century they were being grown in the south and west of Ireland, where they gained popularity not so much because of their flavour (which was considered inferior to older potato varieties such as the Irish Apple) but for their productivity: Lumpers produce extremely heavy crops of large, if eponymously lumpy potatoes. In the days when there was little food of any kind, a small field of Lumpers represented the difference between subsistence and starvation. The grinding poverty of nineteenth-century Ireland is hard to imagine. Even into the twentieth century, as Claudia Kinmonth records in her fascinating history *Irish Country Furniture* from 1994, some families were so poor they had to make chairs out of cut peat and cups from seashells or hollowed-out potatoes. Lumpers were a godsend to families like these, but as they came to rely on Lumpers more and more they ultimately became hostages to fortune – and that fortune ran out in 1845, when potato blight first entered Ireland. By September that year the blight was reported in the counties of Waterford and Wexford, just when the potato harvest was about to begin, and within weeks the entire crop was lost, at a time when around three million people relied on potatoes simply to survive. An official investigation put the cause down to 'wet rot', but there were plenty of other theories, one of the more exotic being that the blight had been caused by 'mortiferous vapours' from volcanic eruptions, or static electricity given off by trains, still something of a novelty in 1845. Since the Irish famine the Lumper's reputation has not, understandably, been high, but reports of its inedibility are best taken with a pinch of salt. It may not be a gourmet potato, but according to the food historian William Woys Weaver, the Lumper tastes better than many better-known 'heritage' varieties, and anyway it was often used as an ingredient in recipes for colcannon and potato bread (a kind of potato-based scone), in which role it performs admirably well. Although rarely grown today, Lumpers can sometimes be bought at events such as Garden Organic's annual Potato Day.

Pink Fir Apple
c. 1850

For many people this is *the* historic potato, but its popularity is well deserved: the Pink Fir Apple has long, narrow tubers, waxy yellow flesh and a deliciously nutty flavour, excellent in salads and wonderful as chips. It is odd that so little is known about it. It has been grown in Britain for well over a century, yet no one seems to know where it came from, although France or Germany are the most likely candidates. Fir Apples once came in three different colours – white, red and pink – but only the pink-skinned kind has survived, largely thanks to the efforts of dedicated gardeners. Today they are enjoying a renaissance, especially in restaurants, and a few enterprising farmers have planted them on a commercial scale. Their main drawback, apart from their slow growth and susceptibility to potato blight, is their eccentrically knobbly shape, which makes them awkward to clean and infuriating to peel. The French variety Ratte (which most probably originated in Denmark) is similar, but has the advantage of producing heavier crops and being far less knobbly.

Sharpe's Express
1900

One of the best-flavoured potatoes of all, Sharpe's Express was introduced by the Lincolnshire seed merchants Charles Sharpe & Co., around 1900. The firm was founded in Sleaford *circa* 1868 by Charles Sharpe, who was born around 1830 and died in 1897, just before Sharpe's Express was launched. By the turn of the century the company was one of the largest employers in the town, and it was trading as recently as 1996; today it is part of a French multinational. Sharpe's potato is an early maturing variety, whose often pear-shaped tubers have pale-cream skin, and it makes a wonderful 'new' potato when cooked immediately after harvesting (although it is better steamed than boiled). Unfortunately it has little blight resistance and gives rather light crops, which hardly recommends it for commercial cultivation, but its flavour is so outstanding that it is well worth growing in the garden.

Charles Sharpe (c. 1830–97)

Shetland Black
before 1923

Like the Pink Fir Apple, the Shetland Black has made something of a comeback in recent years, and it is easy to see why. With its striking looks – purple-black skin and creamy flesh which, when cut in half, reveals a narrow ring of purple colouring inside – and excellent flavour it makes distinctive crisps and an unusual addition to salads. They have relatively shallow roots and can be harvested around July, which makes them worth thinking about for growing in pots or growbags as well as in the garden. They may look primitive, but Shetland Black were only added to the National Collection of potatoes in 1923, and they were most probably developed in the late nineteenth century, possibly as a sport of an American variety called Early Rose.

Witchhill / Snowdrop
c. 1880s

Witchhill is so creamy and delicious that one can only regret its hazy history. It was originally called Snowdrop (which is still grown at the Lost Gardens of Heligan) and came from the Midlands, but some time later Alex Brown, who farmed at Witchhill Farm, Memsie, near the Scottish town of Fraserburgh, seems to have chosen a particularly good form of Snowdrop, which subsequently became known as Witchhill. An early-maturing variety, Witchhill produces large crops of small, oval, pale yellow-skinned potatoes with creamy white flesh.

Radishes

Ah! And here's the surprise, something dainty, some radishes, some pretty little pink radishes. Just fancy! Radishes in March; what a luxury!

Emile Zola, *Paris* (1898)

Radishes might not look like much, but they have been around for a very long time. Our best guess is that they originated in China and Japan, but they were already appreciated in ancient Egypt; and in ancient Greece, according to Pliny the Elder, 'the radish was rated so far above all other articles of food that . . . in the Temple of Apollo at Delphi, a radish modelled in gold was dedicated as a votive offering, though only a silver beetroot and a turnip of lead.' Mind you, the Greeks had less endearing ways with radishes too. Athenian adulterers ran the risk of being punished with *rhaphanidosis*, or 'radishment', which – not to put too fine a point upon it – permitted the outraged husband to conduct what sounds like an extremely uncomfortable operation involving a radish and his rival's bottom.

Given that ancient radishes are thought to have been both larger and longer than the pert little radishes we're accustomed to today, perhaps we should pass rapidly on to the sixteenth century, when the first globe-shaped radishes entered Britain, probably from Germany. They get their first mention in William Taylor's *Names of Herbes*, published in 1548, although even then they were the size of small turnips. Black-skinned radishes arrived a little later, at least according to Henry Lyte, who wrote in his 1586 translation of *Dodoens Herball*: 'The radish with a black root has of late years been brought into England and now biginnith to be common.' For the next 200 years the standard radish was slender and long. The button-sized radishes we eat today seem to have been an Italian invention which British gardeners only began growing in the late eighteenth century, but it wasn't long before these crunchy little morsels became wildly popular. Market gardeners loved these smaller radishes, since they took up little space and were remarkably quick to grow, which made them perfect for interplanting between other crops. London alone had over 4,000 hectares (around 10,000 acres) of market gardens in the early nineteenth century, and although none of them survives today, radishes, asparagus, strawberries and garlic still come up in Brompton cemetery, which stands on the site of an older market garden.

The pink baby radish is the only one seen in most shops today, but other types can still be found, and are easy to raise from seed. In fact the only kind that seems to have disappeared is the turnip-sized radish of ancient Greece – although one suspects that adulterers are unlikely to mourn their passing.

Black Spanish Round
before 1548

Arguably the oldest variety of radish we have, and one of the oldest vegetables in the garden, the Black Spanish Round (or Round Black Spanish) has been grown in Britain since at least the sixteenth century, and may date back to the 1400s. Its rather coarse skin, as its name suggests, is a charcoal black, and its crisp interior startlingly white, with a tongue-bitingly pun-gent taste. Unlike spring radishes it is slow to mature: seed should be sown from June to August, giving a harvest of fat, round radishes from October to December. Its younger cousin, the Black Spanish Long, was first mentioned in 1707. Both varieties keep well through winter if stored in cool, dark conditions, ideally in slightly damp sand.

Black Spanish Round turnip radish

China Rose
c. 1845

Given that China is thought to be the home of ur-radishes, the story that this variety was brought back to Europe by Jesuit missionaries seems perfectly plausible, especially since French Jesuits (like the famous Pères David and Delavay) introduced many species of flowers to the West. China Rose seems to have arrived around 1845, and by the end of the nineteenth century it was widely grown, both in Britain and America, often under its alternative name of Chinese Rose. Like the Black Spanish it is a winter variety, to be sown in July and August. Its smooth tap-roots grow from fifteen to twenty centi-metres (six to eight inches) long,

China Rose radish

with bright-pink skin and firm white flesh. Like many old varieties it is strongly flavoured and sharp to the taste.

French Breakfast
c. 1865

This attractively coloured radish, which has a short tubular root that flushes from rose pink to white at its tip, is renowned for both its appearance and its taste: mild yet refreshingly sharp, with crisp and crunchy flesh. Unlike the Black Spanish or the China Rose it is an early-season radish, and can mature in as little as a month. French Breakfast has long been a favourite for forcing in late winter in a cold frame or greenhouse, and like many radishes it grows best in cool conditions and is best harvested as soon as it is mature – left too long in the ground its roots become unappetisingly woody. There are several related varieties, including White Breakfast, which is regularly grown in the kitchen garden at the Lost Gardens of Heligan.

French Breakfast radish

Icicle
before 1819

Radishes have few drawbacks, but one thing they don't like is hot weather; most of them grow best when it's cool, which makes them an excellent winter vegetable but not so reliable in the summer. The aptly named Icicle, though, is an exception to the rule, keeping its cool even when the heat is on, and rarely turning woody. It resembles a stubby icicle in shape as well as in colour, although by rights it should be translucent rather than white. Icicle grows to fifteen centimetres (around five inches) long, but its mild flavour is at its best when harvested young.

Scarlet Globe
before 1883

Looking more like an earthbound cherry tomato than a regular radish, Scarlet Globe is a fast-growing early variety that can be grown under glass or outside. With a mild flavour and juicy, crisp white flesh, it is a reliable all-rounder that can grow to full size in less than a month and is tolerant of poorer soil.

Rhubarb

Sustained snores came from the cart-house, where some
of the men were lying down; the grunt and squeal of
sweltering pigs arose from the still further distance. The
large-leaved rhubarb and cabbage plants slept too, their
broad limp surfaces hanging in the sun like half-closed
umbrellas.

Thomas Hardy, *Tess of the D'Urbervilles* (1891)

T he fact that we eat rhubarb at all can be put down to the
imagination and perseverance of one man: Joseph Myatt,
the godfather of modern rhubarb. In the early years of the
nineteenth century Myatt owned two market gardens in south
London, one on Lewisham Road, Deptford and the other at
Loughborough, then a hamlet between the villages of Brixton and
Camberwell, growing strawberries and vegetables for the London
markets. In those days rhubarb was grown mainly for medicinal
purposes and taken as powerfully purgative pills, but a few brave
souls had tried cooking the stems, and in 1810 Myatt decided to try
selling them commercially. In 1851 the American *Magazine of
Horticulture, Botany and All Useful Discoveries and Improvements in Rural*

Affairs recorded that 'Mr Joseph Myatt, of Deptford, who is cele-brated for his fine rhubarb, was the first to cultivate it on a large scale. It is now nearly forty years since he first sent his two sons to the Borough Market with five bunches, of which they could only sell three.' It was not a great start, but as the *Atlantic Monthly* noted in 1865, 'Still he persisted in keeping it before the people, although he seemed only to lose rhubarb and to gain ridicule, being desig-nated as the man who sold "physic pies."'

Myatt was obviously a born optimist as well as a canny business-man, and his persistence finally paid off. In 1837 he introduced Myatt's Victoria (now usually known simply as Victoria and still one of the finest varieties), in honour of the Queen's accession, followed in 1840 by the inevitable Prince Albert. Myatt was now the country's leading rhubarb producer and nobody was guffawing about physic pies any more, although Edward Hawkes' nursery, just a little further along Lewisham Road, gave him a run for his money with the launch of another perennial favourite, Hawkes' Champagne.

For all its comparatively recent history as a pudding, rhubarb entered cultivation several thousand years ago. Its name is probably Roman, a conflation of Rha – the ancient name for the Volga river – and *barbarum*, the Latin word that gives us 'barbarian': the barbarian plant from the River Volga. Their geography was a bit hazy: some species of wild rhubarb (whose botanical name is *Rheum*) do grow in Siberia and the Caucasus, but its real heartland is in western China, where the roots of the inedible *Rheum palmatum* and *Rheum officinalis* have been dried and used as purgative pills since ancient times. The Romans don't seem to have grown rhubarb themselves, and in its powdered form it remained an expensive import right up to the eighteenth century, when high costs and declining quality encouraged Europeans to try cultivating it closer to home. Unfortunately they chose the wrong rhubarb: *Rheum rhaponticum*, a species from central Asia, whose purgative properties proved pretty pathetic. Yet the apothecaries' loss turned out to be the pie-makers' gain, for further experiment revealed that its stems were rather tasty, as long as they were cooked with plenty of sugar. (The first recipe we have for cooked rhubarb dates from 1783, when John Farley, in *The London Art of Cookery*, suggested combining it with gooseberries.) Unfortunately, sugar was expensive too, which goes some way to explaining why it wasn't until the mid-nineteenth century, when sugar prices dropped, that rhubarb caught on as a dessert.

The nineteenth century also gave us forced rhubarb, thanks to another accident of history. The story goes that, during the winter of 1815, some workmen dug a trench in Chelsea Physic Garden and chucked the rubble, in traditional fashion, on an apparently empty flower bed. Of course it wasn't empty at all: beneath the clods and broken brick was the Physic Garden's rhubarb patch. Come spring, though, when the rubble was removed, what should be revealed but long, tender rhubarb shoots, whose taste was far superior to the usual tougher stems. (A less romantic version of the story suggests that soil had simply been heaped around the dormant rhubarb crowns to protect them from winter frost.) The results were reported in the *Transactions of the Horticultural Society*, and it wasn't long before commercial growers got in on the act, earthing up the stems, covering them with specially created terracotta pots and, in a final burst of inspiration, transplanting the poor things to darkened sheds.

Forcing really took off in the 1880s, when a group of enterprising families in the so-called 'Rhubarb Triangle' between Wakefield, Leeds and Bradford took advantage of the fact that local coal was cheap as chips and started raising rhubarb in specially heated sheds. The old London firms found it increasingly hard to compete, and by the end of the century the focus of British rhubarb production had shifted inexorably north. And not just British: by the time the industry peaked in the early 1930s, the Rhubarb Triangle was responsible for something like 90 per cent of the world forced-rhubarb supply. It wasn't to last. As with so many other crops, cheap post-war imports and rising labour and energy costs decimated the home-grown rhubarb industry. Where once there were 200-odd producers, today there are fewer than twenty. Tastes changed, too. In the words of rhubarb guru Janet Oldroyd Hume of E. Oldroyd & Sons, Rothwell: 'It was an overexposed star. There was a whole generation which was basically force-fed rhubarb. After the war we started to get all kinds of fruit coming into the country and people just stopped eating it' (*Working Lunch*, February 2006).

But the story doesn't end there. The last few years have seen a rhubarb renaissance, as people have rediscovered its subtle flavour and palate-cleansing mix of sweetness and acidity. In the five years to 2006, Oldroyd's (now the leading producer) doubled its output from 500 to 1,000 tons just to keep pace with demand, while Wakefield – whose railway station once boasted a nightly Rhubarb Express – has launched an annual Food, Drink and Rhubarb Festival, which runs for a week each February. To see the widest selection of varieties for yourself, visit the Royal Horticultural Society's gardens at Wisley or Harlow Carr, which both hold National Collections; another excellent selection (including several Scottish cultivars) is maintained by the National Trust for Scotland at Kellie Castle in Fife.

And what of Joseph Myatt, the visionary who started it all? His nursery expanded, but so did London, and in 1852 his son, William, moved operations to twenty-eight hectares (seventy acres) of land near the Worcestershire village of Offenham, just north of Evesham and the mainline railway to London. Although you won't find a monument to the man who sold physic pies anywhere in Deptford or Brixton, you can still tread the site of his nursery at Myatt's Fields, a pleasant little park off Brixton Road which opened in 1889, and contemplate the curious fact that it might well have been from this spot that rhubarb was first introduced to a dubious British public.

Fenton's Special
1930s

An early to mid-season rhubarb with ruby-red stems, white flesh and excellent flavour, Fenton's Special deserves to be better known outside the Rhubarb Triangle, where it seems to have originated, and where it remains a popular forcing variety. Although its parentage is obscure, Barbara Fenton, writing in the Morley Community Archives, remembers her family growing it in the 1930s in fields on Tingley Common, near Morley, south of Leeds, an area of open land now graced by the M62. It was introduced to commercial cultivation in 1952, and was Highly Commended in trials conducted by the Royal Horticultural Society in 1954.

Glaskin's Perpetual
1920s

Glaskin's Perpetual has not one but three claims to fame: it's the only variety of rhubarb that can be cut in its first year (all the others need two to three years before they are robust enough to survive repeated cutting). And it contains less oxalic acid than any other kind, which means less tartness on the tongue and less sugar in the tart. Its other appealing quality is that its long, greenish stems remain tender right through the season, long after other cultivars have become unappetisingly bitter and tough. A good all-round variety: early cropping, easy to grow (even from seed) and quick to settle in.

Glaskin's Perpetual commemorates John Jessie Glaskin, a baker and greengrocer of Eastern Road, Brighton, who was born in 1875. He was a keen cyclist, marksman and gardener, who had an orchard in Kemp Town and grew roses as well developing the rhubarb that bears his name, not to mention winning prizes for his hot cross buns. Mr Glaskin died in 1940, but happily his remarkable rhubarb lives on.

Hawkes' Champagne
1850s

Hawkes' Champagne is recorded as having been introduced by a Mr Hawkes of Loampit Hill, Lewisham, in the mid-nineteenth century. Neither Lewisham archives nor the Garden Museum can find any record of him, though Pigot's 1840 street directory does list Edward Hawkes, market gardener, in nearby Lewisham Road – the same road, intriguingly, where Joseph Myatt's famous rhubarb and strawberry nurseries were to be found. As a name, Hawkes' Champagne might belong to the blatantly optimistic school of Victorian marketing, but the fact remains that while other varieties have come and gone, Hawkes' Champagne continues to attract new fans: in 2003 it even won a coveted Award of Garden Merit from the Royal Horticultural Society. The reason? Well, if it doesn't actually taste like a bottle of 1966 Krug, it is certainly tender and sweet – in fact it is arguably the sweetest rhubarb of all. A medium-sized plant with bright-red stems, it takes a couple of years to get established, but like all real luxuries, the wait is well worthwhile.

Prince Albert
1840

Launched by the patriotic Joseph Myatt in the year of Albert's marriage to Queen Victoria, this is a large, prolific cultivar with long, thick, scarlet stems and robust flavour. One of the hardiest and earliest of all varieties, it is good for forcing and can successfully be grown from seed, although it does have a tendency to bolt. Myatt produced three of the nineteenth century's most popular cultivars in quick succession: Victoria (1837), Prince Albert (1840) and the deep-green, tender Linnaeus (1842). Why Linnaeus? The

Swedish scientist Carl Linnaeus (1707–78) is best known today as the father of botanical taxonomy, but it seems more likely that Myatt was celebrating what Linnaeus himself counted as his greatest achievement: the introduction of rhubarb to Sweden. Once the most important forcing variety, Linnaeus – often misspelled Linneus – is still well known in the United States; in Britain, by contrast, it's now rather rare, having been largely supplanted as a forcing plant by Timperley Early (itself a Linnaeus offspring). Linnaeus can be seen in the National Collection of rhubarb at Wisley and at Kellie Castle in Fife, although it is no longer commercially available.

Timperley Early
1920s

According to *The History of Rhubarb Grown in Yorkshire* by J. D. Whitwell and C. Creed:

Timperley Early, which forces earlier than any other variety, was spotted in a neighbour's field of Linnaeus by a Mr T. Baldwin of Timperley in Cheshire in the early 1920s, but was kept within the family until the Baldwin Brothers sold up in 1947. At the sale many of the crowns were sold to Yorkshire rhubarb growers and it quickly established itself as the main early forcing variety.

As its name suggests its prize characteristic is that, when forced, it can be harvested as early as Christmas; it is also tender enough to be harvested later than many other varieties. It's a favourite with Debs Goodenough, head gardener at Osborne House, Queen Victoria and Prince Albert's palatial villa on the Isle of Wight. She describes it as 'A robust variety which doesn't bolt or get woody quickly. We are still picking it at the end of July. A wonderful combination is a stewed compôte of blackcurrants and rhubarb – though it does require a good measure of added sugar.' Like Hawkes' Champagne, it won an RHS Award of Garden Merit in 2003. Timperley Early has long and often slender stems whose bright-red colour is strongest when forced, although it also grows perfectly happily outside. Around Timperley, which used to be a major growing area, rhubarb was jokingly referred to as 'Baguley Beef' in honour of the neighbouring town.

Victoria
1837

Introduced in the year of Queen Victoria's accession by Joseph Myatt, Victoria (originally known as Myatt's Victoria) is a giant among rhubarbs, not only in size but also in productivity: it's been claimed that the biggest stems can weigh up to a kilo each. The oldest variety still in general cultivation, it is usually the latest to emerge in spring, sending up thick, greenish stems stained or speckled with red. It is not as sweet as, say, Glaskin's Perpetual or Hawkes' Champagne, but Victoria's advantage is its versatility: its juicy green stems are equally good for forcing, cooking, freezing, and making jam or rhubarb wine. Once established, it is an undemanding plant that should produce heavy crops for anything up to twenty years. Like Prince Albert it is easily raised from seed.

Runner Beans

All the Hallorans shoot up tall, like runner beans; and thick
in the bone.

Arthur Quiller Couch, *The Mayor's Dovecot* (1910)

We tend to take the runner bean so much for granted that
it can come as something of a surprise to discover that,
outside Britain, it is regarded as faintly eccentric to eat
them at all. In America, for example, they are sometimes grown as
decorative annuals, whose flowers attract hummingbirds, but their
pods are usually chucked on the compost heap; in other countries
they are grown only for their seeds, shelled from the pods like other
beans and used either fresh or dried. Eating the young pods whole,
like mange tout, turns out to be a largely British quirk – although it
seems we may have eaten them that way since at least the early
eighteenth century.

The wild ancestors of our runner bean, *Phaseolus coccineus*, grow in
cool, mixed forests of pine and oak, from 1,800 metres (6,000 feet)
up, in the mountains of Central America. Like the domestic runner
bean they are perennials, with red flowers, and although their pods
are far smaller than modern varieties their taste is said to be

identical. Cultivated varieties arrived in Britain around 1633, and were probably first grown in this country by the famous collectors John Tradescant and his son, also called John.

The Tradescants, both of whom gloried successively in the title of Keepers of His Majesty's Gardens, Vines and Silkworms, lived in Turret House, south London, which they filled with such an astonishing range of curiosities that it popularly became known as The Ark. Their garden, too, was packed with rare and exotic plants, many of which had never been grown in Britain before: apart from runner beans the Tradescants first planted Virginia creepers, tulip trees, phlox, Michaelmas daisies, rudbeckias and the plant that bears their name, tradescantia. Part of their collection of objects survived their deaths to form the core of Oxford's Ashmolean Museum, but of their gardens not a trace survives: the house was demolished in 1881, and the gardens built over. They lie under Tradescant Road and Walberswick Street, between Vauxhall and Stockwell, just off the South Lambeth Road.

Runner beans were also grown by the pioneering botanist Philip Miller, head of the Chelsea Physic Garden from 1721 to 1770 and author of the best-selling *Gardener's Dictionary*. Under his direction Chelsea became famous across Europe, most notably for its North American plants, and it may well be Miller we have to thank for first advocating the idea of cooking runner beans whole (although it is possible that Miller may have been referring to a variety of what we would now call a climbing French bean). The runner bean has one other eccentricity of its own: it is a clockwise climber – all the other climbing beans twine in an anticlockwise direction.

Czar
c. 1885

As their Latin name (*Phaseolus coccineus*) suggests, most runner beans
have red flowers, but Czar is unusual in that its flowers are white,
as are the seeds inside its pods. It was bred in the late nineteenth
century by Thomas Laxton of Bedford, whose nursery introduced
many notable varieties of apples, plums and peas. Czar has two
advantages over other runner beans. One is that its white flowers
seem to be less attractive to birds, which sometimes attack red-
flowered kinds. The other is that, while its long pods are good for
cooking whole when young, the beans they contain are worth
eating on their own, if left on the stem to develop until the pods are
dry. They are quite like butter beans. Why Laxton called it Czar is
not clear: the Czar plum, bred by Laxton's rival Thomas Rivers,
commemorated a rather disastrous visit to England by Tsar
Alexander II, but that was back in 1874. The Czar runner bean first
seems to have been exhibited at a Shropshire Horticultural Society
show in August 1885, which was reported in that month's *Gardener's
Chronicle*, although without any explanation of its intriguing name –
could it have commemorated Alexander III's twentieth wedding
anniversary, which fell in that year?

Painted Lady
1633?

The most decorative of all runner beans, Painted Lady may have
been among the first varieties to been sent from America to Britain
around 1633. Its flowers have both white and scarlet petals, which
explains its alternative name, York and Lancaster – after the
opposing sides in the Wars of the Roses, whose heraldic colours
were respectively white and red. Andrew Widd, head gardener at

the historic Essex gardens of Audley End, grows Painted Lady occasionally, 'Just,' as he says, 'because I like the name.' That seems to me as good a reason as any, although it also bears good crops of tender, medium-length green bean-pods.

Prizewinner
1892

Raised by Sutton's of Reading and introduced in 1892, Prizewinner has long, straight pods with an excellent flavour. The modern variety, Enorma, is an 'improved' (that is, more vigorous and disease-resistant) form of Prizewinner. Prizewinner is still sold by Sutton's Seeds today.

Scarlet Runner
1633?

Widely grown and deservedly popular, the Scarlet Runner may, like Painted Lady, have been one of the first kinds of runner bean to arrive in Britain. Andrew Widd of Audley End notes that it crops over a longer period than modern varieties, and he also prefers its flavour; it freezes particularly well. The closely related Scarlet Emperor, which dates back to the 1890s, is probably an 'improved', early-maturing form of the Scarlet Runner. It was first known as the Mammoth Exhibition bean, but was renamed Scarlet Emperor in 1906, when it was sold by Carter's Seeds.

Strawberries

'Doubtless God could have made a better berry, but
doubtless God never did.'

Dr William Butler (1535–1618)

This chapter is haunted by ghosts: the ghosts of strawberries past. We have lost more old varieties of strawberries than any other kind of fruit, with one single exception – the raspberry, which has suffered so many losses that there is not one 'heritage' variety currently available. Were strawberry breeders so careless, and so little concerned with history? Not a bit of it. They would have been as happy as anyone else to see their carefully nurtured creations still on our tables, but for the sad fact that strawberries, like most soft fruit, have a genetic Achilles heel: their susceptibility to viral infection. All plants, of course, suffer from pests and diseases, and long-lived cultivars tend to be those that are most resistant to them. But soft fruit suffer more than most, with viral infections building up so quickly that, even today, virus-free stock has to be jealously guarded (by the alarmingly named Nuclear Stock Association, based at Terrington St Clement near King's Lynn) and it is not uncommon for new varieties to be superseded every two or three years.

Strawberries have always been popular, but their cultivated history is surprisingly short. Until the eighteenth century they were almost invariably gathered from the wild, just as we pick hedgerow blackberries today. Native strawberries (*Fragaria vesca*) can still be found growing wild in many areas of the country if you know where to look, but their fruit is far smaller and much less juicy than cultivated forms, and since larger hybrid varieties supplanted them they have largely been forgotten. Yet before the introduction of new species from continental Europe and, later, from North and South America, they were the only strawberries we had, and if you wanted to grow strawberries in your garden you first had to dig up some wild plants from the woods – or pay somebody to collect them for you, as Henry VIII did in 1533 for his new gardens at Hampton Court, not long after he appropriated it from Cardinal Wolsey.

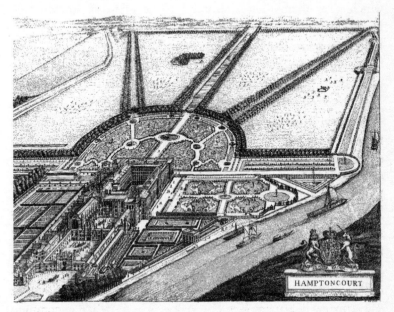

Hampton Court

The sixteenth century also saw the introduction of the first non-native strawberry, the hautbois or moschatel, whose botanical name is *Fragaria moschata*. Named after the oboe-like musical instrument that its tall flower-stems were said to resemble, the hautbois (often anglicised to hautboy) is another wild species, whose natural habitat is the forests of Scandinavia, western

Common Hautbois, or Musky, strawberry

Russia and central Europe. Although it bears less fruit than the British species, its tiny berries have a far more intense flavour, with hints of pineapple and raspberry, and a deliciously musky scent, which gave them their alternative name of musk strawberries. Hautbois strawberries became especially popular in France and Italy, and several varieties were developed, the earliest and most famous being Le Chapiron, or Capron, first mentioned in 1576 and, remarkably, still cultivated on a small scale today.

In the 1620s the hautbois was followed by the first American species, the Virginian strawberry (*Fragaria virginiana*), which was sent from New England by the first European settlers. Its fruit was only marginally larger than native British strawberries, but it was far more flavoursome, and over the years several cultivars were bred; among the best known was Grove End Scarlet, which was raised by William Atkinson of Grove End in London, an area now subsumed within St John's Wood (its location is commemorated by Grove End Road, not far from Lord's Cricket Ground). Pure, small-fruited Virginian strawberry cultivars are rarely encountered today, although one of the finest-tasting varieties, Little Scarlet, is still grown at Tiptree in Essex by Wilkin & Sons for the eponymous conserve. Little Scarlet, incidentally, is the only strawberry variety

The kitchen gardens at Osborne House, Queen Victoria's summer house on the Isle of Wight, were restored in the year 2000 and include many varieties of fruit and vegetable that were named after both Prince Albert and the Queen.

The Scarlet Emperor runner bean – also below with pink asters and in flower at the Lost Gardens of Heligan – was introduced in the 1890s, but it derives from a much older variety, the Scarlet Runner, which seems to have arrived in Britain around 1633.

Traditional radishes, like many other old varieties, were far more varied than their modern counterparts, both in colour and in shape. This selection, grown at the Lost Gardens of Heligan, includes the bright pink China Rose, which was introduced around 1845.

The fact that we expect our strawberries to be brilliant red is largely thanks to Royal Sovereign, which caused a sensation when it was launched by Thomas Laxton in 1892, at a time when strawberries were far more deeply coloured than they are today. It is the only Victorian variety to have survived into the present day.

Despite being one of the most popular tomatoes of the twentieth century, the origins of Ailsa Craig (centre left) remain rather obscure. It originated in Scotland around 1908, but the fact that it has the same name as the famous onion may be coincidence; in fact it may conceivably have been named after a yacht.

This family portrait of the south London nurseryman Joseph Myatt (1771-1855) shows him holding a basket of the strawberries he was best known for in his time, but he is most likely to be remembered as the godfather of the British rhubarb industry.

Two of the finest nineteenth century turnips: Manchester Market (left), whose alternative name of Green Top Stone is fairly self-explanatory, and the immortal Orange Jelly (right), which was introduced by George Chivas of Chester in 1853.

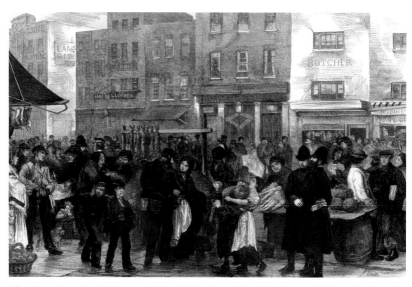

Victorian markets offered a far greater choice of fruit and vegetable varieties than any British market does today – or for that matter any British supermarket. London's New Cut market, pictured here in 1872, still takes place on the site of earlier market gardens, which were destroyed when Waterloo Station was built in 1848.

so far to have entered the annals of popular culture, thanks to Ian Fleming, who named it as James Bond's favourite jam in *From Russia With Love*.

The introduction of *Fragaria virginiana* represented a major advance in strawberry cultivation and ultimately led to the development of the large, juicy strawberries that fill supermarket shelves today. But they would never have come into existence had it not been for the discovery, in the early eighteenth century, of a second species of American strawberry, this time from south of the Equator. Its discovery was made by one of the most colourful figures in horticultural history, a French spy and fireworks enthusiast named Amédée-François Frézier. In July 1712 Frézier sailed to the Chilean port of Concepción, then under Spanish occupation. Posing as a merchant, he spent the following year studiously sketching its military defences without, apparently, attracting any particular attention. Luckily for us he was as interested in plants as he was in espionage and Roman candles (his *Treatise on Fireworks*, written before his Chilean adventures, was the standard work of its day), and while he was staking out the surrounding countryside he was excited to find a native strawberry – now called *Fragaria chiloensis* – which had far larger fruits than any he had seen before. Frézier took as many cuttings as he could fit in his luggage, and when his mission was accomplished, he sailed back to France with the new strawberries on board, arriving in Marseilles on 17 August 1714. Unfortunately only five plants survived the six-month voyage to France (astonishing in itself, given that Frézier's ship almost ran out of supplies and he was reduced to sprinkling them with his own meagre ration of drinking water), and all of them were female, which meant they would never produce fertile seed and could only be propagated by cuttings, but despite these drawbacks they were hailed as an exciting new discovery.

Chilean strawberries entered Britain just thirteen years later, in 1727, courtesy of Philip Miller, director of the Chelsea Physic

Garden. Miller purchased a number of *Fragaria chiloensis* plants from an English grower in Amsterdam, but for all their novelty they proved a culinary let-down. For one thing they were not very productive; nor were they especially hardy, and the little fruit they set was sweet but disappointingly bland. In fact their size appeared to be the only thing going for them, and they seemed fated to fade into obscurity, to be grown (if at all) as an exotic curiosity. And there strawberry cultivation might have stagnated, had French nurserymen not noticed that, when planted alongside the Virginian strawberries they already had, Frézier's new Chilean strawberries had begun setting fertile seed – which meant the two different species could interbreed. The resulting hybrids were not only more vigorous than either of their wild parents, but in a few cases they also combined the fine flavour of Virginian strawberries with the Chilean fruit's larger size. It was a huge step forward, and led to the first recognisably 'modern' cultivars, which began emanating from France during the second half of the eighteenth century. The most successful of these new hybrids was the so-called Pine Strawberry, named for its distinctive pineapple flavour, which became well known in Britain and had the added advantage of coming fairly true from seed.

The Gallic strawberry renaissance turned out to be tragically short-lived, falling victim (like so much else) to the Revolution, whose leaders doubtless considered the aristocratic fripperies of soft fruit to be a far less patriotic field of endeavour than, say, the proletarian potato. But France's loss was Britain's gain, for the knowledge that new hybrid strawberries could be bred successfully from seed rekindled British enthusiasm and led to a number of exciting innova-tions in, of all places, Isleworth.

This west London suburb may be best known today for its proximity to Heathrow airport, but in the early nineteenth century it was noted for its extensive orchards and market gardens, which supplied fruit and vegetables to the London markets. One of the area's most enterprising nurserymen was Michael Keens, who grew fruit on a 24-hectare (60-acre) plot on Worton Lane. (Worton Lane now runs close to the northern boundary of the 48-hectare (120-acre) Mogden sewage treatment plant, begun in 1936 and, more recently, the source of the famous 'Mogden Pong'. The site of Keens' nursery may well lie somewhere beneath its ever-bubbling tanks.) Like most growers Keens raised his strawberry plants from cuttings, but in 1806 he planted the seed of a white Chilean hybrid as an experiment. A motley collection of seedlings came up, but among them was one with large, round, bright-red fruit and a pleasant flavour, which he named Keens' Imperial. This quickly established itself as market leader, but even Imperial was put in the shade by Keens' next major introduction. Keens' Seedling, introduced in 1819, combined prodigious size with incomparable flavour and gained legendary status as one of the finest strawberries ever known.

Keens' success encouraged keen competition among his contemporaries (not least his Isleworth neighbour John Wilmot, begetter of Black Prince and Wilmot's Superb) and won British strawberries a European reputation, so much so that in France all large-fruited cultivars became known as *les fraises anglaises*, which was rather ironic given that it was actually the French who came up with them in the first place. Among the other leading growers of the time were several names we no longer associate with strawberries, for the varieties they introduced have long since disappeared: the gentleman-horticulturalist Thomas Andrew Knight (better remembered today for his cherries), John Williams of Pitmaston House in Worcester (originator of the Pitmaston Pine Apple and the Pitmaston Duchess pear) and Joseph Myatt of Brixton, to whom we owe Victoria rhubarb. Myatt was far better known for his strawberries than his rhubarb in his own day, a fact that is reflected in his family portrait (a copy of which is preserved in the collection of the Lewisham Local History and Archives Centre) in which he is

British Queen strawberry

pictured holding a basket of strawberries. His most famous strawberry, British Queen, was introduced in 1840; it was esteemed by Charles Darwin and was still being grown commercially a century later, although sadly it has since been lost.

All this development was in part, no doubt, inspired by personal ambition and professional pride, but it was also stimulated by jam. The importance of jam in late Victorian Britain is hard to imagine now, but in the days before deep freezers it was impossible to keep soft fruit for any length of time, so bottling, canning, preserving and above all jam-making helped to extend the shelf-life of soft fruit right through the year, and provided a cheap, energy-rich food for the poor. A growing appetite for fresh food of all kinds contributed to the growth of the market, driven by a rapidly growing population and an increasingly efficient rail network. To satisfy the demand from London alone, fruit pickers would begin work at three in the morning in the extensive strawberry fields between Swanley and St Mary Cray in Kent (both of which had direct train connections to the capital); by dawn fragrant punnets of fresh strawberries were being packed on to the shelves of specially designed railway carriages, all bound for the early morning market at Covent Garden. Growers went to extraordinary lengths to ensure that their fruit reached consumers dewy-fresh, often outclassing the much-trumpeted sophistication of twenty-first-century transport logistics with apparently effortless ease. The fruit historian Frederick Roach tells a story about one nineteenth-century firm of growers which claimed that their strawberries were picked overnight, made into jam the same morning and then delivered to the shops in London by lunch-time, presumably still warm. If their claim was true it would be hard to beat even now.

Arguably the greatest British strawberry breeder of the nineteenth century was Thomas Laxton of Bedford, who was responsible for three hugely successful varieties. Noble, a chance seedling, was introduced in 1884 and remained popular in continental Europe as recently as the 1960s; and in 1888 Laxton built on its success with King of the Earlies, which like Noble before it was awarded a highly coveted First Class Certificate from the Royal Horticultural Society. But it was a cross between the two that brought Laxton his greatest triumph, in the form of Royal Sovereign. First sold in 1892, it can still be found today. Of all the hundreds of large-fruited Victorian strawberries it is the only one to survive, and for that – as well as its delectable flavour – it surely deserves to be treasured.

The last century has seen the introduction of many new cultivars, often bred with less of an emphasis on flavour than on resistance to disease, the ability to withstand fairly rough handling during transport and, above all, appearance. Whether any of them approach once-famous varieties like Keens' Seedling and British Queen in quality and taste we will never know, but if Royal Sovereign is anything to go by, for once the stories of a lost golden age are true.

Royal Sovereign
1892

Thomas Laxton was a remarkable nurseryman, whose interests were scientific as well as horticultural. He was in regular correspondence with Charles Darwin, and he conducted many practical experiments on Darwin's behalf, particularly in the hybridisation of peas, experiments that have been compared in importance to Mendel's pioneering work in plant genetics. Laxton began breeding strawberries around 1865, at the height of his long and successful career, and he approached them with characteristic thoroughness. Over the next three decades he grew something like 10,000 seedlings, from which he developed seventeen new varieties. Royal Sovereign quickly established its superiority, primarily on account of the delicious taste and tenderness of its fruit, which could be harvested earlier than most other strawberries of the era, but also for its hardiness and productivity. Even its colour caused a sensation: at a time when the deeper the colour of a strawberry the more enticing it was considered to be, Royal Sovereign's white flesh and brilliant scarlet skin made it instantly recognisable. It may seem odd to think of fashions in fruit, just as there are fashions in music or clothes, but Royal Sovereign's scarlet set a fashion for strawberries that, to a great extent, has held true ever since. The luscious ruby-red Black Prince, now lost, embodied the apotheosis of mid-Victorian strawberries; if we saw it for sale today its colour would probably lead us to

assume that it was bruised or unappetisingly over-ripe – an example of how far our tastes are governed by appearance, and how profoundly they can change (or be changed) over time. For all its fine qualities Royal Sovereign does have some failings: it is not, perhaps, quite as productive as modern varieties, and it is certainly more prone to viral diseases and mildew. Yet Thomas Laxton's revolutionary strawberry is still worth seeking out, for its extraordinary history and matchless flavour.

Thomas Laxton (1830–90)

Tomatoes

No man of spirit can bear to be pelted with over-ripe tomatoes for any length of time without feeling that if the thing goes on much longer he will be reluctantly compelled to take steps.

P. G. Wodehouse, *Mike at Wrykyn* (1908)

Deemed bizarre, exotic and quite possibly deadly, the tomato was regarded with great suspicion by our ancestors, who grew it (when they grew it at all) as an ornamental climber: our habit of eating its fruit would have struck them as foolhardy to say the least, if not actively suicidal. Tomatoes have been classed as a curiosity, a poison and even an aphrodisiac, but in Britain until at least the mid-eighteenth century their fruit was considered too disgusting (and possibly dangerous) to eat – and even when we began using them to cook with they were boiled for hours first, just to be on the safe side.

Tomatoes began life as South American weeds, and their wild relatives can still be found growing in Ecuador and Peru. The Aztecs cultivated a plant they called a *tomatl*, which was first noted by a Spanish priest in 1529. (In Nahuatl, the Aztec language, *tomatl* was actually a generic term for any kind of large, soft fruit: small tomatoes were used to make a kind of ketchup, but the Aztecs apparently preferred the taste of another *tomatl*, which we now know as physalis or the tomatillo.) By the 1540s, tomatoes had been introduced to Spanish colonies around the world, from the Philippines and the Caribbean (where the word 'tomato' appears to have been coined), as well as to Naples, then under Spanish rule, and of course to mainland Spain itself. Compared to our smooth, round modern cultivars these early tomatoes were small, lumpy and misshapen-looking things, and they were more often orange or yellow than red, which explains their Italian name, *pomodoro*, or golden apple.

Although tomatoes were eaten blithely enough by uneducated peasants from the time of their first introduction, botanists soon noticed how similar their flowers were to those of highly poisonous plants like mandrakes and deadly nightshade, and they came to the erroneous (if fairly understandable) conclusion that tomatoes should be approached with great caution. In this they were at least half right, for tomatoes do in fact belong to the same botanical family, the *Solanaceae*, as deadly nightshade and mandrakes – not to mention potatoes, peppers, aubergines and tobacco – all of which are poisonous in part. The botanists' warnings went unheeded by the people of southern Europe, who had already begun the Mediterranean love affair with tomatoes that continues to this day, but in chilly northern Europe, where the relatively tender tomato had yet to gain a foothold, those same warnings went before them – with the result that, outside Italy and Spain, for the next 200 years tomatoes were widely regarded as injurious to health. Successive authors trotted out the same old warnings about tomatoes being 'moist' and 'cold', so perhaps it is not surprising that it was only in the mid-eighteenth century that a few brave British cooks began using tomatoes in the kitchen, although their use was strictly limited to soups and sauces.

These days we are so accustomed to eating tomatoes raw that our ancestors' obsession with boiling them (and just about every other vegetable) to death seems rather puzzling. But in the days before the purity of the water supply could be guaranteed, they were probably only doing what we would be advised to do today when travelling to less developed countries, where cooked food is reckoned to be safer than food that has simply been washed.

Slowly, however, their popularity grew, and by the early years of the nineteenth century tomatoes were starting to be treated as much as a food as a curiosity. By this time there were a number of varieties to choose from, red as well as orange and yellow, although most of them were smaller than modern cultivars, and the majority had the flattened shape and prominent ridges that are only seen today on some beefsteak varieties. The United States led the way in embracing culinary tomatoes (one early adopter was Thomas Jefferson, who first recorded growing 'tomatas' in 1809), and the vast number of American varieties – including such 'heritage' favourites as Brandywine and Mortgage Lifter – reflects this head start. Until recently it was often claimed that Americans overcame their aversion to tomatoes after Colonel Robert Gibbon Johnson munched his way through a basket of them in front of a disbelieving crowd outside the courthouse in Salem, New Jersey, in September 1820, thus proving they were safe to eat. This story turns out to be a suburban myth, but tomatoes were certainly grown widely in the States by the end of the 1820s. Visiting Cincinnati in February 1828, the English travel writer Frances Trollope recorded that 'From June till December tomatoes (the great luxury of the American table in the opinion of most Europeans) may be found in the highest perfection in the market for about sixpence the peck.'

The British market for tomatoes was much slower to take off, probably for the simple reason that, being relatively tender, tomatoes are not naturally suited to the British climate. As late as

1912 in his classic book *English Farming Past and Present*, Lord Ernle could claim that 'Fifty years ago the tomato was as great a rarity in England as an Avocado pear is to-day; a few were imported, a few were grown in private conservatories.' Although this sounds like an exaggeration, tomato cultivation on a major scale would certainly have been difficult, not to say uneconomic, until the later years of the nineteenth century, when the glass needed for commercially sized greenhouses finally became cheap enough. Large-scale cultivation of crops under glass only got under way during the 1860s, at Swanley in Kent, along the Lea Valley in London and, most significantly, around Worthing in West Sussex, where an enterprising market gardener called C. A. Elliott is said to have constructed one of the first commercial greenhouses using glass from Crystal Palace. By the end of the nineteenth century Worthing was the tomato capital of Britain, a position it maintained until the 1950s, when a combination of Spanish imports and pressure from housing development tipped the industry into decline. Today, according to the British Tomato Growers' Association, only around a quarter of the tomatoes we eat are grown in the UK; the rest – some 300,000 tons a year – are imported, mainly from the Canary Islands and Spain, where they have been grown, after all, for almost 500 years.

Ailsa Craig
c. 1908

Despite being one of the most popular red salad tomatoes of the twentieth century, surprisingly little seems to be known about Ailsa Craig. It shares its name with one of the finest British onions, but that seems to be about as far as it goes: the onion dates from 1887, and was raised by the head gardener at Culzean Castle in Ayrshire, which overlooks the Firth of Clyde and the island that gives Ailsa Craig its name. Why the tomato acquired the same name is a bit of a puzzle, especially as (contrary to some claims) it appears to have originated a long way from the Clyde, on the opposite coast of Scotland and far further north. Its date of introduction is equally vague. Some authorities claim it was already known before 1910; several others say 1925, although that seems unlikely, as I believe it won an Award of Merit from the Royal Horticultural Society in 1911. My best guess is that it was introduced in 1908 by Mr Alan Balch of Forres, on the Moray Firth east of Inverness; he was well known locally for his tomatoes, and his family still farms in the area. One (admittedly exotic) possibility is that it was named not after the island but after the first racing motor yacht, *Ailsa Craig*, which won both the 1907 and the 1908 Bermuda Power Boat Race, widely reported events at the time. Why anyone would name a tomato after a yacht may seem peculiar, but then is it any less likely than an onion named after an island?

Whatever its origins, this delicious tomato is still worth growing for its flavour, although it is more susceptible to disease than modern hybrid varieties. Ailsa Craig is ideal for greenhouse cultivation, but it can also be grown successfully out of doors, especially against south-facing walls. It was one of the main so-called 'Scotch Tomatoes' that were once widely planted in the Clyde Valley: tomatoes ripened early in its mild microclimate, giving their growers a useful competitive advantage in the days before year-round availability, when the first tomatoes to reach the market could command a premium price.

Carter's Golden Sunrise
c. 1894

If shop-sold tomatoes were anything to go by it would be easy to believe that all tomatoes were red, but of course that is complete nonsense. Why orange, yellow, purple and striped tomatoes have never caught on commercially is an intriguing question of culinary aesthetics, but if only people could be induced to taste Carter's Golden Sunrise, perhaps that situation would change. A golden-yellow tomato of medium size, it has a richer, sweeter flavour than its red relations, and has been acclaimed as the finest-tasting tomato of any colour or kind. In taste trials of traditional versus modern varieties held over the last few years by the National Trust at Clumber Park in Nottinghamshire, Golden Sunrise beat the competition hands down, and head gardener Neil Porteous still enthuses about its fabulous flavour. It was bred by the long-established firm of Carter's Seeds from Raynes Park, London, in the early 1890s, and sold by Sutton & Sons of Reading from 1896 – an example of how quickly Victorian varieties were 'adopted' by other seed companies and sold nationwide.

Harbinger
before 1910

Contrary to what some heritage enthusiasts would have us believe, not all old varieties of fruit and vegetables taste better than contemporary cultivars – but some do, and few taste better than Harbinger. Like so many apparently well-known old varieties its real origins are frustratingly obscure, but it seems to have been introduced around the start of the twentieth century. Its shiny red fruits look disarmingly similar to modern mass-market tomatoes, but there the resemblance ends: their skin is much finer, and their flavour far more intense. Harbinger does well outdoors, and bears heavy crops of medium-sized fruit, which ripen earlier than most.

Red Currant
1600s

The recent craze for 'currant' tomatoes – so called because they bear masses of currant-sized fruit – is in some ways a happy irony, for it represents the rediscovery of some of the oldest varieties we have, although they were rarely grown in the past for culinary use. I say 'varieties', for there is no one single, true Red Currant cultivar, but rather a group of broadly similar types, yellow as well as red. Apart from their unusual size, what makes currant tomatoes particularly interesting is that they are closely related to one of the original wild species, *Solanum pimpinellifolium*, which sprawls along dusty river-beds near the coasts of northern Peru. They are vigorous, productive and disease-resistant, and their fruit is extremely sweet, if exasperatingly fiddly to pick and prepare.

Yellow Pear
1600s

The large, round red tomatoes we take for granted today were unknown before the nineteenth century. In the days before these 'modern' cultivars, tomatoes came in a wide variety of sizes and shapes, of which the Yellow Pear is a good example. Its date of introduction is unknown, although it may well have been grown as an ornamental climber long before it was grown for its fruits. Like Carter's Golden Sunrise it makes an attractive and unusual addition to salads; its flavour is mild but sweet, and ideal for anyone who finds other tomatoes too acid. Plants grow strongly and can be hard to keep under control, for they tend to spread and generally require careful staking, but like the Red Currant they are resistant to disease.

Turnips and Swedes

On rainy days he sat and talked hours together with his mother about turnips. When company came, he made it his loving duty to put aside everything else and converse with them all day long of his great joy in the turnip.

Mark Twain, *Roughing It* (1886)

Long associated with dirt, soil and the poor, root vegetables have never enjoyed the sophisticated reputation of, say, cherries or strawberries, and few roots have been the butt of more jokes than turnips and swedes. To anyone who has had to endure plates of mashed swede at school their reputation may seem well deserved, yet turnips helped make Britain rich, and without swedes hundreds of thousands of twentieth-century Europeans would have starved to death.

Turnips of one kind or another have been around for several thousand years. The kind we eat, with their swollen stems, seem to have come from the eastern Mediterranean and were known to the Romans, and even then they were considered peasant food. Although the Romans probably brought them to Britain it was another kind of turnip, valued for the colza oil that could be extracted from its seeds, that appears to have been more commonly known; colza oil was widely used for lamps until the mid-nineteenth century. Culinary turnips came in all kinds of colours, sizes and shapes: some had long roots like parsnips or the closely related kohlrabi, while others were closer to the small, spherical varieties we know today. In his famous *Historie of Plants*, first published in 1597, John Gerard recorded that 'The small Turnep growes by Hackney in a sandy ground, and those that are brought to Cheapside market from that village are the best I ever tasted.' He also recorded that it was 'many times eaten raw, especially of the poore people in Wales, but most commonly boiled'.

The apotheosis of the turnip, however, as every schoolchild knows, belongs to the eighteenth century and Charles, Second Viscount 'Turnip' Townshend. Born on the family estate at Raynham Hall in Norfolk, Townshend was Secretary of State under George I and George II, but resigned in 1730 in a huff. He spent the last eight years of his life back at Raynham, improving the agricultural quality of his estate – or to be more specific, concentrating on 'that kind of rural improvement which arises from turnips', according to the incorrigibly waspish Alexander Pope. By all accounts Townshend became obsessed by turnips, which he may have seen being grown on a large scale during his stint as ambassador to the States-General of the Netherlands. Fortunately the sandy soil of north Norfolk proved perfect for their cultivation, and in a remarkably short space of time Raynham's blasted heaths were transformed into prime agricultural land.

It was the start of an agricultural revolution that helped make Britain one of the richest countries in the world, but at first Townshend's experiments were treated with suspicion. As Rowland Ernle wrote in his magisterial *English Farming Past and Present*, 'Outside Norfolk, both landlords and tenants still classed turnips with rats as Hanoverian innovations.' Still, thanks to Townshend's efforts, the turnip finally caught on, and by the late nineteenth century the famous French nursery company Vilmorin-Andrieux was offering fifty different varieties, from flat to long-rooted and yellow to black. Most of them have been lost again since, but a few old varieties survive.

The swede is a newcomer by comparison to the turnip. The two crops are closely related, but swedes have secondary roots below their swollen stems (turnips have a single root), and it seems likely that they originated as a cross between the turnip and the cabbage. Yellow-fleshed swedes were first described in 1620 by the Swiss botanist Gaspard Bauhin, by which time they had already spread across northern Europe from their place of origin – although whether that was in Sweden or Bohemia is still unclear. Their hardiness made them suitable for colder climates, and like turnips they were used both as a vegetable and as cattle fodder. In this latter role they have been credited with revolutionising the northern European diet, for they enabled large herds of cattle to be fed for the first time right through the winter, with the result that more people than ever before had access to fresh meat throughout the year.

Swedes were probably introduced to Britain some time between 1775 and 1780, in what appears to have been an early example of state-sponsored agricultural subsidy. In an intriguing letter dated June 1795, Thomas Jefferson, horticulturalist and soon-to-be American president, sent some swede seeds to a friend, remarking that 'This is the plant which the English Government thought of value enough to be procured at public expense from Sweden, cultivated and dispersed.' Jefferson also noted that 'it has such advantage over the common turnep that it is spreading rapidly over England and will become their chief turnep.' The Scots, meanwhile, embraced swedes with such enthusiasm that they have since supplanted turnips almost entirely, although for maximum confusion the Scots switched the vegetables' names: to this day, Scottish swedes are usually referred to as turnips (the 'neeps' of gastronomic legend), while what the English continue to call turnips were rechristened swedes. In America, of course, the English swede is better known as rutabaga, from the Swedish dialect word *rotabagge*, or 'ram's root', and in France, heaven only knows why, it is sometimes called 'chou de Siam'. The Swedes, understandably enough, do not call them swedes at all but *kålrot*, which translates as 'cabbage root'.

If the turnip's glory days date back to the eighteenth century, the swede briefly took centre stage during the First World War. Mountains of swedes were the only thing that stood between a large part of the German population and starvation during the appalling *Steckrübenwinter* or 'swede winter' of 1916–1917. Almost a century later their reputation has yet to recover, and you will rarely see a German swede on culinary sale.

Champion Purple Top
1850s

One of the best swedes for soups and stews, Champion Purple Top was widely exhibited in the nineteenth century, and remains a popular variety. It is hardy and large in size, purple above and white below, with surprisingly sweet and tender orange flesh.

Manchester Market
before 1857

Also known as the Green Top Stone turnip, Manchester Market appears to be a selected form of Snowball (see below), but with a flatter 'bulb', flushed with green where it is exposed to the light. Larger in size than Purple Top Milan, it has white flesh and a mild flavour, and (unlike some varieties) stores well for winter use. As its name suggests, it was once an important market variety in Cheshire and Lancashire.

Orange Jelly
1853

This delightfully named mid-season turnip is said to have the finest flavour of any variety: nutty and with a hint of bitter almond. It has sweet, tender, delicate yellow flesh, whose lack of fibre gives it an almost jelly-like consistency when boiled – hence the name. Also known as Golden Ball, after its spherical shape and smooth pale-

Orange Jelly turnip

amber skin, it is hardy and keeps well, although it can be rather slow to establish itself. It was raised by George Chivas of Chester and introduced by him in 1853 to great acclaim: among its fans was the *British Farmer's Magazine*, which in 1855 described it as 'almost equal to a melon in shape, and also in sweetness of taste'.

Purple Top Milan
before 1890

With its bright purple shoulders and cream-coloured base, this attractive old early-harvesting turnip still has plenty of fans – among them the head gardener at Audley End in Essex, Andrew Widd, who recommends it as 'good for an early crop in the cold frame and also as a main crop'. It is fast to grow, making it a useful crop to sow between slower-growing winter vegetables, and has an excellent full flavour, especially when harvested young. Purple Top Milan is frost-tolerant and stores well.

Snowball
before 1826

One of the oldest varieties of turnip still easily available, Snowball is noted for its round, all-white roots and mild flavour, which is particularly delicate when picked very young, just four to six weeks after sowing – best done from early summer to late autumn. Unlike Orange Jelly, its flesh becomes tough and pithy if left too long in the ground.

What Can I Do Next?

The best way to preserve old varieties is to do what people have always done: grow them. The following pages include a list of suppliers, some of which specialise in traditional varieties; others sell them alongside their modern counterparts.

But not all of us have the room, or for that matter the time or the inclination, to grow these varieties ourselves. Fortunately there are still many ways in which one can help. One of them is to join one of the organisations, listed in the following pages, that promote and maintain this country's traditional varieties, and encourage people to grow their own.

Of course, there is no better way of appreciating why they are worth growing than seeing them grown by professional gardeners, especially in their original settings. Fortunately the number of gardens growing old-fashioned varieties has rapidly increased in recent years, led by the brilliant example of the Lost Gardens of Heligan and the enlightened support of English Heritage and the National Trust. Places to Visit (pp. 236–45) contains a selection of the best of them. Volunteers are often very welcome, so if you live locally and would like to become more involved, it's well worth asking.

In the end, though, unless there is a demand for old varieties, there will be little incentive for anyone to preserve them in the first place. Happily, the last few years have seen a huge growth of interest in local and traditional food, fuelled by farmers' markets, enlightened cooks and restaurateurs and enthusiastic food writers. But there is still a long way to go: many old varieties are still threatened with extinction, and far too few of them are found in supermarkets, on market stalls, on menus and in cookery books. The more people ask for old and genuinely local varieties in shops and restaurants, the more likely they are to survive.

Organisations

Common Ground
Gold Hill House, 21 High Street, Shaftesbury SP7 8JE
Tel: 01747 850 820
www.commonground.org.uk and www.england-in-particular.info

Garden Museum
Lambeth Palace Road, London SE1 7LB
Tel: 020 7401 8865
www.museumgardenhistory.org
Open Tuesday to Sunday, 10.30 a.m. to 5 p.m.

Garden Organic
Ryton, Coventry CV8 3LG
Tel: 024 7630 3517
www.gardenorganic.org.uk
Gardens open 9 a.m. to 5 p.m. daily.

Lindley Library
Royal Horticultural Society, 80 Vincent Square, London SW1P 2PE
Tel: 020 7821 3050
www.rhs.org.uk/Learning/Library
Open Monday to Friday, 10 a.m. to 5 p.m. excluding Bank Holidays
(Tuesdays 10 a.m. to 7 p.m.).

National Council for the Conservation of Plants and Gardens
Home Farm, Loseley Park, Guildford GU3 1HS
Tel: 01483 447 540
www.nccpg.co.uk

National Fruit Collection, Brogdale
Brogdale Road, Faversham, Kent ME13 8RZ
Tel: 01795 535 286
www.brogdale.org
Open daily 10 a.m. to 5 p.m. (4.30 p.m. in winter).

National Society of Allotment and Leisure Gardeners
O'Dell House, Hunters Road, Corby NN17 5JE
Tel: 01536 266 576
www.nsalg.org.uk

National Trust
Heelis, Kemble Drive, Swindon SN2 2NA
Tel: 01793 817 400
www.nationaltrust.org.uk

National Trust for Scotland
Wemyss House, 28 Charlotte Square, Edinburgh EH2 4ET
Tel: 0131 243 9300
www.nts.org.uk

Royal Horticultural Society Fruit Group
Curator's Office, RHS Garden Wisley, Woking GU23 6QB
Tel: 01483 212 342
www.rhs.org.uk/plants/fruit_group.asp

Westmorland Damson Association
Lile Yaks, Cartmel Fell, Windermere, Cumbria LA23 3PD
www.lythdamsons.org.uk

Suppliers

Fruit

Bernwode Plants, Buckinghamshire
Kingswood Lane, Ludgershall HP18 9RB
Tel: 01844 237 415
www.bernwodeplants.co.uk
Several hundred rare and traditional varieties of fruit, including apples, pears, plums, gages, cherries, vines, medlars, quinces, mulberries and some soft fruit.

Blackmoor Nurseries, Hampshire
Blackmoor, Liss, GU33 6BS
Tel: 01420 473 576
www.blackmoor.co.uk
Excellent apple selection, plus a wide range of other fruit.

Brogdale Orchards, Kent
Macknade Natural Garden Centre, Selling Road, Faversham ME13 8XF
Tel: 01795 858 140
www.brogdale.org

Trees from the National Fruit Collection: a different selection each year, including many old varieties, but almost all the varieties not on sale in the plant centre can be grafted from the trees in the National Fruit Collection, at a cost of £38 per tree.

Charlton Orchards, Somerset
Charlton Road, Creech St Michael, Taunton TA3 5PF
Tel: 01823 412 959
www.charltonorchards.com
Fresh apples in season by mail order, including many old varieties, which are also sold at the farm shop, along with single-variety apple juices.

Conwy Trees, Conwy
Ffordd Ty Gwyn y Graig, Eglwysbach LL28 5RN
Tel: 01492 650 464
www.conwytrees.com
Small selection of rare old Welsh varieties, including Bardsey and Anglesey Pig's Snout apples, Aber damson, Denbigh plum and Snowdon Queen pear.

Deacon's Nursery, Isle of Wight
Moor View, Godshill PO38 3HW
Tel: 01983 840 750
www.deaconsnurseryfruits.co.uk
Good range of classic British plums and pears.

East of England Apples and Orchards Project, Norfolk
The School House, Rougham, King's Lynn PE32 2SE
www.applesandorchards.org.uk
Dedicated to preserving and promoting the orchards of Bedfordshire, Cambridgeshire, Essex, Hertfordshire, Lincolnshire, Norfolk and Suffolk, the East of England Apples and Orchards

Project also sells around 170 traditional varieties of apples and pears, some so rare they are not even in the National Fruit Collection at Brogdale.

John Tweedie Fruit Trees, Dumfriesshire
Maryfield Road Nursery, Terregles DG2 9TH
Tel: 01387 720 880
Unusually wide choice of gooseberries and rhubarb, as well as fruit trees and bushes, by mail order and by appointment from the nursery.

Keepers Nursery, Kent
Gallants Court, East Farleigh, Maidstone ME15 OLE
Tel: 01622 726 465
www.keepers-nursery.co.uk
Fantastically wide choice of apples, cherries, pears and plums, as well as a good choice of soft fruit.

Rougham Hall Nurseries, Suffolk
Ipswich Road (A14), Rougham, Bury St Edmunds IP30 9LZ
Tel: 0800 970 756 or 01359 270 577
www.roughamhallnurseries.co.uk
Excellent selection of old British gooseberry varieties, which forms one of the two National Collections (the other is at Brogdale).

R.V. Roger, North Yorkshire
Malton Road (A169), Pickering YO18 7JW
Tel: 01751 472 226
www.rvroger.co.uk
Good choice of classic apples, plums and pears; supplies old-fashioned standards and half-standards for full-size orchards, as well as ready-trained fans, espaliers and cordons for walls.

Thornhayes Nursery, Devon
St Andrew's Wood, Dulford, Cullompton EX15 2DF
Tel: 01884 266 746
www.thornhayes-nursery.co.uk
Specialist in old apple varieties from Devon, Somerset and Cornwall, many of them rare; good range of other trees, including old plums such as the Bryanston Gage and Dittisham Ploughman.

Yorkshire Orchards, North Yorkshire
White House Farm, Bolton Lane, Wilberfoss, York YO41 5NX
Tel: 01759 380 375
www.yorkshireorchards.co.uk
Apple varieties from Yorkshire and the north.

Vegetables

Association Kokopelli UK, Kent
Ripple Farm, Crundale, Canterbury CT4 7EB
Tel: 01227 731 815
www.organicseedsonline.com
The French-based Association Kokopelli specialises in organically produced traditional varieties of seed, mainly from continental Europe. Membership is optional and starts at £12, but includes discounts on seed purchases.

Carroll's Heritage Potatoes, Northumberland
Tiptoe Farm, Cornhill-on-Tweed TD12 4XD
Tel: 01890 883 060
www.heritage-potatoes.co.uk
Around twenty different classic British varieties of potatoes available to order online, including Arran Victory and Sharpe's Express, both ready grown and as seed.

Chiltern Seeds, Cumbria
Bortree Stile, Ulverston LA12 7PB
Tel: 01229 581 137
www.chilternseeds.co.uk
Increasing number of old varieties, mainly British.

Heritage Seed Library, Warwickshire
Garden Organic, Ryton, Coventry CV8 3LG
Tel: 024 7630 3517
www.gardenorganic.org.uk/hsl
In its previous incarnation as the Henry Doubleday Research
Association, Garden Organic set up the Heritage Seed Library in
1975 to preserve old varieties of vegetables that were in danger of
being lost. The HSL concentrates on those 'heirloom' varieties that
have been handed down through families, but also includes some
former commercial varieties. For a £20 yearly subscription
members receive six seed packets of their choice plus one lucky dip.

Mr Fothergill's, Suffolk
Gazeley Road, Kentford, Newmarket CB8 7QB
Tel: 01638 751 161 or 0845 166 2511
www.fothergills.co.uk
Good choice of traditional varieties, such as The Student parsnip
and Musselburgh leeks.

Organic Gardening Catalogue, Surrey
Riverdene Business Park, Molesey Road, Hersham KT12 4RG
Tel: 0845 130 1304
www.organiccatalog.com
Offers a good range of older varieties alongside modern cultivars,
mostly organically grown.

Simpson's Seeds, Wiltshire
Walled Garden Nursery, Horningsham, Warminster BA12 7NQ
Tel: 01985 845 004
www.simpsonsseeds.co.uk
Good selection of older vegetable (and some fruit) varieties,
including Purple Top Milan turnips and Alderman peas.

Thomas Etty Esq, Somerset
Seedsman's Cottage, Puddlebridge, Horton, Ilminster TA19 9RL
Tel: 01460 57934
www.thomasetty.co.uk
The leading specialist in traditional, mainly Victorian vegetable
varieties: outstanding list backed up by years of research and lots of
useful information.

W. Robinson & Son, Lancashire
Sunny Bank, Forton, Preston PR3 0BN
Tel: 01524 791 210
www.mammothonion.co.uk
Famous for its large 'exhibition' vegetables, W. Robinson also sells
a good selection of older varieties, such as Black Spanish radishes
and Martock broad beans.

Places to Visit

Audley End Organic Kitchen Garden, Essex
Audley End, Saffron Walden CB11 4JG
Tel: 01799 522 148
www.gardenorganic.org.uk/gardens/audley.php
The walled kitchen garden at Audley End is the result of an enlightened partnership between English Heritage, which owns the site, and Garden Organic, which since 1999 has restored the gardens to something like their original glory. Of particular interest is the formal Historic Garden, largely planted with Victorian varieties (many of them from Garden Organic's Heritage Seed Library) and managed using nineteenth-century methods under the inspired direction of head gardener Mike Thurlow.

Calke Abbey, Derbyshire
Ticknall, Derby DE73 7LE
Tel: 01332 863 822
www.nationaltrust.org.uk
Calke's acre and a half of working kitchen garden features traditional vegetable varieties such as Long Red Surrey carrots and Bunyard's Exhibition broad beans, plus old-fashioned gooseberries and other soft fruit, some of which are harvested for sale. The orchard includes regional apples, including the famous Newton Wonder, discovered around 1870 in nearby King's Newton.

Cannon Hall, South Yorkshire
Bark House Lane, Cawthorne, Barnsley s75 4at
Tel: 01226 790 270
www.barnsley.gov.uk
One of the finest collections of pear trees in the country can be found within the walled gardens of Cannon Hall, once the grand eighteenth-century home of the Spencer-Stanhope family but owned since 1951 by Barnsley Metropolitan Borough Council. Begun in the 1760s, the collection now includes almost forty varieties, celebrated with an annual Pear Day each September, which features music, tastings and sales.

Clumber Park, Nottinghamshire
Clumber Park, Worksop s80 3az
Tel: 01909 476 592
www.nationaltrust.org.uk
The triumphant restoration of Clumber's vast kitchen gardens, laid out on a suitably ducal scale for the Duke of Newcastle in 1772, offers a rare chance to compare modern hybrids mixed with pre-1910 varieties such as Oxheart carrots and January King cabbages. The seemingly endless greenhouse, 135 metres (440 feet) long, contains vines, peaches, figs and nectarines, and seasonal garden produce is used in the restaurant and sold in the gardens.

Cogges Manor Farm Museum, Oxfordshire
Church Lane, Witney ox28 3la
Tel: 01993 772 602
www.cogges.org
Popular with families and schools, this working historic farm includes a walled garden planted with traditional varieties of fruit and vegetables, which are prepared and cooked in the farmhouse kitchen.

Cotehele, Cornwall
St Dominick, Saltash PL12 6TA
Tel: 01579 351 346
www.nationaltrust.org.uk
In the nineteenth and early twentieth centuries the Tamar valley around Cotehele was thickly planted with daffodils, apples, cherries and plums, its mild climate providing early produce for the London market. Although the industry was killed off by cheap imports and the Second World War, Cotehele's beautiful gardens preserve many old Cornish and Devon varieties, including around a hundred local apples, as well as cherries, pears and plums.

Down House, Kent
Luxted Road, Downe BR6 7JT
Tel: 01689 859 119
www.english-heritage.org.uk or www.darwinatdowne.co.uk
The orchard at Charles Darwin's former home is planted entirely with fruit varieties that pre-date his death in 1882, while the vegetables in the half-acre kitchen garden all pre-date 1896, when his wife Emma died. Head gardener Toby Beasley explains that 'having this later cut-off date enables us to grow a wider range of vegetables, which makes selection a bit easier and also creates a more interesting display'. Darwin used the kitchen gardens in his experiments, and some specific varieties are mentioned in his work. He was particularly interested in peas, comparing forty-one different varieties, and Toby has grown over twenty of them in the garden – 'about all that we can find'. Down House also runs a Heritage Seed Library garden for Garden Organic.

Fyvie Castle, Aberdeenshire
Turriff, Fyvie AB53 8JS
Tel: 0844 493 2182
www.nts.org.uk
Although the great triple-walled kitchen gardens of this imposing Scottish baronial pile are no longer used, the National Trust for Scotland has redeveloped the nineteenth-century kitchen garden with a growing collection of specifically Scottish fruit and vegetables, including Musselburgh leeks, Ailsa Craig onions, the Green Pear of Yair and famous potatoes such as Duke of York.

Garden Organic, Warwickshire
Ryton, Coventry CV8 3LG
Tel: 024 7630 3517
www.gardenorganic.org.uk
A selection of vegetables from Garden Organic's pioneering Heritage Seed Library is grown in the organisation's four hectares (ten acres) of popular organic demonstration gardens, which also host an annual Potato Day and seed swap in early February.

Helmsley Walled Garden, North Yorkshire
Cleveland Way, Helmsley YO62 5AH
Tel: 01439 771 427
www.helmsleywalledgarden.org.uk
These enormous kitchen gardens once supplied fresh produce for nearby Duncombe Park, itself the subject of a heroic programme of restoration since 1986. The walled gardens were begun in 1758 and cover an area of two hectares (five acres) beside the spectacular ruins of Helmsley Castle (worth a visit in its own right); their restoration began in 1994, conducted largely by volunteers. Among other highlights is a large collection of Yorkshire apples and Victorian varieties of vine.

Hughenden Manor, Buckinghamshire
Hughenden, High Wycombe HP14 4LA
Tel: 01494 755 573
www.nationaltrust.org.uk
The Victorian walled kitchen gardens at Disraeli's former home
were restored in 2005, and feature over fifty old apples, including
local Buckinghamshire varieties.

Kellie Castle, Fife
Kellie Castle and Garden, Pittenweem KY10 2RF
Tel: 0844 493 2184
www.nts.org.uk
The organically gardened fruit and vegetable beds at Kellie Castle
contain both traditional and modern varieties, including more than
thirty pre-1930s varieties of potatoes, a good selection of Scottish
apples and over twenty kinds of rhubarb, all maintained by the
National Trust for Scotland in a beautiful setting.

Little Moreton Hall, Cheshire
Congleton CW12 4SD
Tel: 01260 272 018
www.nationaltrust.org.uk
Small but interesting collection of seventeenth-century vegetables,
including leaf beet, winter radishes, marrowfat peas and early kinds
of cabbage or colewort.

Lost Gardens of Heligan, Cornwall
Pentewan, St Austell PL26 6EN
Tel: 01726 845 100
www.heligan.com
Heligan led the way with its faithful restoration of the nineteenth-
century kitchen gardens, and there is still no better place to see
traditional varieties being grown in a traditional way. Many pre-date

1918 but, as productive-gardens manager Sylvia Travers points out: 'The majority are very much earlier. Some newer varieties have snuck in, but they have been chosen for an exceptional trait, be it flavour or productivity. As a rule, we garden to late Victorian principles and varieties. Most of the varieties we have are not grown commercially, although since the garden's restoration in 1991 there has been a resurgence in "heritage" crops. So much so that varieties whose seed we once saved can be bought now from commercial seed merchants.'

Lyveden New Bield, Northamptonshire
Oundle, Peterborough PE8 5AT
Tel: 01832 205 358
www.nationaltrust.org.uk
Years of painstaking archaeological and documentary research went into recreating the Elizabethan orchards around Lyveden New Bield. One of the largest orchards owned by the National Trust, it now includes ancient apples such as Catshead and Winter Queening as well as pears, plums, cherries and walnuts, all laid out roughly as they might have been before the orchard was grubbed up in 1609.

National Fruit Collection, Kent
Brogdale Road, Faversham ME13 8RZ
Tel: 01795 535 286
www.brogdale.org
Not just a remarkable scientific resource but also an excellent place to buy unusual varieties (see Suppliers). The largest collection of fruit varieties in the world, it includes over 2,300 different varieties of apple, more than 500 pears, 350 plums, over 200 varieties of cherry and 320 kinds of bush fruits, as well as smaller collections of nuts and vines. The future of the Brogdale site and the complicated ownership of the National Fruit Collection is currently under discussion; see the website for the latest information.

Normanby Hall, Lincolnshire
Normanby, Scunthorpe DN15 9HU
Tel: 01724 720 588
www.northlincs.gov.uk/normanby
Owned by North Lincolnshire Council, the one-acre (0.4 hectare)
kitchen garden at Normanby Hall was restored in 1997, and now
forms what is said to be 'the only totally period-correct Victorian
walled garden in Britain'. Head gardener Sue Hoy grows a wide
selection of pre-1901 varieties of fruit and vegetables, as far as
possible using nineteenth-century methods.

Osborne House, Isle of Wight
East Cowes PO32 6JX
Tel: 01983 200 022
www.english-heritage.org.uk
The grand walled garden that once supplied Queen Victoria and
Prince Albert's summer home was restored in the year 2000 as part
of English Heritage's Contemporary Garden Initiative. Although
the garden design (by Rupert Golby) is contemporary, it includes
many varieties of fruit and vegetables associated with the royal
couple, including Lane's Prince Albert apples and Victoria rhubarb.

Pershore, Worcestershire
Pershore Tourism Association, Town Hall, 34 High Street, Pershore
WR10 IDS
Tel: 01386 556 591
www.visitpershore.co.uk
Each August Bank Holiday the town celebrates its annual Plum
Day, with many different varieties for sale, alongside plum wines
and chutneys, as well as a plum identification service.

Quarry Bank Mill, Cheshire
Styal, Wilmslow SK9 4LA
Tel: 01625 527 468
www.quarrybankmill.org.uk
The Apprentice House Garden once provided food for the children who worked at Quarry Bank Mill, and the recreated garden features many nineteenth-century varieties such as Painted Lady runner beans, Champion Purple Top swedes and French Breakfast radishes, as well as a selection of apples such as Irish Peach and Lady's Finger of Lancashire.

Rode Hall, Cheshire
Scholar Green ST7 3QP
Tel: 01270 873 237
www.rodehall.co.uk
Head gardener Kelvin Archer grows a fine selection of nineteenth-century gooseberries in the kitchen garden at Rode Hall, the oldest being the red Crown Bob, which pre-dates 1812. An award-winning gooseberry exhibitor himself who grew the world champion gooseberry in 1993, Kelvin admits that he also has 'lots more modern varieties which usually produce much heavier berries than the old varieties. It's the modern types that our show members tend to grow. They don't even think about growing the old ones any more'.

Tatton Park, Cheshire
Knutsford WA16 6QN
Tel: 01625 374 400
www.tattonpark.org.uk
The extensive walled gardens at Tatton Park have been carefully restored over the last few years, as have the buildings around them, and now contain varieties of fruit and vegetables that might have been grown here in Edwardian times, while the orchards contain many northern and Cheshire varieties of apples, pears, cherries and plums, some of which are sold in season.

Threave Garden, Dumfries and Galloway
Castle Douglas DG7 1RX
Tel: 0844 493 2245
www.nts.org.uk
The gardeners' training school for the National Trust for Scotland has its own fine gardens, in which can be found an excellent collection of venerable Scottish pears saved from ancient orchards in the Carse of Gowrie, as well as a number of Scottish apples such as the East Lothian Pippin and Tower of Glamis.

Tintinhull Garden, Somerset
Farm Street, Tintinhull, Yeovil BA22 8PZ
Tel: 01935 823 289
www.nationaltrust.org.uk
The 1930s vegetable garden at Tintinhull has been planted with rare and unusual varieties from the Garden Organic Heritage Seed Library.

Wakefield, West Yorkshire
Wakefield Tourist Information Centre, 9 The Bull Ring, Wakefield WF1 1HB
Tel: 0845 601 8353
www.wakefield.gov.uk
The annual Wakefield Festival of Food, Drink and Rhubarb celebrates the town's place at the heart of the Yorkshire Rhubarb Triangle, and takes place in the second week of February. The four-day event includes rhubarb-related floral arrangements, rhubarb-wine tastings, a rhubarb-farmers' market and tours of the candlelit forcing sheds.

West Dean, West Sussex
West Dean College, West Dean, Chichester PO18 0QZ
Tel: 01243 811 301
www.westdean.org.uk
The huge and sumptuously restored walled gardens at West Dean offer a superb example of how a grand Victorian kitchen garden might have looked at its height. But this is no slavish recreation, as garden manager Sarah Wain explains: 'When the kitchen gardens were redeveloped between 1993 and 1994 we did a lot of research into nineteenth-century varieties of fruit and vegetables, but it was never our intention to turn the garden into a museum. We do grow a lot of traditional varieties, but only those that are fairly widely available and which have good disease resistance.' Peas and beans are grown for the Heritage Seed Library, and there is a notable collection of fruit trees, including many Sussex varieties.

Wisley, Surrey
Wisley Lane, Wisley, Woking GU23 6QB
Tel: 0845 260 9000
www.rhs.org.uk/wisley
The Royal Horticultural Society's immaculate show gardens by the A3 include one of the two National Collections of rhubarb, with 112 varieties, many of them rare (the other collection is at Harlow Carr, the RHS's northern gardens at Harrogate). Wisley also owns what is arguably the oldest collection of fruit trees in the country, transplanted from the society's nineteenth-century London gardens, grafts from which form the core of the National Fruit Collection at Brogdale.

Gazetteer

Writing in 1948, the fruit expert H. V. Taylor professed himself puzzled that 'the breeders of the new plums seem to have less sentiment for plums than for apples, for whilst pilgrimages are made to see the original trees of Beauty of Bath, Ribston Pippin, Bramley's Seedling, Newton Wonder, etc., no attempt was made to preserve the original trees of important plum varieties, and we do not know with certainty the actual place where the Victoria or the Pershore were first found. Our good fruits deserve more consideration, and furthermore such pilgrimages are most enjoyable.'

What seems most surprising today about H. V. Taylor's lament is not so much his point that plums were thought less of than apples but that, as recently as 1948, people were still making pilgrimages to see them. Such pilgrimages are indeed 'most enjoyable', but the idea of making them seems about as exotic, now, as walking to Santiago de Compostela. More so, in fact, since the Santiago pilgrimage has enjoyed a considerable revival, while the only fruit tree to attract even a passing interest, these days, is the remarkable Bramley apple that still survives in the garden where it was originally raised in Nottinghamshire. Our loss of interest may, perhaps, be ascribed to the fact that the other trees that Taylor mentions have subsequently been lost, victims of age or mindless vandalism (although happily an offshoot of the original Ribston Pippin may still exist).

And yet we go to see many places simply for their associations with a particular event or person. When we visit Dove Cottage, for example, we're not expecting to meet Wordsworth, or when we go to Charleston, Vanessa Bell. Yet literary shrines are hugely popular, while the sites of important culinary discoveries have been almost entirely forgotten. Which is odd, for it would be a fairly safe (if possibly contentious) bet that Cox's Orange Pippin, say, has given more pleasure to more people over the years than the works of William Wordsworth, and is probably known to more people too. But while Wordsworth's homes in Grasmere, Rydal and Cockermouth have been preserved for posterity, the house and garden where Richard Cox lived were swept away long ago, with not even a local plaque to commemorate their site. The idea of visiting somewhere associated with a particular vegetable, mean-while, would be considered eccentric, if not bordering on the insane, by most people. Which seems an excellent reason to start doing it.

Here, then, is a map and gazetteer of the varieties whose stories appear in this book, and the places that they came from, in the cause of stimulating local pride, as well as offering some intriguing destinations for a most enjoyable pilgrimage. For ease, I've used the well-known county boundaries from before the 1974 shake-up.

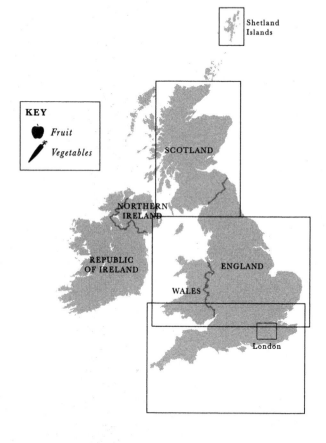

KEY

Fruit

Vegetables

Shetland
Islands

SCOTLAND

NORTHERN
IRELAND

REPUBLIC
OF IRELAND

WALES

ENGLAND

London

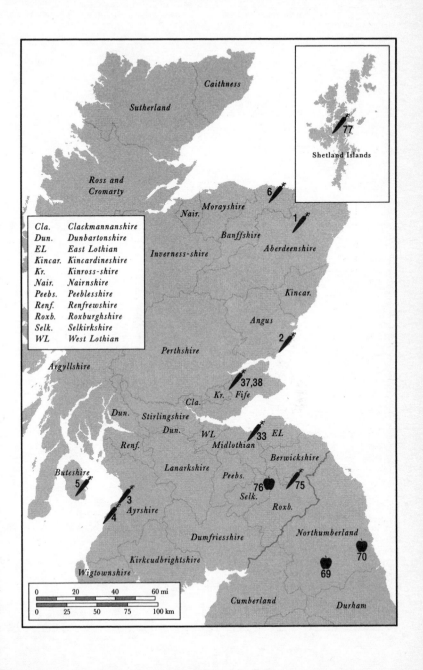

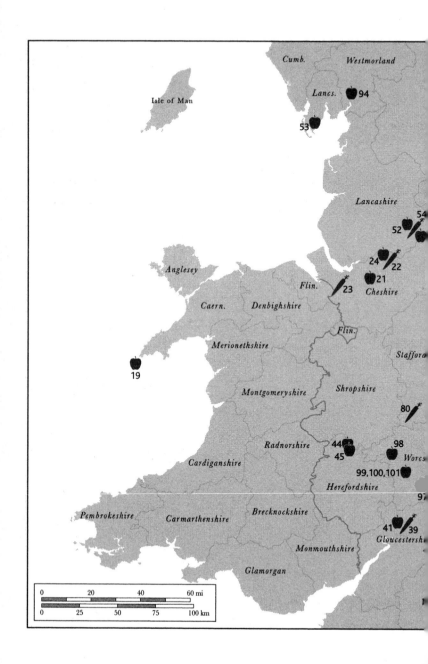

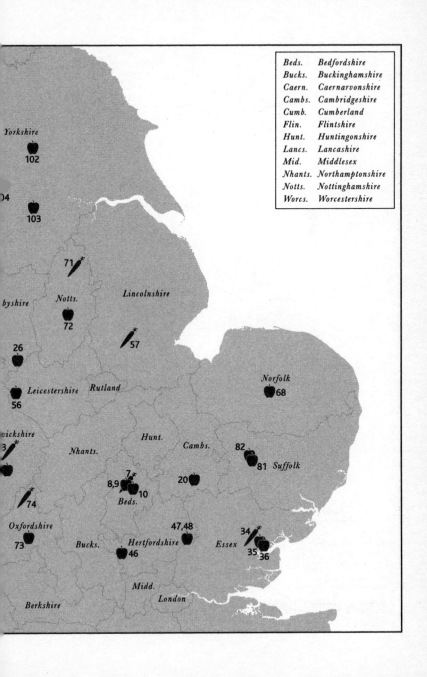

Beds.   Bedfordshire
Bucks.   Buckinghamshire
Caern.   Caernarvonshire
Cambs.   Cambridgeshire
Cumb.   Cumberland
Flin.   Flintshire
Hunt.   Huntingonshire
Lancs.   Lancashire
Mid.   Middlesex
Nhants.   Northamptonshire
Notts.   Nottinghamshire
Worcs.   Worcestershire

Yorkshire
102

04
103

71

Notts.
72

Lincolnshire

byshire

26

Leicestershire
56

Rutland

57

Norfolk
68

vickshire
3

Nhants.

Hunt.

Cambs.

82
81   Suffolk

74

7
8,9
10

20

Beds.

Oxfordshire
73

Bucks.

47,48

Hertfordshire
46

34

Essex

35   36

Midd.

Berkshire   London

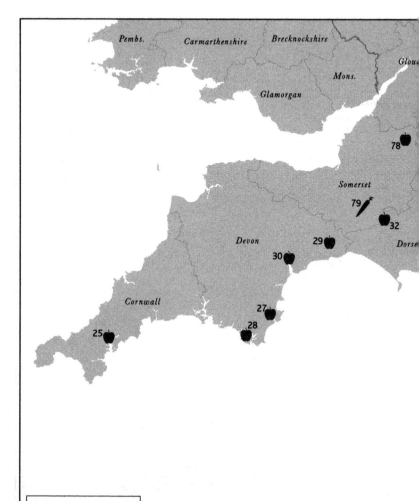

0   20   40   60 mi

0   25   50   75   100 km

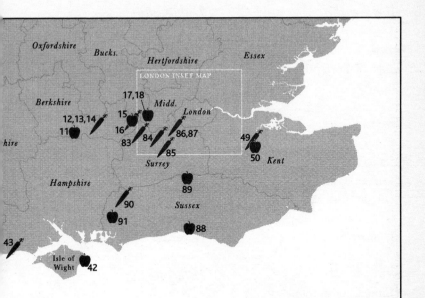

Oxfordshire Bucks. Hertfordshire Essex

LONDON INSET MAP

Berkshire Midd. London

12,13,14 17,18

11 15

16 84 86,87

83 85 49

Surrey Kent 50

Hampshire 89

90 Sussex

91

88

43

Isle of
Wight 42

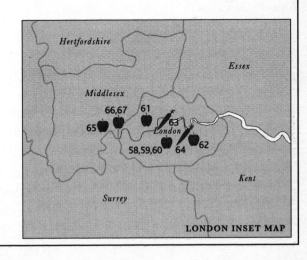

Hertfordshire

Essex

Middlesex

66,67 61

65 63

London

58,59,60 64 62

Kent

Surrey

LONDON INSET MAP

Aberdeenshire

FYVIE
Duke of York potato,
1891 (1)

Angus

ARBROATH
Golden Wonder potato,
1906 (2)

Ayrshire

AYR
Home Guard potato,
1942 (3)

CULZEAN CASTLE
Ailsa Craig onion,
1887 (4)

LAMLASH, ISLE OF ARRAN
Arran Victory potato,
1918 (5)

Banffshire

CORNHILL
Kerr's Pink potato,
1907 (6)

Bedfordshire

BEDFORD
Bedfordshire Fillbasket sprout,
before 1925 (7)
Laxton's No. 1 redcurrant,
c. 1914 (8)
Royal Sovereign strawberry,
1892 (9)

WARDEN ABBEY
Warden pear,
1100s? (10)

Berkshire

ALDERMASTON
Williams' Bon Chrétien /
Bartlett pear,
1770 (11)

READING
King George cucumber,
1911 (12)
Sutton's Globe (aka
Bedfordshire Champion)
onion,
1869 (13)
The Sutton broad bean,
1923 (14)

WINDSOR
Frogmore Early cherry,
c. 1864 (15)
Green Windsor broad bean,
before 1754 (16)

Buckinghamshire

COLNBROOK
Cox's Orange Pippin apple,
c. 1825 (17)
Cox's Pomona apple,
c. 1825 (18)

Caernarvonshire

BARDSEY ISLAND
Bardsey apple, before
1998 (19)

Cambridgeshire

Cambridge Gage plum,
1800s (20)

Cheshire

ACTON BRIDGE
London gooseberry,
1831 (21)

ALTRINCHAM
Altringham carrot,
1880s (22)

CHESTER
Orange Jelly turnip,
1853 (23)

TIMPERLEY
Timperley Early rhubarb,
1920s (24)

Cornwall

TRURO
Cornish Gilliflower apple
c. 1800 (25)

Derbyshire

KING'S NEWTON
Newton Wonder apple,
c. 1870 (26)

Devon

DITTISHAM
Dittsham Ploughman plum,
1700s? (27)

GALMPTON
Bascombe Mystery apple?
before 1827 (28)

GITTISHAM
Tom Putt apple?
1700s (29)

TOPSHAM
May Duke gooseberry,
1900 (30)

Dorset

BRYANSTON
Bryanston Gage plum,
c. 1800 (31)

TRENT
Tom Putt apple?
1700s (32)

East Lothian

MUSSELBURGH
Musselburgh leek,
before 1834 (33)

Essex

KELVEDON
Kelvedon Wonder pea,
1925 (34)

TIPTREE
Cambridge Gage plum,
1800s (35)

TOLLESHUNT D'ARCY
D'Arcy Spice apple,
c. 1785 (36)

Fife

AUCHTERMUCHTY
British Queen potato,
1894 (37)
Up to Date potato,
1894 (38)

Gloucestershire

CHELTENHAM
Cheltenham Green Top
beetroot, before 1883 (39)

CIRENCESTER
The Student parsnip,
1859 (40)

GLOUCESTER
Ashmead's Kernel apple,
c. 1700 (41)

Hampshire

BEMBRIDGE, ISLE OF WIGHT
Howgate Wonder apple,
1915 (42)

CHRISTCHURCH
Epicure potato,
1897 (43)

Herefordshire

DOWNTON CASTLE
Waterloo cherry,
1815 (44)

ELTON
Elton Heart cherry,
1806 (45)

Hertfordshire

BERKHAMSTED
Lane's Prince Albert apple,
before 1841 (46)

SAWBRIDGEWORTH
Conference pear,
1885 (47)
Early Rivers cherry,
1872 (48)

Kent

ALLINGTON
Bunyard's Exhibition broad
bean, before 1880s (49)

EAST MALLING
Wellington XXX blackcurrant,
1913 (50)

Lancashire

ASHTON UNDER LYNE
Leveller gooseberry,
1851 (51)

BLACKLEY (MANCHESTER)
Howard's Lancer gooseberry,
1831 (52)

GLEASTON
Keswick Codlin apple
c. 1790 (53)

MANCHESTER
Manchester Giant Red celery,
before 1835 (54)
Manchester Market turnip,
before 1857 (55)

Leicestershire

SHACKERSTONE
Dumelow's Seedling apple,
c. 1790 (56)

Lincolnshire

SLEAFORD
Sharpe's Express potato,
1900 (57)

London

BRIXTON
Prince Albert rhubarb,
1840 (58)
Victoria plum (first sold),
before 1838 (59)
Victoria rhubarb,
1837 (60)

BROMPTON
Kirke's Blue plum,
1820s (61)

LEWISHAM
Hawkes' Champagne rhubarb,
1850s (62)

LOWER MARSH, WATERLOO
James' Longkeeping onion,
c. 1793 (63)

NEW CROSS
Prince Albert pea,
c. 1842 (64)

Middlesex

BRENTFORD
Black Tartarian cherry
(via St Petersburg)
c. 1796 (65)

TURNHAM GREEN
Dumelow's Seedling apple
(first sold),
c. 1790 (66)
Williams' Bon Chrétien /
Bartlett pear (first sold),
1770 (67)

Norfolk

Norfolk Beefing apple,
before 1780 (68)

Northumberland

HUMSHAUGH
Houghton Castle redcurrant,
c. 1820 (69)

MORPETH
Whinham's Industry
gooseberry,
c. 1835 (70)

Nottinghamshire

CLAYWORTH
Clayworth Prize Pink celery,
1870s (71)

SOUTHWELL
Bramley's Seedling apple,
c. 1813 (72)

Oxfordshire

WOODSTOCK
Blenheim Orange apple,
1781? (73)

WROXTON ABBEY
Wroxton sprout,
1895 (74)

Roxburghshire

KELSO
Lyon / Prize Taker leek,
c. 1883 (75)

Selkirkshire

YAIR
Green Pear of Yair,
before 1814 (76)

Shetland

Shetland Kale,
1600s? (77)

Somerset

BATH
Beauty of Bath apple,
before 1864 (78)

MARTOCK
Martock broad bean,
1200s? (79)

Staffordshire

WORDSLEY
Webb's Wonderful lettuce
1864 (80)

Suffolk

BURY ST EDMUNDS
Coe's Golden Drop plum,
before 1800 (81)

HENGRAVE
Green Gage plum,
c. 1724 (82)

Surrey

CHERTSEY
Long Red Surrey carrot,
before 1821 (83)

COBHAM
Cobham Improved Marrow
parsnip, 1940s? (84)

GREAT BOOKHAM
Purple Cape cauliflower,
before 1808? (85)

RAYNES PARK
Carter's Golden Sunrise
tomato
c. 1894 (86)
Duke of Albany pea
1881? (87)

Sussex

BRIGHTON
Glaskin's Perpetual rhubarb,
1920s (88)

CRAWLEY (TILGATE)
Crawley Beauty apple,
c. 1870 (89)

MIDHURST
Brown Goldring lettuce, before
1923 (90)

WALDERTON
Victoria plum,
before 1838 (91)

Warwickshire

Warwickshire Drooper plum,
before 1900 (92)

LEAMINGTON SPA
Leamington cauliflower,
c. 1873 (93)

Westmorland

LYTH VALLEY
Westmorland Damson plum,
before 1800 (94)

Wiltshire

WARMINSTER
Wheeler's Imperial cabbage,
before 1846 (95)

Worcestershire

OFFENHAM
Myatt's Offenham cabbage,
c. 1897 (96)

PERSHORE
Pershore Yellow Egg plum,
c. 1833 (97)

WITLEY COURT
Pitmaston Pine Apple apple
(raised),
1785? (98)

WORCESTER
Pitmaston Duchess pear,
1841 (99)
Pitmaston Pine Apple apple
(first sold),
1785? (100)
Worcester Pearmain apple,
c. 1870 (101)

Yorkshire

GREAT RIBSTON
Ribston Pippin apple,
c. 1709 (102)

HESSLE
Hessle pear,
before 1827 (103)

MORLEY
Fenton's Special rhubarb,
1930s (104)

Bibliography

For anyone interested in the history of fruit and vegetables, the richest vein of material for the nineteenth century lies in the thousands upon thousands of pages of gardening magazines, most notably John Claudius Loudon's *Gardener's Magazine*, which he founded in 1826, Joseph Paxton's *Horticultural Register*, founded in 1831, and, arguably the most important of all, the *Gardeners' Chronicle*, which ran from 1841 to 1969. The solutions to some of the mysteries in this book may still lie within its pages, and I could easily have spent another two or three years going through every issue in the hope of finding them.

Some of the books in this list are worth reading from cover to cover, such as Charles Darwin's *Variation of Plants and Animals Under Domestication* and Jonathan Roberts' attractively illustrated *Cabbages and Kings*; many others have yielded useful nuggets. Some (like Fred Roach's *Cultivated Fruits of Britain*) are classics of their kind, referred to (and deferred to) by almost every other writer on the subject. Among the most useful of all were the deeply obscure, such as R. A. Redfern's *Gooseberry Shows of Old*, privately printed in 1972 from a manuscript written at some time during the 1940s. Many of them are, sadly, no longer in print, but virtually all of them can be consulted at the Royal Horticultural Society's inimitable Lindley Library in London.

Anderson, James (ed.), *The New Practical Gardener and Modern Horticulturalist* (William Mackenzie, 1875); edited and enlarged edition of Charles McIntosh's classic work, *The New and Improved Practical Gardener*

Arbury, Jim, and Pinhey, Sally, *Pears* (Wells & Winter, 1997)

Beavington, Frank, *The Development of Market Gardening in Bedfordshire 1799–1939* (*The Agricultural History Review*, 1975)

Bradley, Richard, *New Improvements of Planting and Gardening, Both Philosophical and Practical* (London, 1739)

Brown, Catherine, and Mason, Laura, *The Taste of Britain* (Harper Press, 2006)

Bunyard, Edward, *The Anatomy of Dessert* (Chatto & Windus, 1933; repr. Random House, 2006)

Bunyard, Edward, *A Handbook of Hardy Fruits More Commonly Grown in Great Britain* (Murray, 1925)

Burr, Fearing, *The Field and Garden Vegetables of America* (Crosby & Nichols, 1863)

Campbell, Susan, *A History of Kitchen Gardening* (Frances Lincoln, 2005)

Clifford, Sue, and King, Angela, *The Apple Source Book* (Hodder & Stoughton, 2007)

The Common Ground Book of Orchards (Eco-Logic Books / Worldly Goods, 2000)

Darrow, George M., *The Strawberry: History, Breeding and Physiology* (Holt, Reinhart & Winston, 1966)

Darwin, Charles, *The Variation of Plants and Animals Under Domestication* (John Murray, 1868)

Earley Local History Group, *Suttons Seeds – A History 1806–2006* (Earley Local History Group, 2006)

Ernle, Rowland, *English Farming Past and Present* (Longmans, Green & Company, 1912; revised 1936)

Etty, Thomas, *The Roots of Vegetables: Being at Once a Dissertation and Gardener's Vade-mecum Upon Those Vegetable and Small Salad Seeds Known from Medieval Times Until the Death of the Late Queen Victoria* (Thomas Etty, 1997–2006)

Evelyn, John, *Acetaria, A Discourse of Sallets* (London, 1699)

Foust, Clifford M., *Rhubarb: The Wondrous Drug* (Princeton University Press, 1992)

Gerard, John, *The Herball, or General Historie of Plantes* (London, 1597; revised edition 1633)

Greenoak, Francesca, *Forgotten Fruit: The English Orchard and Fruit Garden* (André Deutsch, 1983)

Greenoak, Francesca, *Fruit and Vegetable Gardens: The National Trust Guide to the Productive Garden* (Guild Books, 1990)

Grubb, Norman H., *Cherries* (Crosby Lockwood & Son, 1949)

Harvey, John, *The Georgian Garden: An Eighteenth-Century Nurseryman's Catalogue* (Dovecote Press, 1983)

Heath, Philip, *Conservation Area Histories: King's Newton, District of South Derbyshire* (South Derbyshire District Council, 2005)

Hedrick, U. P. (ed.), *Sturtevant's Edible Plants of the World* (Dover, 1972)

Hogg, Robert, *British Pomology, or The History, Description, Classification and Synonymes of the Fruits and Fruit Trees of Great Britain* (London, 1851; republished in 1860 as *The Fruit Manual*)

Hudson, T. P. (ed.), *A History of the County of Sussex* (Volume 6, Part 1) (Victoria County History, 1980)

Jabs, Carolyn, *The Heirloom Gardener* (Sierra Book Club, 1984)

Juniper, Barrie E., and Mabberley, David J., *The Story of the Apple* (Timber Press, 2006)

Laws, Bill, *Spade, Skirret and Parsnip: The Curious History of Vegetables* (Sutton Publishing, 2006)

Life Cycle Modelling CO_2 Emissions for Lettuce, Apples and Cherries (Department for Transport, June 2002)

Lindley, George, *A Guide to the Orchard and Kitchen Garden* (Longman, 1831)

Morgan, Joan, and Richards, Alison, *The New Book of Apples* (Ebury Press, 2002)

Mudie, Robert, *A Description and History of Vegetable Substances used in the Arts and in Domestic Economy* (Charles Knight, 1829)

Nottingham, Stephen, *Beetroot* (http://ourworld.compuserve.com/homepages/Stephen_Nottingham/beetroot.htm, 2004)

Petherick, Tom, and Eclare, Melanie, *Heligan: A Portrait of the Lost Gardens* (Weidenfeld & Nicolson, 2004)

Petherick, Tom, and Eclare, Melanie, *The Kitchen Gardens at Heligan: Lost Gardening Principles Rediscovered* (Weidenfeld & Nicolson, 2006)

The Plum Project Book (Once, 2006)

Prince of Wales, Charles, and Donaldson, Stephanie, *The Elements of Organic Gardening* (Weidenfeld and Nicolson, 2007)

Redfern, R. A., *Gooseberry Shows of Old* (manuscript, 1944; privately printed, 1972)

Rivers, Thomas, *Catalogue of Fruits* (Rivers, October 1859)

Roach, F. A., *Cultivated Fruits of Britain: Their Origin and History* (Blackwell, 1985)

Roberts, Jonathan, *Cabbages and Kings: The Origins of Fruit and Vegetables* (HarperCollins, 2001)

Romans, Alan, *The Potato Book* (Frances Lincoln, 2005)

Sanders, Rosanne, *The English Apple* (Phaidon, 1988)

Shand, Morton, *A Book of Food* (Jonathan Cape, 1927)

Sidwell, R. W., *A Short History of Commercial Horticulture in the Vale of Evesham* (Vale of Evesham Historical Society Research Papers, 1969)

Smith, Andrew F., *False Memories: The Invention of Culinary Fakelore and Food Fallacies*, from *Proceedings of the Oxford Symposium on Food and Cookery 2000* (Prospect Books, 2001)

Spiers, Virginia, *Burcombes, Queenies and Colloggetts: Makings of a Cornish Orchard* (West Brendon, 1996)

Stickland, Sue, *Back Garden Seed Saving: Keeping Our Vegetable Heritage Alive* (Eco-Logic Books, 2001)

Stickland, Sue, *Heritage Vegetables* (Gaia Books, 1998)

Taylor, Craig, *Return to Akenfield* (Granta Books, 2006)

Taylor, H. V., *The Apples of England* (Crosby Lockwood & Son, 1936; second and third editions 1945–48)

Taylor, H. V., *The Plums of England* (Crosby Lockwood & Son, 1949)

Twiss, Sally, *Apples: A Social History* (National Trust, 1999)

Uglow, Jenny, *A Little History of British Gardening* (Chatto & Windus, 2004)

Vilmorin-Andrieux company (ed. William Robinson), *The Vegetable Garden* (John Murray, 1905)

Watson, Benjamin, *Taylor's Guide to Heirloom Vegetables* (Houghton Mifflin, 1996)

Watson, William, *An Orchard Survey of the City of Worcester* (Worcester Biological Records Centre, 1999)

Weaver, William Woys, *Heirloom Vegetable Gardening: A Master Gardener's Guide to Planting, Seed Saving, and Cultural History* (Henry Holt, 1997)

Weaver, William Woys, *100 Vegetables and Where They Came From* (Algonquin Books of Chapel Hill, 2000)

Wilson, Alan, *The Story of the Potato Through Illustrated Varieties* (Alan Wilson, 1993)

Acknowledgements

Among the many people who have helped me during the writing of *Forgotten Fruits* I would particularly like to thank:

My editor Sophie Lazar at Random House, for her steadfast encouragement, enthusiasm and good humour over a long and occasionally stressful project; her colleagues Nigel Wilcockson, Louise Campbell, Dinah Drazin and Emily Rhodes; and Caroline Pretty, for her painstaking copy-editing. They have all been a total pleasure to work with.

Lisa Darnell from Guardian Books, who gave me the original commission.

Lorna Tremayne and Sylvia Travers at the Lost Gardens of Heligan for their incredibly generous help with photographs.

Ray Warner from Thomas Etty, who kindly allowed me to make use of his own years of research into traditional vegetable varieties.

Brent Elliott and the staff of the RHS Lindley Library in London, who patiently answered my obscurest queries.

Anna Pavord, whose astonishment that I had originally been given six months to write this book was matched by my happiness in discovering that her last one had taken her six years, and who suggested I took as long as I needed to write something I was content with. Her wise advice may not have pleased everyone, but it was a great encouragement to me.

Joanna Morland, for dragging me away from my computer for coffee and Dorset apple cake.

Claire Wrathall, for entertaining me with regular despatches from the big city.

And last but not least, to Roy and my parents, without whose unfailing personal and financial support I could never have completed this book.

Many other people have helped me, but for their generous advice and encouragement I would particularly like to thank Jim Arbury and Jim English at RHS Wisley; Kelvin Archer and Sir Richard Baker-Wilbraham at Rode Hall; Toby Beasley at Down House; Andrew Bennett, Brighton and Hove Archivist at East Sussex Records Office; Mike Calnan and Kristy Jones at the National Trust; Richard Childs, county archivist, West Sussex Record Office; Sue Clifford at Common Ground; Leah Colthorpe at the Royal Horticultural Society; John Coulter, Local Studies Librarian at the Lewisham Local History and Archives Centre; Charles Cowling and Sharon Phillips; Professor Alan Davison at Newcastle University; Graeme Edwards at the Somerset Record Office; Susan Farr, Worcestershire County Council; Marcus Field and Andrew Wilson; Professor Mick Fuller at Plymouth University; Helen Garrett at the Bishop's Palace and Gardens, Wells; Jane Garrett at Brogdale Horticultural Trust; Deb Goodenough, now head gardener at Highgrove; Hans-Peter Grunenfelder at the SAVE Foundation, St Gallen, Switzerland; Sue Hoy at Normanby Hall; Dr Thomas Kiely at the British Museum, Department of Greek and Roman Antiquities; Mark Nesbitt and Anna Quenby at the Royal Botanic Gardens, Kew; Philip Norman at the Museum of Garden History; Neil Porteous at Clumber Park; Kim Robinson at Wells Civic Society; Susan Russell, head gardener at Culzean Castle; Maria Scholten in Edinburgh; Sandra Slack at Garden Organic, for her generous help at the inception of this project; Andrew Smith, editor in chief of *The Oxford Encyclopedia of Food and Drink in America*; Stephanie at the Isle of Portland Underhill Library; Kate Thomas at Worcestershire Wildlife Trust; Steve Townsend; Paul Verdeyen at Worcestershire Education Business Link, Pitmaston House, Worcester; Sarah Wain, Shirley Tasker, Jim Buckland and Karon Read at West Dean Gardens; Andrew Widd, head gardener at Audley End; Sinclair Williamson, head gardener at Kellie Castle; Gayle Wilson at Visit Scotland; Kate Woods at English Heritage; and Marilyn Wright at Stoughton Parish Council.

A book of this kind will always have to rely, to a certain extent, on other printed sources of reference, and while every attempt has been made to cross-check each story as far as possible, my apologies if I have inadvertently perpetuated any previous authors' mistakes.

The author is grateful for the following permissions:
Quotation from *Those Barren Leaves* by Aldous Huxley © Aldous Huxley 1952. Reprinted by kind permission of the estate of Aldous Huxley. Quotation from *The Tale of the Flopsy Bunnies* by Beatrix Potter © Frederick Warne & Co., 1909. Reproduced by kind permission of Frederick Warne & Co. Quotations from *Mike at Wrykyn / Indiscretions of Archie* by P. G. Wodehouse, published by Barrie & Jenkins. Reprinted by kind permission of The Random House Group Ltd.

Illustrations:
Black and white portraits (pp.68, 86, 161, 185, 221) © RHS Lindley Library
Inset: Bramley's Seeding apple tree (© John Glover / Alamy); Pitmaston Pine Apple apples at Normanby Hall (© Sue Hoy at Normanby Hall); Pitmaston House, Worcester (by kind permission

of Worcestershire County Council); Benary Egyptian Turnip-Rooted Beetroot and Rouge Crapaudine (© RHS Lindley Library); Bunyard's Exhibition broad bean flowers (© Heligan Gardens Ltd); Edward Bunyard (© RHS Lindley Library); Shetland Kale (© Maria Scholten); Wroxton Abbey, Oxfordshire (by kind permission of Wroxton College); Walled garden at Heligan (© Heligan Gardens Ltd); James' Scarlet Intermediate carrots (© Charles Francis – supplied by Heligan Gardens Ltd); Cauliflower Teapot, from Burlem, Staffordshire, c.1759–66 (lead glazed cream earthenware, slip-cast, English School, 18th century Fitzwilliam Museum, University of Cambridge, UK / The Bridgeman Art Library); The taking of Marshall Tallard and pushing 4000 Horses into the Danube at the Battle of Blenheim in 1704, c.1760 (coloured engraving, Laguerre, Louis 1663–1721 (after) / Courtesy of the Council, National Army Museum, London, UK / The Bridgeman Art Library); May Duke Cherries (from *Pomoua Britannica* London / 1812 – private collection); Lemon Apple cucumber (© Sue Hoy, Normanby Hall); John Tradescant the Elder (1570–c.1638, oil on canvas, Neve, Cornelius de c.1609–78 (attr. to) / © Ashmolean Museum, University of Oxford, UK / The Bridgeman Art Library); Laxton's No. 1 redcurrant (© RHS Lindley Library); Vegetable plot at Normanby Hall, Scunthorpe (© Sue Hoy, Normanby Hall); Egton Bridge Annual Show exterior (© Mike Kipling Photography/ Alamy); Egton Bridge Annual Show interior (© TravelStock Collection – Homer Sykes / Alamy); Whinham's Industry goose-berries (© Heligan Gardens Ltd); Welsh Guards (© PCL / Alamy); Marvel of the Four Seasons lettuce (© Heligan Gardens Ltd); Ailsa Craig island (© Holmes Garden Photos / Alamy); Down House, Darwin's home (© David Ball / Alamy); Williams' pear (© Lynne Evans /Alamy); Pershore Plum tree (© Heligan Gardens Ltd); Dittisham village, Devon (© Stephen Bond / Alamy); Duke of York potatoes in bag (© Heligan Gardens Ltd); Duke of York potato flower (© Heligan Gardens Ltd); Parmentier's tomb (© Guichaoua/

Alamy); Osborne House (© Jinny Goodman /Alamy); Scarlet Emperor runner beans (© Charles Francis – supplied by Heligan Gardens Ltd); Scarlet Emperor runner bean plants (© Heligan Gardens Ltd); China Rose radish (© Dawn Runnals – supplied by Heligan Gardens Ltd); Royal Sovereign strawberry (© Claire Travers – supplied by Heligan Gardens Ltd); Ailsa Craig tomato (© Martin Hughes-Jones / Alamy); Joseph Myatt portrait (Reproduced by kind permission of Brian Myatt – supplied by Lewisham Local History and Archives Centre); Turnips (© Charles Francis – supplied by Heligan Gardens Ltd); Sunday Morning in the New Cut, Lambeth (The Print Collector / The Heritage Image Partnership).

Maps (pp.248–253) © Darren Bennett

Index

ANDREA WULF

The Brother Gardeners
Botany, Empire and the
Birth of an Obsession

Longlisted for the Samuel Johnson Prize for
Non-fiction 2008

'Wondrous . . . I have learned so much from her book'
JON SNOW, CHANNEL FOUR NEWS

One January morning in 1734, cloth merchant Peter
Collinson hurried down to the docks at London's Custom
House to collect cargo just arrived from John Bartram in the
American colonies. But it was not bales of cotton that awaited
him, but plants and seeds…

Over the next forty years, Bartram would send hundreds of
American species to England, where Collinson was one of a
handful of men who would foster a national obsession and
change the gardens of Britain forever: Philip Miller, author of
the bestselling *Gardeners Dictionary*; the Swede Carl Linnaeus,
whose standardised botanical nomenclature popularised
botany; the botanist-adventurer Joseph Banks and his
colleague Daniel Solander who both explored the strange flora
of Tahiti and Australia on Captain Cook's *Endeavour*.

This is the story of these men – friends, rivals, enemies, united
by a passion for plants. Set against the backdrop of the emerging
empire and the uncharted world beyond, *The Brother Gardeners*
tells the story of how Britain became a nation of gardeners.

'Absorbing and delightful'
JENNY UGLOW, SUNDAY TELEGRAPH

HILLARY JORDAN

Mudbound

Winner of the Bellwether Prize for Fiction

'*A page-turning read that conveys a serious message without preaching*'
OBSERVER

When Henry McAllan moves his city-bred wife, Laura, to a
cotton farm in the Mississippi Delta in 1946, she finds herself
in a place both foreign and frightening. Henry's love of rural
life is not shared by Laura, who struggles to raise their two
young children in an isolated shotgun shack under the eye of
her hateful, racist father-in-law. When it rains, the waters rise
up and swallow the bridge to town, stranding the family in a
sea of mud.

As the Second World War shudders to an end, two young men
return from Europe to help work the farm. Jamie McAllan is
everything his older brother Henry is not and is sensitive to
Laura's plight, but also haunted by his memories of combat.
Ronsel Jackson, eldest son of the black sharecroppers who live
on the farm, comes home from war with the shine of a hero,
only to face far more dangerous battles against the ingrained
bigotry of his own countrymen. These two unlikely friends
become players in a tragedy on the grandest scale.

'*This is storytelling at the height of its powers*'
BARBARA KINGSOLVER

'*Jordan builds the tension slowly and meticulously, so that when the
shocking denouement arrives, it is both inevitable and devastating …
A compelling tale*'
GLASGOW HERALD

ANDROMEDA ROMANO-LAX

The Spanish Bow

When Feliu Delargo is born, late-nineteenth-century Spain is a nation slipping from international power and struggling with its own fractured identity, caught between the chaos of post-empire and impending Civil War.

Feliu's troubled childhood and rise to fame lead him into a thorny partnership with an even more famous and eccentric figure, the piano prodigy Justo Al-Cerraz. The two musicians' divergent artistic goals and political inclinations threaten to divide them as Spain plunges into Civil War. But as Civil War turns to World War, shared love for their trio partner – an Italian violinist named Aviva — forces them into their final and most dangerous collaboration.